DRAMA and
PHILOSOPHY

The right of the
University of Cambridge
to print and sell
all manner of books
was granted by
Henry VIII in 1534.
The University has printed
and published continuously
since 1584..

CAMBRIDGE UNIVERSITY PRESS

CAMBRIDGE

NEW YORK   PORT CHESTER   MELBOURNE   SYDNEY

Published by the Press Syndicate of the University of Cambridge
The Pitt Building, Trumpington Street, Cambridge CB2 1RP
40 West 20th Street, New York, NY 10011, USA
10 Stamford Road, Oakleigh, Melbourne 3166, Australia

First published 1990

Printed in Great Britain at The Bath Press, Avon

British Library Cataloguing in publication data
Themes in Drama, 12
1. Drama – History and criticism – Periodicals
809.2'005 PN1601

Library of Congress catalogue card number 82–4491

ISSN 0263–676x
ISBN 0 521 38381 1

Themes in Drama

An annual publication

Edited by James Redmond

12

DRAMA AND PHILOSOPHY

SUBSCRIPTIONS The subscription price to volume 12, which includes postage, is £35 (US $67.00 in USA and Canada) for institutions, £20.00 (US $40.00 in USA and Canada) for individuals ordering direct from the Press and certifying that the annual is for their personal use. Airmail (orders to Cambridge only) £6.00 extra. Copies of the annual for subscribers in the USA and Canada are sent by air to New York to arrive with minimum delay. Orders, which must be accompanied by payment, may be sent to a bookseller, subscription agent or direct to the publishers: Cambridge University Press, The Edinburgh Building, Shaftesbury Road, Cambridge CB2 2RU. Payment may be made by any of the following methods: cheque (payable to Cambridge University Press), UK postal order, bank draft, Post Office Giro (account no. 571 6055 GB Bootle – advise CUP of payment), international money order, UNESCO coupons, or any credit card bearing the Interbank symbol. Orders from the USA and Canada should be sent to Cambridge University Press, 40 West 20th Street, New York, NY 10011.

BACK VOLUMES Volumes 1–11 are available from the publisher at £30.00 ($69.00 in USA and Canada).

Contents

	page
Themes in Drama volumes and conferences	vii
List of contributors	ix
List of illustrations	xi
Editor's preface	xiii

The ancient quarrel between poetry and philosophy
  by THOMAS GOULD   I

Drama and Aristotle
  by VICTOR CASTELLANI   21

Faith, reason and the Prophets' dialogue in the Coventry *Pageant of the Shearmen and Taylors*
  by PAMELA M. KING   37

Shakespearian self-knowledge: the synthesizing imagination and the limits of reason
  by WILLIAM R. MORSE   47

Shakespeare's problem comedies: an Hegelian approach to genre
  by SHAWN WATSON   61

Self-undoing paradox, scepticism, and Lear's abdication
  by WILLIAM O. SCOTT   73

'His legs bestrid the ocean' as a 'form of life'
  by BRIAN CHEADLE   87

'A curious way of torturing': language and ideological transformation
in *A King and No King*
    by DAVID LAIRD   107

Dialogue into drama: Socrates in eighteenth-century verse dramas
    by K. J. H. BERLAND   127

Theatre as temple in the 'New Movement' in American theatre
    by WILLIAM F. CONDEE   143

Images of women and the burden of myth: plagues on the houses
of Gorky and O'Neill
    by PATRICIA FLANAGAN BEHRENDT   161

Bruno and Beckett: coincidence of contraries
    by JAMES E. ROBINSON   171

The Devils and its sources: modern perspectives on the Loudun
possession
    by JANE GOODALL   185

Drama and philosophy: *Professional Foul* breaks the rules
    by MICHAEL ELDRIDGE   199

FORUM
The puzzle of Tadeusz Różewicz's *White Marriage*
    by HALINA FILIPOWICZ   211

Index   225

Themes in Drama volumes and conferences

Volumes already published in the series

  1   *Drama and Society*
  2   *Drama and Mimesis*
  3   *Drama, Dance and Music*
  4   *Drama and Symbolism*
  5   *Drama and Religion*
  6   *Drama and the Actor*
  7   *Drama, Sex and Politics*
  8   *Historical Drama*
  9   *The Theatrical Space*
 10   *Farce*
 11   *Women in Theatre*
 12   *Drama and Philosophy*

Forthcoming

 13   *Violence in Drama* (pub. 1991)
 14   *Melodrama* (pub. 1992)
 15   *Madness in Drama*
 16   *National Theatres*

Themes in Drama *conferences*

Annual conferences are held at the University of London and at the University of California, Riverside. The subject in 1991 will be 'Madness in Drama' and this title has been proposed and accepted for the annual journal *Themes in Drama* (volume 15). The subject for the 1992 conferences will be 'National Theatres' and this title will be proposed for publication. Details of the conference held in California may be obtained from: *Themes in Drama* Conference, University of California, Riverside, CA 92521. Details of the conference held in London may be obtained from the Editor.

   Potential contributors are asked to correspond with the Editor at an early date. Papers for volume 15 should be submitted in final form to the Editor before 1 September 1991.

James Redmond, Editor, *Themes in Drama*, Queen Mary and Westfield College, University of London, Hampstead, London NW3 7ST.

Contributors

Patricia Flanagan Behrendt, *Theatre Arts, University of Nebraska*
K. J. H. Berland, *Pennsylvania State University*
Victor Castellani, *Department of Foreign Languages, University of Denver*
Brian Cheadle, *Department of English, University of Witwatersrand*
William F. Condee, *School of Theatre, Ohio University*
Michael Eldridge, *Discipline of Philosophy, Spring Hall College*
Halina Filipowicz, *Department of Slavic Languages, University of Wisconsin*
Jane Goodall, *Department of Drama, University of Newcastle, New South Wales*
Thomas Gould, *Department of Classics, Yale University*
Pamela M. King, *Department of English, Queen Mary and Westfield College, University of London*
David Laird, *Department of English, California State University, Los Angeles*
William R. Morse, *Department of English, College of the Holy Cross*
James E. Robinson, *Department of English, University of Notre Dame*
William O. Scott, *Department of English, University of Kansas*
Shawn Watson, *Department of English, Ohio University*

Illustrations

		page
1	Wyndham's Theatre, London (1899)	149
2	Edward Gordon Craig: *Macbeth* (1906)	150
3	Robert Edmond Jones: Arnold Schönberg's *Die glückliche Hand*	151
4	Norman Bel Geddes's plans for a theatre fit for the new spirit in drama	152
5	Norman Bel Geddes's plan for an intimate theatre	153
6	Norman Bel Geddes's sketch for an intimate theatre	154
7	Frank A. Waugh's plan for the Butterick Memorial Theatre	155
8	'The coincidence of contraries', Willie and Winnie (Tristan Middleton and Tiffany Murray) (photo: Keith Roughton)	177

Editor's preface

This is the twelfth volume of *Themes in Drama*, which is published annually. Each volume brings together articles on the theatrical activity of a wide range of cultures and periods. The papers offer original contributions to their own specialized fields, but they are presented in such a way that their significance may be appreciated readily by non-specialists.

Each volume indicates connections between the various national traditions of theatre by bringing together studies of a theme of central and continuing importance. The annual international conferences (see p. vii) provide an opportunity for scholars, critics and theatrical practitioners to exchange views, and many of the papers in the volumes are revised versions of papers read and discussed at the conferences. The present volume reflects the range and quality of the 1988 conferences on 'Drama and Philosophy'. Contributions are invited for volumes 14, 15 and 16; they should follow the style of presentation used in this volume, and be sent to

James Redmond
Editor *Themes in Drama*
Queen Mary and Westfield College
University of London
Hampstead
London NW3 7ST

The ancient quarrel between poetry and philosophy*

THOMAS GOULD

'Pathos' is our name for the power of some events to stir us to a mysteriously agreeable sadness. It is also our name for the emotions awakened by such an event, a mixture of tenderness and sympathy. When the occasion is some turn or observation in our own lives, pathos may be associated with a sense of loss; even then, however, it is thought to be of value and hardly painful at all. And when it is created by a drama or story, or by music or art, it may be esteemed for its ability to ennoble us or to deepen our understanding. Still it is a minor pleasure, and we do not think about it much.

The Greek *pathos*, on the other hand, distant ancestor of 'pathos' (via Aristotle, Longinus, and Pope, among others[1]), was a very different sort of thing. The *pathos* was cherished by some Greeks as the most vital moment in religion and art, feared by others as an enticement to sacrilege and irrationality. When the term first gained currency (it is not found before the fifth century), it was the right name for the operative event in stories essential to popular religion and to tragedy: catastrophic suffering, undergone by some great figure, man or god, far in excess of the sufferer's deserts. Modern readers regularly miss this almost technical use of the word *pathos*. That failure then contributes to serious misunderstandings, not only in our interpretation of the tragedies and of key passages in them, but also in our attempt to evaluate the tradition of hostility to exploitation of the *pathos*, what Plato called 'the ancient quarrel between poetry and philosophy'.[2]

The weight given the idea of *pathos* in the fifth and fourth centuries can be appreciated if we link the word, not with our 'pathos', but with our 'Passion'. Paul and other writers of the New Testament tended to speak of Christ's god-caused unmerited suffering as his *pathēmata*,[3] a different nominal formation from the same verb, *pathein*, 'to suffer'. And the idea is still the same: a lamentable victimization by and for God and also for the benefit of mankind. Jerome translated *pathēmata* by the Latin *passiones*, at that time a little-used noun but correctly formed from the verb *patior*, to have something done to one.[4]

* A draft of this paper was read at the *Themes in Drama* International Conference held at the University of California, Riverside, in February 1988.

From *passiones*, of course, comes our 'passion'. So Greek popular religion and the Biblical religions both concentrated on the same paradoxical spectacle, the *pathos* or *pathēmata*, 'passions' in the sense of the Passion of Christ. In the Pagan as in the Christian tradition the pious cherished the *pathos* and were grateful for it; but the Greeks worried about this strange phenomenon. As the dancers say in *Oedipus the King*, the revelation of a *pathos* makes one shudder and want to turn away, even as it makes one yearn to look, to feast one's eyes and try to understand.[5] The dancers' aversion and abhorrence at the sight of the blinded Oedipus is almost as strong as their intense fascination. The same is true of the audience. This is very strange: we are taking a grim kind of pleasure in what horrifies us. Worse yet, as the dancers reason in *Agamemnon*, gods can give man a revelation through a *pathos* only if they are capable of perpetrating monstrously unjust events, which is surely what the sacrifice of Iphigeneia was. Should we be thankful to gods like that, the dancers ask.[6] The Socratics are even more blunt. The first mark of true piety, they insist, is the realization that divinity never condones, and certainly does not perpetrate, injustice toward anyone, man or god. Instruction and revelation through the spectacle of a *pathos*, therefore, is not compatible with the nature of divinity, and any religion that moves its followers by *pathē* (the plural of *pathos*) is necessarily false and inimical to true piety. But we have lost the Greeks' clarity on this issue, especially in Christian theology. It rarely occurs to Christians that their theologians are playing a trick on them when they call the Passion an instance of justice, not injustice.

It is probable, but not entirely certain, that *pathein*, from which *pathos*, *pathēma*, and other new nouns were formed in the fifth century, meant, from the beginning, 'to suffer', 'to undergo a calamity'. The verb's etymology is obscure. Chantraine suggests a relation to *pēma*, 'misery', *talaipōros*, 'distressed', and *penomai*, 'to toil'.[7] But the etymologies of these words are also obscure. In favor of an original meaning 'to be made miserable' is the fact that the first nominal form of the verb was *penthos*, which never lost its earliest attested meaning, 'grief', 'misery'. Also, in the epic tradition *pathein* seems always to denote an experience the victim deplores. There are only two or three passages open to a different interpretation.[8] Shortly after the epic period, however, we get two instances, Archilochus 14.2 and Tyrtaeus 12.38, where *pathein* means experiencing something good. This may be a development from a common formula for reciprocal justice: do evil and you must expect to suffer evil. This formula, which appears in a Hesiodic fragment,[9] may have suggested a corollary: do good and you may expect to experience good. Except for an occurrence in Solon, however, in a line which may not be by Solon,[10] and several occurrences in the Theognidea, a collection of verses from different periods, *pathein* as the experience of good does not appear again until the fifth century.

The use of *pathein* so familiar to readers of classical literature and philosophy, to have something done to one – good, bad, or indifferent – its employment, in other words, as a functional passive for *erdein* and other words meaning 'to do', is surprisingly late, to judge from our records. This may be an accident, but it may indeed point to a late development, either from greater familiarity with *pathein* for good experiences, or from the Socratic habit of referring to emotions and sense experiences as *pathē* since such things were thought by them to be harmful as often as not.[11] This Socratic idiom is, of course, the origin of our other use of the Latinate 'passion' – passions in the sense of rage, sexual arousal, and the like. Yet no Greek writer, not even Aristotle, forgot the use of *pathos* derived from what was once the most widely recognized meaning of *pathein*, to suffer a major catastrophe.[12] And Plato was very sensitive to the old belief that a holy *pathos* required a terrible injustice perpetrated by a god.[13]

Is it an accident that we have no occurrence of *pathos* before Aeschylus? We cannot explain its absence from our record on metrical grounds.[14] Still, we cannot be sure that this formation was not older than it seems. We do have *ainopathēs*, 'suffering terrible things', at *Odyssey* 8.201. Yet the earlier record hardly prepares us for the many appearances of *pathos* in the fifth century. And unlike *bathos*, 'depth', which also began appearing about the same time in place of *benthos* but with the same meaning as *benthos*, *pathos* was reserved for some uses not attested for *penthos*. *Penthos* continued to mean 'grief', or 'mourning'; *pathos* almost always means the occasion for grief, especially a god-caused catastrophe largely or entirely undeserved by the victim.

It is certainly possible to find old uses of the verb *pathein* that could have led to the new technical meaning of *pathos*. Odysseus was often called *polla pathōn* and the like, meaning that he suffered many calamities; and those calamities were, by and large, far beyond what he deserved. Also, ultimately his troubles were mostly god-caused; many were brought about by Poseidon, for instance.[15] And at Callinus 1.17 *pathein* is used of the death of a great warrior, one on whom his fellow citizens should now gaze with wonder. But the fifth-century use of *pathos* in connection with initiatory and hero religions, enthusiasms only rarely referred to in our earlier records, may point to a different origin for the word's new popularity. It could be that new interest – or more articulate interest – in the special suffering of revered gods, like Dionysus and Demeter, or of heroes, like Ajax or Adrastus, required a term that would denote the victimization of the revered figure, not the grief that was an obvious consequence of the victimization. It is possible that *penthos*, 'grief', was no longer universally known to be the nominal form of *pathein*, since the 'n' in the noun appeared in no longer recognizable guises in most forms of the verb. But *penthos* would in any case have been inadequate as a name for the god-caused unmerited suffering of a god or hero.

The use of *pathos* in talk about some of the initiatory religions can be seen in Herodotus. At 2.170–1 he refers cryptically to the *sparagmos* (dismemberment) of Dionysus as the god's secret *pathos*. He then likens it to a comparable secret about the suffering of Demeter and Persephone. Centuries later *pathos* reappears as a technical term for these Passions in the accounts of Plutarch, Pausanias, and others.[16] The use of *pathos* in explanations of hero religion can be seen in Herodotus and Pindar. At 5.67 Herodotus describes the celebrations at Sicyon, early in the sixth century, of the *pathea* of the hero Adrastus. Herodotus tells us that these *pathē* were celebrated by 'tragic dances', a claim often dismissed as unhistorical, though some scholars defend the description as correct in one sense or another.[17] In any case it is easy enough to find phrases in the surviving tragedies which echo the use of *pathos* by Herodotus in this passage.[18] There appears to be no great difference between the *pathē* of Demeter or Dionysus on the one hand, and those of Ajax and Adrastus on the other. What is needed above all, as Pindar makes clear in the Seventh Nemean, is a genuine and obvious gap between the sufferer's deserts and what happens to him. A hero is entitled to veneration only if he is the victim of a genuine injustice. Odysseus, Pindar complains, was much too guilty (too unscrupulous and sophistic) to merit veneration. Ajax, on the other hand, was a true victim and so deserves his hero honors.[19]

The *pathos* in a holy story can in fact be followed by a victory – as in the great compromise won by Demeter, the vindictive triumphs of Dionysus born again, the deification of Heracles, the heroization of Adrastus and Ajax, and so on. This is a pattern we also find in fifth-century tragedies: a fair number either end in the restitution of justice or hint at justice to come at some later date. And even those that end in bleak misery and complete defeat may allude to future benefits mankind will receive from all this suffering. The *pathos* need not be the final event in the story, therefore. All that is needed is a prominent and genuine *pathos* at an important moment in the drama; the ending can seem almost to cancel it out. Consider the parallel in Christianity. Paul tells his readers to concentrate on the cross, the terrible and utterly undeserved suffering of the blameless Christ, a painful injustice ordered by God himself.[20] This does not feel like blasphemy, because there is always the resurrection, whether it is mentioned or not. And in any case, mankind cannot but be grateful for the *pathos*. Nevertheless, the event itself is a monstrous injustice.

Jews and Christians have lived for centuries with the idea that their deity benefits mankind by causing largely or entirely unjustified suffering for certain individuals or generations. However, few rely on that thought when they themselves suffer a loss. A mourner, if he is pious, will not assume that a victim of, say Auschwitz or leukemia, must have deserved his suffering. His grief may be quite terrible. Yet he may assume that some higher justice is being done, despite appearances. The thoughts with which he will comfort himself are in fact quite like those in some Greek tragedies: divinity's ways are not our ways, on a higher plane or in the distant future it may yet be possible to discern the true benevolence of divinity, the very incomprehensibility of the event shows that it is not the work of man alone, and so on. The Greeks, however, seem never to have been without thinkers who demanded that *pathē* cease to be the focal point of holy stories, and that intelligible justice be looked for in every event, whether in a holy story or in life.

When the gods first came to be envisaged as human agents, greater and less vulnerable than we are yet ourselves as we should like to be, religion-based morality became hopelessly difficult. Are we required to venerate gods who act like human rulers, proud, competitive, vindictive, pleasure-loving? Or do true gods act only as we would have our rulers act? Must we accept divine intervention according to a moral order we would condemn in a purely human society? Or do gods act in strict conformity to an enlightened human code? The Greeks never reached a consensus until the triumph of Platonized theology in post-classical times.[21]

The *Iliad*, for instance, gives us a universe in which the most splendid men and women can expect to experience terrible suffering at the hands of gods. The poet of the *Odyssey*, by contrast, insists that by and large justice is done and men who deserve happiness will experience it eventually.[22] Solon suggests that apparent injustices in divine punishment can be explained by the absence of quick anger in the gods' decisions; as a consequence of Zeus' timeless composure there is often a delay in his actions, even into subsequent generations.[23] Aeschylus dismisses this solution as inadequate. He insists that there is a difference between the old order and a new order. Once there was indeed a rule by Divine Injustice, as can be seen in the *pathē* of Iphigeneia, the children of Thyestes, Cassandra, Agamemnon, and so on; but now true justice prevails, even in individual lives.

In the latter half of the fifth century, opinions about *pathos* religion were ever more sharply divided. Sophocles brought the thrilling *pathē* of hero religion right into the theatre and evidently felt that no explanation or apology was needed. Meanwhile Socrates was going around Athens insisting that his fellow citizens reject as dangerously false any story that moves men with depictions of Divine Injustice. Sophocles would obviously have to be banned if Socrates had his way. It must make us pause that it was Sophocles who was revered as exceptionally pious and Socrates who was put to death for his rejection of the city's religion. Euripides, like Socrates, was also held in suspicion by some Athenians, perhaps in part because he made men think about the moral puzzle inherent in *pathē*. He tended to bring the peripheral victims of earlier tragedy, the women and children, into center stage – which underlined the innocence of the victims and therefore the guilt of their divine tormentors. He then made the gods explain themselves – but with such dubious logic and in such a flat-footed tone that many of the pious in the audience must surely have been annoyed or distressed.

Plato accepted Socrates' evaluation of *pathos* religion. He obviously believed that his own view of gods and men was in harmony with that of his teacher. First, the gods are always good. As Plato has Socrates argue in the *Euthyphro*, 'good' for divinity is not only the same as 'good' for man, it is known to us solely through good for man.[24] Secondly, only if men are truly good do they approach the happiness of the gods. Men must therefore make themselves good like the gods in order that they will be blessed like them. It follows that excellence is, not only a necessary, but also the sufficient condition for happiness. The gods see to it that this will always be so, in the life of every individual as well as in the long run for mankind as a whole.[25] Obviously, then, divinity could never teach through *pathē* as that idea was traditionally interpreted, genuine unhappiness suffered by genuinely good persons. In the *Apology* Plato does indeed have Socrates call his own unjust condemnation a *pathos*, but he then insists that Socrates, because he was good, experienced no diminution of his happiness whatsoever.[26] A less good man does not even know how truly to harm a good man, he argues. If Plato's strictures against tragedy had not come down to us, only the essence of Socratic morality, we would have had to conclude nevertheless that he must surely have been bitterly opposed to Attic drama.

In the *Republic* much is made of the fact that large-scale justice and injustice spring ultimately from justice and injustice within the citizens' individual personalities. Plato's theory of tragedy is therefore given in both an outer and an inner version. The public version comes first, in Book II. Here Plato treats tragedy as part of the religious tradition, as the tragedians and their audiences had also. The gods cause only good, 'Socrates' complains. Stories that show gods acting otherwise ought long ago to have been declared impious. Plato's first examples come from the epics, then he moves on to tragedy. In a rational and truly pious society, he says, a dramatist would not be permitted to present 'the *pathē* of Niobe', as Aeschylus had done, or 'the *pathē* of the children of Pelops', or 'the Trojan *pathē*'.[27] If the unhappiness is real, then the cause of the misfortunes must be shown to be, not gods, but the sufferers themselves. Better yet, the cause should be gods but the sufferers must be seen to deserve and need their punishment. In the long run divine intervention is always for men's benefit; our holy stories must make this clear, Plato thought. A third plot is suggested in the description of the death of Socrates at the end of the *Phaedo*: a victim of real injustice is seen to die happily, whatever the world had intended for him, because he was truly good. But it was the plot Plato disapproved of, the traditional *pathos*, that fueled the greatest of the Attic plays. Plato was right about that.

The interior analogue to this analysis must be postponed until Plato has given a full account of the tripartite psyche. He says as much at the very beginning of Book x: now that we have distinguished the parts of the psyche we have even clearer reasons for objecting to tragedy (595a5–b1). A *pathos* may give pleasure, he says, but it does so by gratifying the lowest and most irrational part of our souls. This is the part that is in command in the behavior of dictators, madmen, and criminals, also of neurotic and compulsive people. Indeed, it is the part that is dominant in all of us whenever we are asleep and dreaming. In Book ix 'Socrates' had explained that when we sleep a part that had formerly been asleep (i.e. unconscious) while we were awake now 'awakens' (571c3). Plato's catalogue of phantasies which this part then fulfills in dreams is drawn from some of the best-loved tragedies, especially the stories of Oedipus and Thyestes.[28] In Book x he suggests that a moral citizen, when he permits himself to be moved by a tragedy, allows this same part of his soul to be 'awakened' once again (605b3). That is the real reason why stories like those of Oedipus and Thyestes win prizes: they gratify a part of us that is denied all gratification, even in phantasy, when our reason is in full command.

The lowest part of the psyche, Plato says (606a3), is normally held forcibly in check, that is repressed: *biāi katechomenon*. But except for the rare instances when the personality is very well trained and the intellect exceptionally strong, attendance at a tragic *pathos* will cause this darkest element to come unstuck again and exercise its strength. Strange things happen. We weep, yet we enjoy the experience profoundly. We think we are weeping for the hero undergoing the *pathos* down there on the stage, yet we are actually weeping for our own *pathos*, Plato insists. (We suffer with the wretched hero, *sympathein*, he says: 605d3–4.) The experience is enjoyable, it seems, because the lowest part of the psyche is getting exactly what it wants. What it yearns to believe is just what Socrates insists we should never accept as the truth: that monstrous *pathē*, true victimizations, are not only possible in this universe, they are the essence of divine rule. A part of us is by its nature anti-Socratic, Plato concluded; it wants a universe full of genuinely good men and women who are made genuinely unhappy nevertheless, through no fault of their own.[29]

What exhilarates us, then, when we watch a *pathos* of the traditional sort, is not the proof that the suffering is real and intense, although that is necessary too, but proof that this is a true injustice. That is, by suffering along with the hero we are able to accept his innocence as well. This is something we find difficult to believe of ourselves. However much we rail against enemies or bad luck, deep down we suspect that we would now have everything we want if only we were not so lazy, so morally weak, or so limited intellectually. By accepting a world ruled by Divine Injustice we can forgive ourselves – if only for the duration of the story. A pious person may well attribute his new sense of moral cleanness to the god whose presence he feels in the event. A vivid example of this kind of self-forgiveness, issuing in religious feelings of the strongest sort, may be found in Carl Jung's reminiscences about his boyhood struggles with the dark and unjust God of the Bible.[30]

But it is surely Freud who has the missing key to this puzzle. Plato's 'middle part' of the psyche, which functions much like Freud's superego, is itself a major cause of human misery, Freud discovered.[31] Guilt, the pain inflicted on us by our own superegos, is not harmless, as Plato had supposed. The superego is often irrational, unrealistic, and life-poisoning. A strong middle part is necessary – it encourages virtuous behavior, just as Plato had said – but it may also make inner peace impossible. Indeed, it is often the better kind of person who has the greatest sense of guilt. Saints have more, not less difficulty than the rest of us in achieving inner peace.[32] This is a paradox never suspected by Plato. Had he understood it, he might not have been so uncompromising in his condemnation of activities, like attendance on a *pathos*, that cleanse us of such guilt. But of course, acceptance of religion and art based on the *pathos* would have necessitated the abandonment of Socratism. The latter is based, after all, on belief that there is no true injustice in the experiences of god or man.

That Plato should have underestimated the danger of a strong superego is not really surprising. Freud came to this discovery by his study of paranoia, a condition in which the tormenting superego is so imperious that it is not infrequently felt to exist as a hostile voice or voices from without. But the most dramatic example of paranoia among Plato's close associates was that of Socrates, who assumed that his always nay-saying 'voice' was divine and wonderful.[33]

Aristotle had a problem. On the one hand, he was still a Socratic. That is, he thought that by and large true excellence brought genuine happiness. No truly happy man, he says, can ever be reduced to misery – although he might indeed be less than completely happy if he is made to suffer, say, the fate of Priam (*Nicomachean Ethics* I, chapters 9–11). In any case a religion based on Divine Injustice would make no sense to Aristotle. He ought, therefore, to have gone along with Plato's rejection of tragedy. On the other hand, he eventually developed Plato's theory of *erōs* into a thoroughgoing teleology. All events, human or cosmic, are explained as caused by good of various sorts being striven for, formal-final causes. Tragedy, he believed, was no exception. There is the form (the imitation of a serious action...), matter (direct speech, dance, spectacle...), and an agent (the good tragedian), also a function (the arousal of certain kinds of pain, especially pity and fear, in order to effect their very pleasurable purgation). Tragedy must therefore be a source of good for mankind. It must be an aid in our pursuit of philosophy, not a hindrance.

Like Plato, Aristotle accepts the need for *pathos* in tragedy: 1452b10. 'It is not tragic,' he says of one possible plot, 'because there is no *pathos*', 1453b39, *ou tragikos, apathes gar*. He also accepts the fact that pity, our initial reaction to a *pathos*, comes from the perception of an injustice, not justice: 1453a4. Although this is an unpleasant perception, he believes (*Rhetoric* 1385b13–14), it does lead to a pleasurable elimination. Plato was wrong to suppose that there was something in even a good man that took pleasure in victimizations; but a painful sight can trigger a reaction which is itself quite pleasurable. There must be an element of injustice, then, because the cleansing cannot be engineered without first rousing pity; hence the need for a *pathos*. Yet there must also be some justice, Aristotle insists.[34] The pleasure from the element of true justice in all good tragedies is in fact the true key. If there is no justice at all there will be no pleasure at all.

Still, Aristotle accepts the traditional place that *pathos* in the old sense had always had in tragedy, and he adds, quite correctly, that perpetrator and victim are usually related by blood in the most famous plays (1453b19–20). The poet (efficient cause), if he is to achieve the pleasurable cleansing of pity and fear (final cause), cannot afford to neglect '*pathē* within the family circle', he says. This is helpful. Such *pathē* touch us all and at the point where our need for self-forgiveness is most acute. Aristotle also observes, correctly again, that the *pathos* need never actually occur; it is sometimes enough if the harm is intended or attempted. But whether the harm is actually carried out or is intended merely, the perpetrator must be ignorant of his or her blood kinship with the other victim. The discovery of their kinship should come later. In the cases where the subject of the *pathos* is really the perpetrator of the terrible act (Oedipus in the parricide, Thyestes eating his young sons, Iphigeneia about to sacrifice her brother) foreknowledge of the blood ties would obviously have turned the distressing event into a mere crime. A Socratic would hardly be expected to accept such a criminal as a person for whom we should feel compassion. The perpetrator–victim must therefore be entirely ignorant of the all-important blood ties as he does the deed. In one passage Aristotle praises as best of all the plot in which the gods step in and prevent actual fulfillment of the polluting deed (1454a4–8). More characteristically he praises plots in which the blood ties are discovered too late to prevent the violation (1453a14–15).

Aristotle's hesitation on this last point may be traced to his impossible desire to reconcile tragedy and Socratism. In plays in which the discovery comes too late, *Oedipus the King*, for instance, the pleasurable elimination of pity and fear is thrilling. The *pathos* is allowed its full force and the play can end in an apparent defeat – a prominent peculiarity of tragedy. But plays in which the gods refuse to permit innocent suffering, as in *Iphigeneia Among the Taurians*, depict a world entirely congenial to a Socratic.

Aristotle insists, however, that, at least in stories in which the *pathos* is carried out in full, the perpetrator–sufferer must not be entirely blameless, however far he may also have been from having had complete knowledge of the circumstances. Indeed, he must be responsible in some large and obvious ways for the consequences of his ignorant act. Otherwise a good Socratic in the audience would feel 'polluted'. (Aristotle uses Plato's word, *miaron*.[35]) This is in fact a major blunder on Aristotle's part, but it is understandable. Once more the explanation is to be found in Aristotle's need to keep Socratism and yet embrace the *pathos* of tragedy as well. The first depends on Divine Justice, the second on Divine Injustice. Pity and *pathos* require injustice; a hero partly responsible for his own downfall, also another virtue of good tragedy, *to philanthrōpon*, 'pleasure in one's kinship with humanity',[36] require justice. It is the idea that the best plays always show heroes acting in such a way that the play will not 'pollute' a Socratic that makes this a blunder, Aristotle's insistence that the sufferer be at least partially responsible for his own catastrophe. The notion does terrible damage to our reading of the plays themselves.

An appreciation of the technical use of the word *pathos*, and of the special phenomenon it denotes, helps us understand what is perhaps the most important of all the ways in which tragedy developed from popular religion. Pleasure in *pathē* is vital to both. There is no doubt that the tragic poets themselves were aware of this special link with religion, and Socrates and Plato were also. Aristotle, on the other hand, approaches this famous idea as a philosophical problem, one to be solved, neatly and without emotion, by fitting it into the grand Aristotelian scheme of things. An intellectual crisis which had lasted more than a century was no longer considered important. Aristotle makes one reference to the function of *pathos* in mystery religion.[37] He accepts it as akin to illumination in philosophy, but makes clear that it is not the highest philosophical illumination. So also in tragedy: the *pathos* has a function, but it needs to be balanced by an awareness of some genuine justice in the events depicted. And the benefit to be expected by the pleasurable 'cleansing' of tragedy is really quite minor, according to Aristotle: potentially troublesome emotions are flushed out so that viewers can get back to more important things, philosophy, for instance.

A sharp awareness of the significance of the *pathos* can help us isolate the features peculiar to the work of each of the three tragedians.

Aeschylus will be seen to want it both ways, like Aristotle. He moves us with traditional *pathē*, those of Iphigeneia, Agamemnon, Cassandra, and so on; but he insists that this kind of religion has been superseded by a rational theology, ever since the famous acquittal of Orestes on the Areopagus. Only in the *Seven Against Thebes* (among the surviving plays) does Aeschylus let the *pathos* work without further explanation.

Sophocles' reputation for orthodoxy and extraordinary favor from divinity, we may suspect, derived from the success with which he produced, by his dramatic *pathē*, emotional responses recognizable from popular piety, especially the hero cults. Only in the *Electra* does he allow intellectual hesitation to complicate the response of the believers.

Euripides constructs memorable dramas out of stark injustices, as Aristotle pointed out. He often chooses victims whose radical innocence is easy to believe. But he regularly permits wit and second thoughts to complicate the solemn enjoyment of the pious in the audience. He sometimes lets the gods explain their reasons for engineering the *pathē* of mortal heroes. Most of their speeches are not calculated to please the pious. The later tradition according to which Euripides and Socrates were good friends is not inherently improbable. Euripides may have set out to undermine literal belief in the old holy stories, just as Socrates was doing.

Armed with our new understanding of *pathos* we should be able to shed new light on certain notoriously ambiguous scenes in the surviving plays.

We will no longer be tempted to sum up Aeschylus' wisdom and his contribution to the debate by the formulas for reciprocal justice (to him who does it shall be done, *pathein*), which the players and dancers in the *Oresteia* sometimes take comfort in, sometimes find ominous or depressing. Nor will we look for it in 'illumination from a *pathos*' (*pathei mathos*), which was guaranteed to men by Zeus, according to the dancers in the *Agamemnon*. First of all, the formula will be seen to mean, not that we learn from our own suffering (a traditional mark of the fool[38]), but that the pious 'learn' from the *pathē* of heroic figures like Iphigeneia. Secondly the formula is not only the subject of agonized doubt on the part of old men themselves, it is also rejected in favor of a new, just covenant at the end of the trilogy.

When the newly self-blinded Oedipus steps forward in Sophocles' play, the dancers, like the dancers in the *Agamemnon*, are troubled by the fact that they do not find the *pathos* merely revolting and horrifying. The *frisson* caused by the sight of their blind king has two components, repulsion and a longing to stare and to 'learn'. But the moral question is quickly cut short. Oedipus insists that he had to put out his eyes; he had no choice. After those two far greater *pathē* engineered by Apollo himself, the parricide and the incest, what other course could he have taken (1329–35, cf. 1369 ff.)?

The philosophers were understandably troubled by this latter scene. Plato identifies the play's plot as a whole as the most shocking and lawless of the archetypical wishes of the lowest part of the psyche (*Republic* 9.571c9). Aristotle, who regularly praises the play as an admirable producer of pleasurable cleansing of the right sort, nevertheless objects to this particular scene. The *frisson* ought to have been produced by the sequence of events, he says, not by a spectacle (1453b1–11). Shocks produced by spectacles are troubling, perhaps, because they seem to be instances of mere suffering; the Socratic in the audience is not given a chance to find an element of justice in the event. It is almost certain that Aristotle was thinking of the spectacle of the newly blinded Oedipus in the passage where he denigrates visual *pathē*, not only because of the mention of this play in the context and by his concentration on *pathos* and *frisson* (*phrikē* in the play, *phrittein* in the *Poetics*), but also because he switches from his usual words for 'pity' and 'fear' to the words used by the messenger and dancers in the *Oedipus* (*oiktron* instead of *eleos*, *deinon* instead of *phobos*.)[39]

As happens in any tradition that invites poets to compete as individuals, the Greek poet often found himself struggling all his life against the power and achievements of his predecessors, or of some one great predecessor. Sophocles tells us that in his case it was Aeschylus. He had to free himself from the bulk and angularity of Aeschylean language, he says (Plutarch, *moralia* 79b–c), ultimately by learning to make a joke of these qualities. He also narrowed his vision from the epic sweep of his predecessor and concentrated on the presentation of simple *pathē*. From justice that must await another generation, as in Aeschylus, Sophocles turned to unexplained, mysterious justice to be felt, but not understood, in every suffering. He was obviously proud of the new direction he had given to tragedy.

In the case of Euripides, the agonizing competition was not with Sophocles, as we might expect, but with Aeschylus once again. Allusions to Sophocles in Euripides' plays are few and problematical; those to Aeschylus are many and famous. But Euripides' quarrel with Aeschylus was quite different from Sophocles' with the same poet. Sophocles had reproduced the traditional *pathē* (with greater enthusiasm for hero religion and less attention to the initiatory cults) but had then just left out the older poet's theological hedging. The *pathē* were allowed to work, unencumbered by any explanations. Euripides, by contrast, attacked the Aeschylean explanations head on. He made the gods explain themselves, as Aeschylus had, but in deliberately unsatisfactory ways, for the most part.

Aeschylus said that he served up mere fish slices from Homer's great banquet (Athenaeus 8.347e). There are in fact a number of different ways in which he is obviously in debt to Homer. None is more important, however, than his adoption of Homer's attitude toward the traditional holy stories. Both poets (or all three if the *Iliad* and *Odyssey* were shaped by different master poets) assume that deep wisdom can be found in these much loved stories, but that it can be revealed clearly only if one suppresses false tales and erroneous versions, then uses one's own intelligence and genius to recreate the truth. Euripides, by contrast, characteristically chooses a particularly grotesque version of the story he is exploiting, one that would have been rejected by Homer or Aeschylus.[40] He then shows his gods and heroes bravely trying to explain away the absurdities. He does not hesitate to show the most august of the gods behaving naively or sophistically. This must have been felt by many as a subversive program. Yet Euripides also had an enthusiastic following. His sharp, intellectual clarity about the *pathos* seems to have contributed to his dramatic power. As Aristotle said, he was, for all his failings, the most truly tragic of the three dramatists (1453a30).

In the post-classical centuries the 'ancient quarrel' reverted to the form it took in Solon and Aeschylus: what are we to make of the well-attested Wrath of God?[41] This has obscured the urgency of the question for secular philosophers. And among the theologians themselves the controversy has been hopelessly complicated by the peculiar honor the Biblical religions have accorded to their holy stories as written texts. Modern theologians accept one of Plato's demands but reject the other. They assume he is right when he insists that divinity is always just, toward every individual as well as toward mankind and the universe; but they refuse to pick and choose among their holy stories and keep only those that manifestly prove what they assume to be true about God. They start with the assumption that all of the holy stories are true in one sense or another.

A recovery of the ancients' clarity about the *pathos* might well bring more clarity to some of our own disputes about the nature and function of tragedy. There are, in particular, two current controversies that might be raised to a higher level if we won a sharper understanding of the ancient debate. One is a large problem that will surely never be completely settled; the other is a specific dispute that might even cease to be seen as a crisis once the Greeks' perspicacity is made our own again.

The general dispute, which engages different critics in different ways, is over the ambition, current since Aristotle, to find a wholly satisfactory explanation for tragedy within the framework of rational behavior. We should start, I think, with Plato's insistence that rationality is one thing and the appeal of tragedy something entirely different, that the 'ancient quarrel', in other words, is a permanent state of affairs. What we want is, not a way to reconcile tragedy and rationality, which is impossible, but a psychological explanation of the counter-rational pleasure we get from tragedy. We should accept the reasoning behind Plato's objections to pleasure induced by a *pathos*, therefore, but then add to his analysis more recent discoveries concerning the sources of life-poisoning guilt and the activities men indulge in to modify such guilt. The result will be a vindication of tragedy, though it will seem like a satisfactory vindication only to those who are already its partisans.

The specific dispute concerns the function of violence in literature and in popular fiction. If the ancients prove to have been right – that the thrill of the *pathos* is vital, not only to many deeply cherished religious dramas, but also to many of our most admired literary stories – then we would do well to distinguish sharply between violence told or shown in such a way as to elicit sympathy only for the victims, true *pathē*, and violence that is depicted with sympathy only for the perpetrators, the staple of popular films and television.[42] The investigation of the possible evil effects of violence could then concentrate on the latter formula, fully justified brutality. We will be able to follow the evidence wherever it leads us, in the secure knowledge that damaging conclusions would nevertheless permit us still to keep our Homer, Sophocles, and all true tragedians down through the centuries.

NOTES

1 The word's meaning in all modern languages was influenced by Longinus' unhistorical understanding of Aristotle's contrast (1459b13–16) between the *Odyssey*, which he describes as *ēthikē*, a story of 'character', and the *Iliad*, which he describes as *pathētikon*, full of *pathē*: *On the Sublime* 9.15. The adjective *ēthikē* was assumed by Longinus to characterize a story that had serene revelations of unchanging principles (cf. Aristotle 1450a25–9 and 1448a1–7), so *pathētikon* carried overtones of the particular, transient, and subjective, as well as of the highly emotional – none of which was intended by Aristotle. Longinus nevertheless attributes to a vehement and god-inspired *pathos* the power to lend sublimity to a story (8.1). *Pathos* could therefore be used in either a bad or a good sense. In English the good sense was given a decisive boost by Pope's heavy-handed travesty of Longinus, *Peri Bathous, the Art of Sinking in Poetry* (1727), in which he contrasted *pathos* with *bathos* ('depth'). The latter term, never used by the ancients for a literary quality, was defined by Pope, quite arbitrarily, as a ludicrous collapse of dignity. Thus 'pathos' is almost always a good thing in English, whereas in French, for instance, the same word means roughly what Pope meant by 'bathos'. Yet *le pathétique* can do duty for the English 'pathos' and English 'pathetic' is often equivalent to the French *pathos*.
2 *Republic* 10.607b5 and c3. Plato supports his assertion that the 'quarrel' is 'ancient' by quoting abuses aimed by un-named poets at philosophers. From *Laws* 12.967c7–d1 we gather that the philosophers' materialistic astronomy was the chief reason for the poets' hostility. From the larger context of the argument in *Republic* x, however, we may define 'poetry' as the enterprise of those who wish to move hearers with accounts of *pathē*, and 'philosophy' as the mission of those who are hostile to this enterprise.
3 E.g. 2 Corinthians 1:5. The plural is preferred to the singular, but see Hebrews 2:9. *Pathēma* was preferable to *pathos*, since the latter now usually meant violent emotion (e.g. at Colossians 3:5), but both forms were known to be from *paschein*. Some learned Alexandrines speculated that *pascha* was also from *paschein*. See N. R. M. de Lange, *Origin and the Jews* (Cambridge University Press, 1967), pp. 94f. (*Pascha* is actually a garbled Hellenization of *pesach*, 'Passover'.)
4 The earliest of the very few occurrences of *passio* in Pagan literature is in Varro, fr. 60 Goetz Schoell, where it means 'passion' in the sense of 'emotion'. In the Vulgate *passiones Christi* translates *pathēmata tou Christou* (2 Corinthians 1:5), *passibilis* translates *pathētos* (Acts 26:23), and so on.
5 As the doors are about to open on the newly blinded Oedipus, the messenger says

(line 1295) that the dancers will now see a spectacle (*theama*) which even those who hate will pity – meaning, not those who hate Oedipus, of course (all present love their king), but those who hate the terrible sight. The dancers respond by singing, 'Fearful *pathos* for men to look at!' They then expand on the messenger's assertion of the double nature of this *pathos*. The shudder (line 1306) may be an element of the fascinating side of the experience, not of the abhorrent side only.

6 Lines 176–83. I take the *pou* at line 184 as an interrogative. See Maurice Pope, *Journal of the Historical Society*, 94 (1974), 100ff.

7 Pierre Chantraine, *Dictionnaire etymologique de la langue Grèque, Histoire des mots* (Paris 1968) s.v. *pascho*.

8 The *peisetai* at *Odyssey* 7.197 is sometimes understood in a neutral sense, but cf. *Iliad* 20.127, which suggests that a grim interpretation is probably right in *Odyssey* 7 also. In the *Theogony*, *hossa pathontes* at line 651 and *anaelpta pathontes* at line 660 have sometimes been interpreted in a good sense. See M. L. West on both lines. But the usual Homeric usage makes perfectly good sense in both passages. Hesiod fr. 198 (West) sounds like a neutral formula: if what is done to a man (*ei ke pathoi*) is what he himself did, there will be true justice; but the preceding line says, if a man sows evil he will harvest evil. *Pathoi* therefore surely means 'suffers'.

9 Hesiod fr. 198 (West). See previous note.

10 Solon 24.4 = Theognidea 722.

11 *Pathos* as emotion appears at Democritus B31, but the text is uncertain; also at Thucydides 3.84.1, although the authenticity of the passage is disputed. Cf. *pathēma* at Gorgias B11.9 and at Xenophon, *Cyr.* 3.1.17. Otherwise the evidence points to a Platonic origin for this use of *pathos*. The idea that rage, sex, etc. are afflictions from without is, of course, common in Greek poetry from the *Iliad* on. At *Phaedrus* 265b6 *to erōtikon pathos* is half way between 'affliction' and 'emotion'. In Aristotle 'affection' is often the appropriate translation, e.g. *de an.* 402a9, 403a3, *Nicomachean Ethics* 1109b30; yet 'affliction' is often also implied, e.g. *Poetics* 1455a31–32 and *Rhetoric* 1378a20.

12 See especially the four definitions of *pathos* in *Metaphysics* Delta, 1022b15–21. The first two are developed from *paschein* as one of the Categories. The third, however, is regrettable alterations, especially very painful ones, and the fourth is misfortunes and pains of exceptional magnitude: *eti ta megethē tōn symphorōn kai lypērōn pathē legetai*. Alex. Aphr. omits *kai lypērōn*, so Jaeger brackets these words; Ross, however, accepts them. One of the best MSS has *hēdeōn* instead of *lypērōn*, which Jaeger thinks may preserve a variant tradition, *symphorōn hēdeōn kai lypērōn*, but that presumably resulted from puzzlement experienced by a generation which really had forgotten the technical use of *pathos*.

13 See especially *Republic* 2.380a5, discussed below.

14 E. Frisch, *Homerische Wortbildung und Flexion* (Berlin 1974), lists words with the same metrical form as *pathos*, pp. 84–7.

15 *Pathein* is attached to Odysseus in several formulas, first in the invocation (1.4), then many times thereafter, in the mouth of Odysseus himself and as observed by others, both mortals and gods. Only Poseidon implies that the hero's suffering was richly deserved (5.377).

16 Walter Burkert, *Ancient Mystery Cults* (Cambridge, Mass.: Harvard University

Press, 1987), p. 156 n. 46, lists occurrences in Diodorus, Dionysius of Halicarnas-
sus, and Plutarch (three times). To this list should be added Aristotle, *De Phil.* fr.
15 (Ross), mentioned briefly by Burkert, p. 891 and p. 153 n. 13, also Pausanias
8.37.5 (the *pathēmata* of Dionysus), Athenagoras, *Legatio* 32.1, the 'Orphic Gold
Leaves' A4 (Zuntz), and possibly many more. Burkert (pp. 75–6) warns, quite
sensibly, against the Frazarian belief in a single pattern to be found in all stories
of 'suffering' (and sometimes 'resurrected') gods. In *Greek Religion*, tr. John
Raffan (Cambridge, Mass.: Harvard University Press, 1985), pp. 260–4, he
describes the power of initiatory religions without reference to sympathy for the
gods' suffering; but see p. 277 of the same book.

17 See A. W. Pickard-Cambridge, *Dithyramb, Tragedy, and Comedy* 2nd edn, revised
by T. B. L. Webster (Oxford University Press, 1962), pp. 101–7, Albin Lesky,
Die tragische Dichtung der Hellenen (Göttingen, 1972), p. 43, Ettore Cingano,
'Clistene di Sicione, Erodoto e i poemi del ciclo tebano', *Quaderni Urbinati di
Cultura Classica*, 20.2 (1985), 31–40, and Emily Vermeule, 'Baby Aigisthos and
the Bronze Age', *Proceedings of the Cambridge Philological Society*, NS 33 (1987),
122–52.

18 Some tragedies climax or end with what looks like a formula, e.g. *PV* 1093,
eshorāis m' hōs ekdika paschō and *Antigone* 940–2, *leussete ... hoia ... paschō*. Older
writers, e.g. Carl Robert, *Oidipus* (Berlin, 1915), vol. 1, p. 142, occasionally went
too far in equating the role of a hero's suffering with that of a god's, but that is still
preferable to the more recent habit of interpreting Adrastus' *pathea* as his
'experiences' rather than his calamities, e.g. J. A. Davidson, *From Archilochus to
Pindar* (London 1968), pp. 5–68.

19 7 Nem. 20–1. Pindar complains that 'for myself I hold that Odysseus' reputation
(*logos*) exceeds his *patha*.' As Kirkwood notes in his commentary, the *patha* is not
the contest with Ajax for Achilles' armor, but the years of suffering described in
the *Odyssey*. Pindar may have felt that it was an irritating paradox for Homer to
emphasize the great victimizations (*polla pathōn ...*) of the one hero who was
eventually given a rousing fulfillment of all his desires. Odysseus was in any case,
as Pindar notes, famous for using language, not to tell the truth, but to achieve
his own ends at any cost. Pindar contrasts him with Ajax, who, because he acted
without recourse to clever language, suffered a genuine *pathos*, one which ought
to earn him even more veneration than he has received.

20 Paul and Timothy (Philippians 3:10) use the arresting phrase *koinōnia pathēmatōn
autou*, translated in the Vulgate as *societas passionum illius*.

21 The pious in post-classical times usually assume (1) ultimately God causes
everything that happens, (2) *pathē* do in fact occur, yet (3) God causes only good.
Only step 3 is Platonic. Cf. John Paul II in his letter to the National Conference
of Catholic Bishops in America: 'With our hearts filled with this unyielding hope,
we Christians approach with fearsome respect the terrifying experience of the
extermination, the *Shoah*, suffered by the Jews during the Second World War,
and we seek to grasp its most authentic, specific and universal meaning'
(released to the press 18 August 1987). On 25 July 1988 the Pope called the
extermination of the Jews (and others) 'a gift to the world'. He did not explain.

22 See *Iliad* 4.1–27, *Odyssey* 1.32, ff. The exoneration of the gods in the *Odyssey* is not
quite sweeping: what Zeus complains of is that mortals blame all their miseries

on the gods even though, because of their own reckless insolence, they suffer more than is alloted to them. Odysseus is offered as a counter-example: a god has made him suffer far more than he deserves. Zeus is reassuring: Odysseus will now, at long last, get all the good he so richly deserves. This series of speeches reads like a complaint against the poet of the *Iliad*. See Wolfgang Kullmann, 'Gods and Men in the *Iliad* and *Odyssey*', *Harvard Studies in Classical Philology*, 89 (1985), 1–23, esp. pp. 5–6 and note 11, for the current state of thinking on the separate authorship of the two poems.

23 Fr. 13 (West) 25–42: sometimes 'people who are not responsible pay, / either their children or a still later generation.'

24 A thing is not holy because divinity approves of it, says Socrates: divinity approves because it is holy. One cannot infer the will of the gods from the traditional holy stories, therefore, in the manner of fundamentalists like Euthyphro; the authority of the story must first be established – by demonstrating that it implies a known truth about the will of divinity. At 6a–c Plato has Socrates say that his difference with other Athenians on this point is the essence of the charge against him.

25 E.g. *Apol.* 41c–d. Plato's fullest statement of this very basic Socratic idea is found at *Theaetetus* 176a–177a.

26 At *Apol.* 41b Socrates looks forward to meeting Palamedes and Ajax in Hades, 'or if there's anyone else who lost his life as a consequence of an unjust judgement': what a joy it might be, he says, to compare his own *pathē* with theirs! *Pathē* cannot mean 'suffering', because Socrates, at least, has not and will not suffer. It could mean 'experiences'; but the phrase to lose one's life as a consequence of an unjust judgement seems to define *pathos* here, and that meaning clearly fits the most common usage in the heroic stories as told by the tragedians.

27 380a5–7. Readers dependent on translations can hardly be blamed for failing to see what Plato is saying here. Not only is there no single word in any modern language that instantly communicates the sense of *pathē*, translators regularly feel compelled for stylistic reasons to vary the word from example to example. (For once Allan Bloom's notion of 'literal' translation stands him in good stead.) The passage following this list of examples (380a7–c3) offers, by implication, a full definition of *pathos* in epics and tragedies as Plato understood the term: *pathē* are god-caused catastrophes that are neither deserved nor therapeutic.

28 The third category of bad dreams, 'refraining from no food', has puzzled readers, ancient and modern, because it seems to fit ill with incest and pollution-causing murder. If it refers to Thyestes unknowingly eating his own sons, however, it is indeed a dream of the same order as the other two.

29 This is an interpretation, not a simple report, of what Plato says in *Republic* 10.605e–606b. (a) The lowest part of the psyche, which is the part gratified by tragedy, by its nature desires to weep and gets its pleasure this way. (b) It is ostensibly reacting to the *pathē* of other people (*allotria pathē*, 606b1), namely those of the sufferers in the tragic story. In fact, however, pleasure in other people's *pathē* stimulates pleasure in one's own *pathē* – if one's own *pathē* were not indeed the real source of pleasure from the beginning. Therefore (c) it is the nature of the lowest part of the psyche to take pleasure in the idea that we ourselves are all victims of *pathē* – an un-Socratic, even an anti-Socratic idea.

30 *Memories, Dreams, Reflections,* trans. and ed. Aiela Jaffe (US edition, New York, 1965), ch. 2. When Jung first realized that he was a victim of God's incomprehensible cruelty ('I understood religion as something God did to me'), he 'wept for happiness and gratitude'.

31 Freud's developed theory can be found, for instance, in 'Dissection of the Psychical Personality', lecture 31 in *New Introductory Lectures on Psychoanalysis.* The function of the super-ego as censor can be found in Plato's analogy with the white horse in the *Phaedrus.* Its function as preserver of traditional social virtues can be seen in *Republic* 9.590c–591a.

32 *Civilization and its Discontents,* ch. 4.

33 Down through the centuries there has been much speculation concerning this voice. See L.-F. Lélut, *Du démon de Socrate, spécimen d'une application de la science psychologique à celle de l'histoire* (Paris 1836). There are theories in Plutarch (*de genio Socratis*), Descartes (letter to Princess Elizabeth, Nov. 1646), Voltaire (*Poème sur la loi naturelle,* 1752), Nietzsche (*Das Problem des Sokrates,* 1888), and in many other writings. The idea that it is an abnormally strong 'conscience' has recurred in several guises.

34 We may conclude this from the fact that Aristotle rejected as polluted and therefore polluting the plot that has no reassuring justice at all: the story of the fall into wretchedness of a thoroughly deserving person. (On the word *miaron,* 'polluting', 1452b36, see the next note.)

35 1452b36. Since Aristotle uses this word nowhere except here, in *Poetics* ch. 13 and 14, and since Plato uses it often (in a serious, semi-literal sense, not as a general insult as in comedy and oratory) we should probably assume that Aristotle has a Platonic discussion in mind. In passages like *Republic* 9.589e4 and 621c2, for instance, 'polluted' means corrupt as opposed to being enlightened by Socratic truth. Aristotle's usage in ch. 13 and 14, however, is also obviously influenced by the very common literal usage in tragedy. In any case, the word cannot reasonably be supposed to mean merely 'upsetting'.

36 E.g. at 1452b38. Liddell–Scott–Jones ('LSJ'), *Greek–English Lexicon,* 9th edn (Oxford University Press, 1940) defines it as *'appealing to human feelings',* then adds, '(less prob. *satisfying the sense of poetic justice)'.* But at 1453a3, for instance, Aristotle says that the story of the fall of an abominable person does at least have *to philanthrōpon.* The term would therefore seem to mean satisfaction at proof of Socratic truth, the meaning tentatively rejected by LSJ. On the other hand, as John Moles observes, *'Philanthropia* in the Poetics', *Phoenix,* 38 (1984), 328, 'poetic justice' usually implies that the suffering is 'particularly fitting'. This is not an essential feature of Aristotle's *philanthrōpon.*

37 Fr. 15 (Ross) of 'On Philosophy'.

38 *Works and Days* 218: 'a fool understands only after he has first suffered the consequences of his former ignorance.' See H. Doerrie, *Leid und Erfahrung: die Wort- und Sinn-Verbindung pathein-mathein* (Wiesbaden, 1956), p. 13.

39 Aristotle speaks of being affected (*haper an pathoi tis*) by 'hearing' (*akouōn*) the *mythos* of Oedipus: on *akouein* meaning reading (aloud) see G. C. Hendrikson, 'Ancient Reading', *Classical Journal,* 25 (1929–30), 182–90. Aristotle says that a thrill caused by a spectacle is dependent on the arts of productions, not on poetic

composition; but these arts are also the responsibility, after all, of the poet: directions, costume and mask making, etc.

40 Compare, for example, the story of the Python in *Eumenides* 5 and in the *I T*, 1244ff.

41 See, for instance, Lactantius, *De ira dei* (c. AD 314), although the controversy was already old by then. For an overview of current thought see *The Interpreter's Dictionary of the Bible* (Nashville, 1962), 'Wrath of God', 903ff., bibl. 908.

42 The plot preferred by the Greeks, in which the perpetrator is the real victim, hardly exists today. The stories of Othello and Macbeth may come to mind; but these sufferers are not kept in total darkness and there are other candidates for 'the perpetrators'.

Drama and Aristotle*

VICTOR CASTELLANI

Theatre and dramatic literature significantly influenced Aristotle's philosophy. Werner Jaeger and Eric Havelock have clarified the literary or, more precisely, the *poetic* culture during the earlier centuries of Hellenic civilization after the post-Mycenaean Dark Age.[1] Values and habits of thought from their epic myths guided, even determined Greeks' behavior and thinking to 500 BC and far beyond. Not only did the fifth-century playwrights and other intellectuals belong to this culture, participate in it, and reshape it, but so did the philosophers and rhetoricians of the earlier 300s BC. By the time of Aristotle's prime (the middle decades of the fourth century) Homer, Hesiod, and the early lyric poets had not left the scene, yet three new trends of culture had come to the fore, which Jaeger identifies as bourgeois realism, rhetoric, and philosophy. The first of these redirected the development of drama profoundly, with the result that relatively serious 'Middle' and 'New' Comedy arose; the other two, rhetoric and philosophy, affected poetry, dramatic and otherwise, even more profoundly – in the view of some, all but killing it.[2] It is a commonplace that poetry influenced other modes of thought and expression during their beginnings, then they, once evolved some distance, cast irresistible influence back upon poetry. In the *Poetics* of Aristotle and the *Characters* of his disciple Theophrastus intellectual historians find only the most self-conscious examples of philosophers *telling* playwrights *what* to treat and even *how* to go about it.[3] A well-founded conjecture is that, unless, like Plato, they rejected existing poetry almost entirely, other philosophers, too, were advising poets (and may have held their attention more closely than the Peripatetics appear to have done). What seems *not* to have been appreciated, on the other hand, is how in one very important case, that of the same Aristotle, the 'new' poetry in and of the theatre directly and fruitfully influenced a leading thinker. Euripides, quite properly treated at *Themes in Drama*'s 'Philosophy and Drama' conferences in his own right, and the fourth-century comedians,

* Drafts of this paper were read at Brigham Young University in November 1987 and at the *Themes in Drama* International Conference, held at the University of California, Riverside, in February 1988.

themselves more or less philosophical, thus made their mark upon philosophy. The nature and consequence of this counter-counterinfluence upon Aristotle's work in human and social studies – that is, in his *Nicomachean Ethics*, *Politics*, and *Rhetoric* – are the subject of this study.[4] It will also touch upon the neglected question of why Aristotle should have undertaken the research, contemplation, and composition of a dramatological 'poetics' at all in the midst of his work on much more general moral–practical matters.

At the outset it ought to be established that his extensive reading of plays, with many attentive and receptive hours watching them, did indeed give Aristotle more than mere matter for decorative allusion or for incidental illustration in his treatises on interpersonal behavior. Allusions there are, to be sure, in abundance, and they show us important things about The Philosopher and what he was reading. These will be treated below. For the present it is essential to understand that what he read in the dramatic texts he knew so well, what he saw – and felt – in the contemporary theatre he so thoroughly enjoyed, furnished him with data about human action and passion (and their causes) upon which he relied in posing questions and in answering them, in finding, analyzing, and solving basic problems of the good life, society, and communication. These data fall into two categories that it is convenient to distinguish: human motivation and human typology. Let us consider motivation first.

Aristotle's view that thinking-through (what he called διάνοια) and choosing (προαίρεσις), the causes of action, are indispensable indications of ἦθος, character, in drama is well known; so is his prescription that a tragic protagonist ought to suffer not because of moral viciousness but rather because of a mistake or mistakenness (ἁμαρτία).[5] Well known, too, is his program of emotional purificaiton, involving above all the emotions pity and fear. *All* of these notions, which appear to have occurred to him from his study and experience of drama, play major roles in the *Ethics* and *Politics*, works that internal evidence indicates to have preceded the *Poetics*.[6]

When discussing moral action in the third book, second chapter of the *Ethics* (111b5–1112a17) he carefully distinguishes between the 'choosing' that reveals moral character and, on the one hand, passion that can also lead to action, and, on the other hand, opinion or personal judgment (δόξα) that may be helpless to control our actions. Through passion, therefore, or through viciousness we may do something bad even though in some sense we should and do 'know' better. This possibility, which contradicts the Socratic–Platonic optimism about knowledge and behavior, is nothing other than the mechanism of Euripidean tragedy and of those morally earnest sorts of fourth-century comedy whose spiritual father Euripides was. *Video meliora proboque*, 'I see and find good the better course', *deteriora sequor*, 'I follow the worse': the speaker is Ovid's Medea (*Metamorphosis* VII, 20–1), yet the sentiment is that of hero after hero in

Euripides, of heroine after heroine (his Medea and Phaedra, for example, say much the same thing), and of conscience-ridden young men without number in Greek Middle and New Comedy – Aristotle's contemporary comedy – and in Roman imitations. The 'facts' of these dramatic characters' unedifying performance appear to have made a deep and decisive impression upon Aristotle.[7]

Aristotle, moreover, treated both emotions and more rational (though often *speciously* rational) motives for action in ways that strongly suggest his acquaintance with them through other literature, yet above all through plays, whether seen in the Theatre of Dionysus or read in the Lyceum or during his sojourn in northern Greece. His concern with good intentions that lead to disastrous deeds and events, particularly when these result from mistakes, with sensational crimes against kin, and, in his *Politics*, with the (historically obsolescent) figure of the tyrant can more easily be explained from his books than from his biography; while his incidental statements in *Nicomachean Ethics* VII, 3 (1147a22–4) about how the stronger emotions produce striking physiological changes *and that incontinent people should be regarded like actors* (evidently because they are not 'themselves') may indicate that he learned about these moral phenomena in the theatre, *through* actors, more impressively than elsewhere or otherwise. When he discusses civic education near the end of the *Politics* (VIII, 7 [1341b32– 1342b34]), he calls for a general application of music that corresponds closely to the moralizing catharsis by tragedy, at least, and possibly also by comedy such as he will go on to prescribe in *Poetics*.[8] In fact, he refers his reader explicitly (1341b39–40) to a more thorough discussion of catharsis that he promises in that other, soon forthcoming work. Furthermore, we find similar concerns in (probably) his last 'political' work, the *Rhetoric*, which he evidently composed in its existing form after *Poetics*. As our moral judgment of a basically 'good' and sympathetic dramatic character should not be determined by his mistake, so, Aristotle now advises us, in equity and its adjudication, the 'errors' (ἁμαρτήματα) of a real person must not be confounded with crimes that would condemn him by our indignant votes (*Rhetoric* II, 13 (1374b4–9; cf. 1372b16–18 in chapter 12]). Moreover, in his discussion of the rhetorical function ὑπόκρισις early in Book III (1403b15– 1404a18), Aristotle points out how this activity, which here must be translated 'delivery' or the like *but which is also the proper word for an actor's in-character utterance*, can arouse desirable emotions, pity above all, in a courtroom. He observes, in fact, that epic reciters (rhapsodes) and tragedians have naturally and perforce developed this skill.

Dramatic literature, then, was never far from Aristotle's thoughts, nor the stage from his imagination, as he reviewed the nature and quality of what men do, by decision or by passion.

From motivation we must now move to human *types*. Persons Aristotle

presents as typical in feeling and act because of their age, or their social
standing, or simply because they are recognizably one sort of person rather
than another are an important device of Aristotle's ethical exposition in all
three of the non-'poetical' works here under discussion, above all in his
Ethics. These types are the aspect of his systematic ethical work to which the
drama of his own day is most obviously related. Indeed, several of the moral
types he describes, placing them at one extreme or the other from his
median virtues, are comic stock characters familiar to anyone who is
acquainted with post-Aristophanic comedy at Athens.[9] Needless to say, the
'types' go beyond comedy, to include ethnic classes (like the luxurious
women of Sparta) and individual roles (for example, the tyrant) that
Aristotle would have encountered in tragedy (Spartan women in Euripides'
Andromache [594–601], tyrants notably in Euripides' *Suppliants*, *Heracles*, and
Phoenician Women). Most, however, are from recent or contemporary *comedy*.

Book IV of the *Ethics* is uniquely rich in these, though they may be found
in Books II, III, and VIII. Different from these, yet on the same level of
generalization, are 'the young', 'the old', and 'slaves' as classes (which
Aristotle also treats, though at less length and with fewer circumstantial
comments, in *Politics* and *Rhetoric*) and also, though even less important,
'women'. His numerous type names and the circumstantial details of
behavior he provides for many of his types go well beyond what he needs for
his demonstration about moral excesses and deficiencies, echo Middle and
New (and Roman) comic character and scenario, and receive, from
Aristotle himself, the designation 'silly' (μάταιος or, more often,
ἠλίθιος). A few, for example pimps and usurers (both cited as glaring
embodiments of αἰσχροκέρδεια, 'shameful profit-making' at 1121b31–
1122a3 in *Nicomachean Ethics* IV, 1), are stock minor roles in the later comedy.
Others seem to defy his efforts to explain their behavior rather than, with
amusement, simply to describe it.

In the latter category is the unseemly bashful and abashed *old man*, whose
improbability Aristotle notes (since only the young are supposed to be
bashful), but whom students of Roman comedy will recognize instantly – in
the Chremes of Terence's *Phormio* for instance (whose model, however, is
third-century). And at least one person, a certain memorable gourmand
(ὀψόφαγος, literally 'sauce-eater') whom the philosopher describes in
Book III of the *Ethics*, may be a specific comic character from a specific,
though unknown, comic play. Some manuscripts of *Nicomachean Ethics* give,
to the epicure who prayed that his throat might exceed a crane's in length to
increase his gustatory delight, a personal name that is surely comical:
Philoxenos Eruxios, 'Loving-guest son of Belch' (*Nicomachean Ethics*
1118a32–b1).[10] Conceivably we have here an historical *parasite*, like
Plautus' memorable Artotrogos, 'Bread-muncher', of the *Miles Gloriosus*, or
else just a Gargantuan slob; yet, whatever he was in precise character, his

vividness owes not just to awareness that gluttons exist (or, in Aristotle's own language, that 'belly-crazies' do: γαστϱίμαϱγοι, III, 11 [1118b19], itself an amusing compound that goes back to Pindar's lyric) but owes also, and much more, to Old and/or Middle Comedy's caricature of a fifth-century Athenian whom history would otherwise have soon forgotten, but whom a Stagirite drama-lover remembered.

Let us enumerate the more striking (and single out the most obviously *comical*) of these pre-Aristotelian types in Aristotle. In the seminal seventh chapter of *Ethics* Book II, when he is just beginning his long and famous disquisition on extremes-means-and-deficiencies, Aristotle introduces (one might almost say, 'brings onto the scene') the Buffoon, the Boor, the Obsequious Man, the Flatterer, the Grouch, the Nervous Wreck, and the Gloater (1108a23–b6). Every one of these personages is significantly connected with comedy. 'Buffoon' in Aristotle's Greek is βωμολόχος, a word whose slang sense 'ribald, coarse-humored' originates, it seems, with Aristophanes; the earliest appearances of the Greek word for 'boor' or 'rustic' (ἄγϱοικος) are in Aristophanes' *Acharnians* and *Clouds*; *The Flatterer* (Κόλαξ) was the name of more than one known comedy; *The Grouch* (Δύσκολος), of course, is the title of a surviving play by Aristotle's young contemporary Menander (though this play was not produced during the philosopher's lifetime); the word translated 'nervous wreck' above (κατάπληξ) is first attested in the fifth-century comedian Theopompus; and one of his fourth-century successors, Anaxandrides or Alexis, seems to have been first to use the epithet 'gloater' (more literally 'rejoicer-over-evil', in Greek ἐπιχαιϱέκακος).[11] Of these, Boor and Grouch will return for important development and refinement later in the *Ethics*, as we shall see presently, while Flatterer will play a notable supporting role in the *Politics* (where he is the 'friend' of tyrants and tyrannical democracies at IV, 4 [1292a17–12] and V, 9 [1313b39–a4]) and in the *Rhetoric* as well (II, 6 [1383b30–33]).

As already stated, *Ethics* IV is rich in this matter, almost a theatre archive in fact. Buffoon, Boor, Flatterer, Obsequious, and Grouch all reappear, here, as classes of persons, in plural numbers.

Buffoons are opposed at one extreme to Boors at the other (chapter 8, 1128a4–9), and the two types receive the further sobriquets 'vulgar' (φοϱτικοί) and 'gruff' (σκληϱοί), respectively. Flatterers encore as a drain on the resources of Prodigals (chapter 1, 1121b5–7), a complementary pairing we know well from New Comedy, and are mentioned yet again later, with Grouches and Obsequious (chapter 6, 1127a8–11). Grouches return twice, first as opposite to the Obsequious in the passage just cited, then in Book VIII's delightful discussion of 'grim and elderly' men, στϱυφνοί and πϱεσβυτικοί (1158a1–3 in VIII, 6) – two words, yet again, that we find first in Aristophanes. Old men, in fact, with various shadings of 'meanness' or 'illiberality' provide several amusing subtypes, with names in apparent slang, at *Nicomachean Ethics* IV, I (1121b21–28): 'Stinters' (φειφωλοί, a word found only once, and not of a person, before the Old Comedy writers Aristophanes and Eupolis), 'Clingers' (γλίσχϱοι, earliest applications with this sense in Aristophanes and his younger colleague Euphron), 'Niggards' (κίμβικες, not attested in Comedy), and, last but hardly least, the 'Cuminseed-slicer' (κυμινοπϱίστης, which is plausibly explained as Aristotle's abridgment of the splendid formation 'cuminseed-slicer cress-dicer', κυμινοπϱιστοκαϱδαμογλύφος from Aristophanes' *Wasps*, where its accusative form makes up most of line 1357).

Aristotle also has uncomplimentary thoughts about *young* men, though nothing age-typical about them appears for quite some time after his very first stereotypic remark in *Nicomachean Ethics* I, 3, where he announces that the young in years *or in character* (this looks like reference to aging playboys from the comic stage) live according to each and every successive emotion (1095a2–9). Finally at Book VIII, chapter 3, however, we read the following account of young friends and lovers: 'The friendliness of the young seems to be because of pleasure, for they live according to emotion and pursue above all what is pleasing and present to themselves. When age changes, what pleases also becomes different. Therefore they quickly become, quickly cease to be friends; for with the pleasant moment the friendship passes away – and quick is the change of the pleasure. And the young are amorous (ἐϱωτικοί), for according to emotion and for the sake of pleasure occurs most of a love-affair. Therefore they love quickly and quickly stop, often changing within the same day' (1156a31–b4). An intended literary description of the typical 'young man' in New Comedy could hardly be more acute, describing as this does his volatile feelings both toward his girl-friend herself and toward his usual allies in pursuing her (clever slave, parasite, complaisant neighbor, et al.).

Several comic character types are, of course, independent of age, like Boor and some others we already met in Aristotle. There are, in fact, too many for me to treat them all here. But those who exceed or come short of the mean in fierceness, in anger, and in veracity are worth noting, especially as the philosopher develops their portraits far beyond the strict requirements of his program. The Coward who falls short of proper fierceness is potentially funny (and is the subject of many a comedy), but funnier by far is his opposite, whom Aristotle in *Nicomachean Ethics* III, 7 (1115b29–33) calls ἀλάζων and whom, with thanks to Plautus, we may call 'Gloriosus'. He is also noted in the *Rhetoric* (III, 6 at 1384a4–6). Yet such fellows are not truly over-fierce, as they *should* be to fit Aristotle's alleged pattern of vice-as-excess, since they prove to be all bluster, no stuffing, when a danger actually appears – 'bold-craven' (θϱασύδειλοι) as Aristotle calls them, apparently minting a compound of his own. But they *are* comic.

The ἀλάζων, in fact, is also, and famously, opposed to the εἴρων, in *Nicomachean Ethics* IV, where we may name the two respectively Boaster and Dissembler (chapter 7, beginning at 1127a20–3). Persons belonging to a subtype of the latter type are among the most amusing of all Aristotle's moral examples, though these, too, go beyond what he really needs to demonstrate: ones whom he terms, by his own coinage again, βαυκοπανοῦργοι, 'humbugs' or, more literally, 'prude-rogues' (1127b26–7), the first element of whose compound name is found by itself only in the early-fourth-century comedian Araros. Aristotle preonounces them 'more contemptible' than other ironists and dissemblers, since they insufferably disclaim trivial and/or obvious attainments.

Concerning the deficient and the excessive in anger, we find Aristotle hard-pressed to name the former at all, whom he nevertheless deems 'foolish' (*Nicomachean Ethics* IV, 5 [1126a4–6]) *and whom we may recognize as a comic type,* the complaisant neighbor or even, like Kallippides in Menander's *Dyskolos,* the complaisant *father* in New and Roman comedies. The excessively angry, on the other hand, prompt him to offer at 1126a13–28 a catalogue of subtypes matched in variety only by that of the illiberal: 'Irascible' (ὀργίλοι, a plain word in general use), 'High-bilious' (ἀκρόχολοι, Aristophanic), 'Bitter' (πικροί, general usage), and 'Difficult' or 'Stern' (χαλεποί, very common usage). These are not, of course, exceptionally laughable in themselves; but they lead the philosopher directly into a striking and acute observation about praise (IV,5 [1126a35–b2]), a matter to which Aristotle returns in Book I of the *Rhetoric* (chapter 9, 1367a36–b3), and the method of Flatterer, Obsequious, and their ilk, developed spectacularly by the most brilliant of comic characters, the clever slaves and the parasites. The method is simply this: to find a complimentary description for a (mildly) vicious person. The advice on how to 'praise' in that *Rhetoric* I passage is insightful, ingenious – and largely comic. Assuming the somewhat similar to be identical, Aristotle advises us, we may regard 'the simpleton [as] a solid person, the emotionless [as] gentle, and always take the best in each case from coincidental features, for example [calling] the irascible and the fanatic person "candid", and the willful one "distinguished and dignified". Those with excesses [we may describe] as having virtues, for example the rash, as "courageous", and the prodigal, as "generous".'

Finally, before we leave characters, let us observe, briefly, that Aristotle, operating as always from the perspective of the mature head of a middle-class household, that is, of a *man* in his forties or fifties, notes as ethical problems some issues that had featured in comedy after comedy: the conflict of husbands against well-dowered wives (*Nicomachean Ethics* VIII, 10 [1161a1–3]), of fathers against sons who may be too close to them in age or appetites (*Politics* VII, 14), and of all against women who are either too poor (and uncontrollable) or too rich (and insufferable; *Politics* IV, 12 [1300a4–8]). But rich *men* do not escape unscathed in Aristotle any more than on the stage; for example in Book IV, chapter 9 of the *Politics* (1295b9–10 and 13–19) the poor are mentioned with less – and less amusing – ethical detail than the unruly rich. At the other social extreme, the behavior of slaves is discussed, again with echoes from drama. In *Nicomachean Ethics* VIII, 11 (1161b5–8) Aristotle begrudgingly allows that master, as human being, and slave, as human being, may occasionally be friends – as they are so often in the plays. In *Politics* I, 2 (1255a4–b4), he describes confusion between slaves and free persons, and at II, 2 (1263a19–21) household slaves clashing with their masters. In *Rhetoric* III, 14 (1415b23–24) Aristotle, using the *literary* word for them (δοῦλοι) asks his reader to recall how slaves typically beat about the bush, presumably when, like almost every comic slave sooner or later, they are in trouble with the master. The most obviously *comic* Aristotelian slaves, however, are the 'quick ones among servants' (οἱ ταχεῖς τῶν διακόνων) who run off before they have heard all their instructions; he mentions them in Book VII of *Ethics* (chapter 6, 1149a26–28), I am sure with a vivid 'running slave' scene or two from comedy in mind.

To sum up the argument so far: although women and slaves receive much less attention in the philosopher's works than they do on the stage, and although their 'virtues' interest Aristotle little if at all, they do not escape his notice in his humane studies; and when he does acknowledge their existence, they, too, like his young men and old men, clearly recall *roles from a play*. Very many of the ethical, personal data that Aristotle used, both the things and the names for them, come from dramatic types, and especially from comedy.

We may proceed now, as promised, into his explicit allusions to the theatre, to playwrights and actors, and to specific dramatic texts, for how these will qualify the demonstrated influence of dramatic literature and performance upon his thinking.

First are allusions to the theatre. We read numerous remarks that show Aristotle's (and presume his reader's) familiarity with theatre-going and theatre production. A few are so simple and so delightful as the observation that spectators will increase their noisy consumption of crunchy sweets in direct proportion to their boredom with the play on stage (*Nicomachean Ethics* X, 5 [1175b11–13]). Others are more complex and more telling, in particular a pair of rather odd comments about love-of-theatre in the *Ethics*. In Book I, 8 (1099a9–10) he lists, among other enthusiasts who love such diverse things as horses, justice, and virtue, the φιλοθέωρος, 'lover of theatre' (itself a comic word, from Alexis); and in Book III, 10 (1118a7–8) for an example of extreme behavior (though not, he says, of true 'intemperance' as he understands the notion) he cites that by persons who 'delight excessively in songs or acting'. What makes these notices odd, the second especially so, is that, although there were more frequent performances at Athens in Aristotle's day than a century before, drama remained a pleasure impossible to pursue so monomaniacally as the Romans could do two or three centuries later. Few of his readers, in fact, were likely to have been such passionate 'theorophiles', and also so eager to read plays, as Aristotle himself! Also betraying his special interest in theatre are references to the performers there, a couple in the *Ethics* to actors, a couple in the *Politics* to choruses. On the one hand, Aristotle advises us to regard those who lack self-control when they speak as being like *actors*, whose words and meanings are not 'real' (*Nicomachean Ethics* VII, 3 [1147a22–24]). On the other hand, in contrast to this almost Platonic disparagement, he reveals something very important about his high regard for actors and acting in a remark intended only for its logical form (*Nicomachean Ethics* VII, 4 [1148b6–9]), namely, that we may not classify a 'bad physician' *or a 'bad actor'* as, simply, 'bad' persons in the ethical sense. Aristotle in the heat of an argument thus mentions acting in the same breath with the very high art of medicine (which his father had practiced and for which all his own writings, and indeed his biological interests, show the highest respect).[12] In Plato we must suspect irony in the juxtaposition, at least if Socrates were the speaker; but in Aristotle we see, I think, inadvertent revelation of where a great part of his great heart lay.

Indeed, he was avidly interested in what we call theatre history, as references to the fifth-into-fourth-century tragic actor Theodorus (in both *Politics* VII, 15 [1336b28–29] and *Rhetoric* III, 2 1404b22–3]) and to the contemporary comic one Philemon (in *Rhetoric* III, 12 [1413b25–8]) make clear, and in the delivery of actors generally, as a model for orators (which he proposes at some length in the opening chapter of *Rhetoric* Book III [1403b16–1404a19]).[13] Aristotle likewise presupposes his reader's knowledge about dramatic choruses in the *Politics*, where (at 1276b4–6 in III, 1) he uses the changing function of the same choreuts, now in comedy, now in tragedy, for analogy with citizens in a changing state; and where (in chapter 8 of the same book, at 1284b11–13) he observes how a chorus-master rejects for his chorus one who sings louder or more beautifully than the rest. In the works we have been looking into are even a pair of references, if only oblique ones, to the making of plays, surely an uncommon enterprise for most of Aristotle's readership, though something he appears to have imagined himself attempting. One occurs when he declares that what happens to a person after death is much less important than sufferings to a character *before* the events of a tragic play (*Nicomachean Ethics* I, 11 [1101a31–b1]); the other when, in the *Rhetoric* (III, 3 [1406b6–8]), he points out the sometimes thin margin between tragic grandeur of language and comical exaggeration or bathos, in instructions ostensibly not for a dramaturge but for a public

speaker – who should presumably avoid *both* those styles as unsuitable.
What is more, he was interested in the personal lives, the biographies, of
those who wrote the plays, as scattered anecdotes of non-poetical incidents
involving Aeschylus, Sophocles, Euripides, and Antiphon the tragedian
demonstrate.[14] In the *Ethics* he discusses the production of plays, *chorēgia*,
for which the expenditure may be proper, improperly low, or improperly
high, like any other important outlay (IV, 2 [1122a24–5 and b22–6]).
According to the *Politics* (V, 7 [1309a17–20]), rich citizens in a democracy
probably should *not* be encouraged to bear production costs at all. Instead,
Aristotle believed that a state ought to have public officials as χοϱηγοί,
'drama producers', whom at 1299a15–20 in *Politics* IV, 12 he lists immediately after priests, and ahead of such important functionaries as heralds and
ambassadors! And he had other views about theatre regarding such things
as who should play the accompanying flute, what modes of melody should
be permitted, and so forth.

Aristotle could misquote lines (as he once does from Sophocles' *Antigone*),
could misrepresent the content of scenes (as he does also for *Antigone*!), and
could misattribute authorship of an entire work (identifying Sophocles as
writer of Euripides' *Meleager*).[15] Frequently he does not bother to mention
the play or its author by name, merely quoting a bit of iambic dialogue or
describing a recognizable dramatic scene or predicament. But quote from
drama he does, and refer, unmistakably, to situations that come from
(usually) tragedies rather than from history or current events; and he does
both with greater frequency even than the reviser of the Penguin *Politics*
would suggest by his remark that 'Like most Greek writers, he delights in
appealing to the poets.'[16] Not only do quotations from dramatic texts
preponderate over those from other poetic genres and from the historians
and orators almost everywhere in Aristotle's *Ethics*, *Politics*, and even *Rhetoric*
(with an important exception in this last work to be discussed below); but
they are also occasionally entered somewhat intrusively, providing far-
fetched examples of what the philosopher is trying to demonstrate. For
instance, in the third book of the *Ethics* (chapter 1, 1111a11–12) when
listing and exemplifying the varous kinds of mistake, he adduces for
mistake-of-person-acted-upon the case of confusing one's *son* with *an enemy*,
'like Merope'. Merope, Aristotle expects his reader to know, is the mother
of Cresphontes in Euripides' (fragmentary) melodrama of that name,
where she nearly makes the unlikely mistake in question. Indeed Aristotle
quite regularly presumes his reader's conversance not only with contemporary drama (tragedies of Chaeremon, Polycrates, and, his favorite
among them, Theodectes; comedies of Anaxandrides) but also with fifth-
century 'classics' (by Aeschylus, Agathon, Antiphon, Carcinus, and, of
course, Euripides and Sophocles in tragedy, by Epicharmus and
Aristophanes in comedy). Often he introduces a phrase or a verse (or two)

with a simple 'it has been said' or 'the poet says/the poets say', especially when he quotes Euripides (whom he cites nearly as often as all other tragedians combined).[17] We know that Euripides was popular in Aristotle's day, yet this casualness is surely worthy of note. Worthy of note, too, is Aristotle's somewhat odd claim that 'Euripides first showed the way' in developing that plain style which he recommends to orators in *Rhetoric* III, 2 (1404b25). Sophocles' style, if a Euripidean may venture the comment, is actually quite as plain as Euripides', often more natural, and often finer in expression; yet Aristotle, like 'Dionysus' in Aristophanes' *Frogs*, clearly loved to read Euripides, whatever his faults as dramaturge!

Finally, there are numerous places where, though we find neither quotation nor explicit reference, the philosopher seems to have a dramatic scenario near the front of his mind. Let me offer three examples. In his discussion of suicide as a crime against the state in *Nicomachean Ethics* V, 11 (1138a9–14) he 'proves' that it is deemed so by the formal dishonor (ἀτιμία) that the state is supposed to inflict upon the self-slayer. But the commentators can explain only that a suicide's hand was buried separately from his or her body – not much of a dishonor, one might feel, and probably seldom really inflicted (since death in the home and burial were, of course, wholly private affairs).[18] May Aristotle not be thinking more of Creon's Thebes or of Agamemnon's camp before Troy than of Demosthenes' and Aeschines' Athens? Second example: in Book VI of the same *Ethics* (chapter 13, 1144b10–12), as an analogy for good disposition without intelligence to guide it, Aristotle describes a powerful man, *deprived of sight* (ἄνευ ὄψεως), who stumbles powerfully. The likeness is itself not especially apt for his point; but, more important, the situation looks suspiciously like a sensational scene from tragedy, perhaps from Euripides' *Hecuba* or the same author's lost *Oedipus* (in which the title character did not blind himself, but was blinded by others), since a person born or grown blind does not blunder about as Aristotle asks us to imagine.[19] A third dramatic allusion is less certain, yet it also deserves mention here: in his *Politics* Aristotle repeatedly discusses the possibility that not merely different persons but even different classes or interest-groups might govern a state 'in alternation' or 'by turns' (ἐν μέρει, κατὰ μέρος, παρὰ μέρος; in II, 1 [1261b2–5], in III, 11 [1288a26–7], and in IV, 10 [1297a4–5]). The idea is surely reasonable, but, as he concedes, it often breaks down; *the idea was reasonable for Oedipus' cursed sons, at mythical Thebes*, but it broke down, fratricidally, according to the old epic narration *and with numerous memorable variations on the tragic stage*. From Aeschylus' *Seven Against Thebes*, from Sophocles' *Antigone* and *Oedipus at Colonus*, from Euripides' *Phoenician Women*, and doubtless from other such plays closer in date to his own time, Aristotle 'knew' the sad story of a famous attempt to share rule not simultaneously, by a division of powers, but successively.[20]

We may now draw some conclusions and add a few final thoughts. Aristotle seems not to have 'worked on' dramatic literature and pondered earlier and contemporary theatre only just before and for the sake of his undertaking to produce a *Poetics*. Rather, drama and the theatre worked on *him*, to give him data of human motivation and behavior, to give him exemplars and even names for things. Aware of this effect upon himself, he once, at least, seems to have tried to suppress it. During the first ten chapters of *Rhetoric*, Book I, he refers not at all to any Attic drama or dramatist or to the theatre (quoting only the Sicilian comedian Epicharmus, once, among many bits of Homeric and other non-dramatic verse); indeed, in the tenth of those chapters he offers a set of decidedly *non-comic* age stereotypes (1369a9–30). After this restraint, however, he quite gives up, so that not only in the third book (which in some ways complements *Poetics*) but in the second as well he cites and quotes Attic *playwrights* even more often than Attic and other *orators* in almost every chapter![21] He must have been aware of drama's effect upon himself, and extrapolated from his own to other intelligent people's experience. Consequently, after completing most of his *Politics* (whose concluding discussion of education and music may well have followed rather than suggested the new and peculiar project) he ventured into the *Poetics*. The unusual fact that Aristotle took the time to research and write such a specialized 'art' too seldom draws proper attention – and astonishment. Why, we ought to ask, should a thinker whose high aims were human happiness, and the best attainable human community, and the right understanding of the world and of the human mind, concern himself with defining and perfecting a form of popular literature that had seen better days? Only if that literary form had impressed him, personally, with its possibilities for the emotional and moral benefit of the individual and the *polis*, I think we might answer. The *Poetics* he undertook to compose would thus prescribe the proper, pro-moral canons of tragedy and (probably) of comedy, which arts were, for Aristotle, evidently more urgent to reform than the morally neutral (though far more widely and lucratively purveyed) art of rhetoric.[22] Even rhetoric could wait, vitally important though it obviously was for a citizen–statesman in Athens or anywhere else in the Hellenic world. Poetics – that is, dramatics – must first be enlightened.

NOTES

1 W. Jaeger, *Paideia: The Ideals of Greek Culture*, 2nd edn, vol. I, trans. G. Highet (Oxford University Press, 1945; paperbound, 1965); and E. A. Havelock, *Preface to Plato* (Cambridge, Mass.: Harvard University Press, 1963), especially Part One, 'The Image-Thinkers' (pp. 3–193), on Homer, Hesiod, and oral poetry/performance.

2 Nietzsche's thesis in *Die Geburt der Tragödie aus dem Geiste der Musik* (1872) and in *Die Philosophie im tragischen Zeitalter der Griechen* (1873) is well known. For a provocative more recent discussion of the relationship of Platonic and Aristotelian philosophy to the arts, in particular to poetry and drama, see two articles by T. Gould, 'Aristotle and the Irrational', *Arion*, 2 (1963), 55–74, especially pp. 70–3, and 'Plato's Hostility to Art', *Arion*, 3, (1964), 70–91, especially pp. 84–8.

3 See W. W. Fortenbaugh, 'Die Charaktere Theophrasts. Verhaltensregelmässigkeiten und aristotelische Laster', *Rheinisches Museum*, 118 (1975), 62–82, for discussion and bibliography.

4 The texts I have used are those in the Loeb Library series (Cambridge, Mass.: Harvard University Press/London: William Heinemann), whose chapter divisions I have followed. These are *The Nicomachean Ethics* (revised edn. 1934) and *Politics* (corrected edn. 1944), both trans. H. Rackham, and *The 'Art' of Rhetoric* (1926), trans. J. H. Freese. All passages are also identified in the standard page+column+line style after the 1831 master edition of Aristotle's works by I. Bekker.

The question of *Nicomachean* versus *Eudemian Ethics* – not to mention the, probably, pseudo-Aristotelian *Magna Moralia*! – is a vexed one; for a comprehensive discussion see *Aristoteles: Magna Moralia*, trans. and commentary by F. Dirlmeier (= vol. 8 of *Aristoteles Werke in deutscher Übersetzung*, Berlin: Akademie Verlag, 1979), pp. 93–147.

Although his argumentation has been properly criticized (notably by T. H. Irwin in *Journal of Philosophy*, 77 [1980], 338–54, and by N. Sherman and M. Presser in *Journal of the History of Philosophy*, 19 [1981], 380–4), the thesis of A. Kenny, *The Aristotelian Ethics* (Oxford University Press, 1978) and *Aristotle's Theory of the Will* (New Haven: Yale University Press, 1979), merits serious attention. Kenny maintains that three books common to manuscripts both of '*Nicomachean Ethics*' (as Books v–vii) and (as Books iv–vi) of '*Eudemian Ethics*' belong properly to the latter, and that the latter is Aristotle's more mature statement of moral philosophy. My own argument does not depend on his correctness; but what I have found supports an hypothesis that the 'common books' and the rest of *Eudemian Ethics* all come from a different Aristotle than wrote the rest of the Nicomacheans, the *Politics*, the *Rhetoric*, and the *Poetics* – from a man less immediately involved with the theatre and drama (though one who, in *Eudemian Ethics* vii, cites drama with some frequency, Euripides especially). That man may certainly be Aristotle in his second Athenian period, viz. from 335 BC to his death in 322. That man is not, however, the developing Aristotle, open to data from real-life experience but also from the vivid though vicarious 'experience' of drama, whom my study examines.

All references to '*Ethics*' will consequently be to their Nicomachean form/phase/edition unless otherwise noted.

5 The authoritative discussion of ἦθος remains E. Schütdrumpf, *Die Bedeutung des Wortes ēthos in der Poetik des Aristoteles* (Munich: C. H. Beck, 1970), now supplemented by G. F. Held, 'The Meaning of ἦθος in the *Poetics*', *Hermes*, 113 (1985), 280–93.

Bibliography on the notorious term *hamartia* in the *Poetics* is formidable. A

34 *Drama and philosophy*

hefty 1984 dissertation at Florida State University, Tallahassee, by D. E. White (available on microfilm) is merely 'A Sourcebook on the Catharsis Controversy'! Nevertheless I must mention the major monograph by J. M. Bremer, *Hamartia: Tragic Error in the Poetics of Aristotle and in Greek Tragedy* (Amsterdam: Hakkert, 1969) and two articles of identical title, '*Hamartia* in Aristotle and Greek Tragedy', by T. C. W. Stinton, *Classical Quarterly*, NS 25 (1975), 221–54, and by S. Østerud, *Symbolae Osloenses*, 51 (1976), 65–80.

6 Chronological questions are, however, unsettled, among portions of each major work relative to one another and among the different ethical treatises (see n. 4 above), so that no simple ordering can possibly win the general agreement of scholars. In fact, Aristotle seems likely to have revised some, at least, of his work even as he compiled the treatises, adding cross-references to fit the present state of his encyclopedia-in-progress. For whatever the evidence is worth, *Politics* IV, 9 (1295a35–9, widely agreed to be a late part of the work) certainly refers back to (some) *Ethics*, and the very end of *Nicomachean Ethics* (though here the text may be post-Aristotelian Peripatetic) looks ahead to a treatment of political–social matters; *Politics* VIII, 7 (1341b38–40) promises a περὶ ποιητικῆς (i.e. a 'Poetic' treatise or handbook), toward which *Rhetoric* III, 1 (1404a39) and 2 (1404b27–8 and 1405a3–6) clearly look *back*.

7 R. A. Gauthier and J. Y. Jolif, in their translation with commentary *L'éthique à Nicomaque* (in the series *Aristote: traductions ét études*, Louvain: Publications Universitaires, 1959), vol. 2, Part One, pp. 177–8, discuss at some length the Euripidean problem of passion versus moral responsibility in connection with Aristotle's remark at 1111a24–25 in *Nicomachean Ethics* III, 1.

8 'Catharsis' is even more nightmarish for the bibliographer than 'hamartia'. A series of articles by L. Golden may, however, be recommended: 'Catharsis', *Transactions and Proceedings of the American Philological Association*, 93 (1962), 51–60; 'Mimesis and Catharsis', *Classical Philology*, 64 (1969), 144–153; 'The Purgation Theory of Catharsis', *Journal of Aesthetics and Art Criticism*, 31 (1973), 473–9; 'Epic, Tragedy, and Catharsis', *Classical Philology*, 71 (1976), 77–85; and 'The Classification Theory of Catharsis', *Hermes*, 104 (1976), 437–52. The more recent A. Ničev, *La catharsis tragique d'Aristote: nouvelles contributions* (Sophia: Éditions de l'Universitaire, 1982), has won much attention (and provoked controversy).

Although there is at least one worthy doubter (R. Cantarella, 'I "libri" della Poetica di Aristotele', *Rendiconti dell'Accademia dei Lincei*, 30 [1975], 289–97), most scholars believe that we have lost at least a second book of Aristotelian *Poetics*, which R. Janko, *Aristotle on Comedy: Towards a Reconstruction of* Poetics *II* (London: Duckworth, 1984), ambitiously undertakes to extrapolate.

9 On the so-called 'Middle' and 'New' Comedy see A. Lesky, *A History of Greek Literature*, 2nd edn, trans. J. Willis and C. de Heer (New York: Thomas Crowell, 1966), pp. 633–7 and 642–64; and E. W. Handley in P. E. Easterling and B. M. W. Knox, eds., *The Cambridge History of Classical Literature*, vol. 1: *Greek Literature* (Cambridge University Press, 1985), pp. 398–425. My paper 'Plautus versus *Komoidia*: Popular Farce at Rome', in vol. 10 (1988) of the *Themes in Drama* series offers a more concise description (pp. 54–5) and further bibliography.

10 The same fellow is mentioned, and named, at the corresponding part of *Eudemian Ethics* (III, 2 [1231a15–17]) and also in the late pseudo-Aristotelian *Problems*

(XXVIII, 7 [950a3]). Although because of his father's improbable proper name Eruxis (genitive Eruxios or Eruxidos), 'Belch', it was not unreasonable for Loeb translator Rackham to pronounce the gourmand 'Apparently a character of comedy, though later writers speak of him as a real person' (pp. 176–7, n. *d*), evidence for an historical Philoxenus whom not only Aristophanes (*Wasps* 84, *Clouds* 686, and *Frogs* 934) but also his Old Comedy rival Eupolis (fr. 235) mentioned suggests that we have not a complete fiction but a caricature. Part of the joke Aristotle repeats for us seems to lie in an invented (?) name Eruxis (whom – or, rather, which – the *Frogs* makes Philoxenos' *son*); but part, I believe, also depends upon a lost comic scene in which Philoxenos must have uttered his grotesque and unforgettable prayer. (There is no non-comic evidence that any person named 'Eruxis' ever existed; four men named 'Eruxias', three of them Athenians, are attested. W. B. Stanford, however, in *Aristophanes: The Frogs*, 2nd edn. [Basingstoke and London, 1963; reprinted with alterations 1968], p. 155, following W. Schmidt, supposes that Citizen Belch was a real person.)

For information and sources on the historical Philoxenos see Pauly-Wissowa, *Real-Encyclopädie der classischen Altertumswissenschaft* (*'RE'*), 20: 1 (1941), 190, 'Philoxenos' number 5. Gauthier and Jolif's commentary, *RE*, vol. 2:1, pp. 241–2, offers some additional information and discussion.

11 I depend for history of word occurrences upon the Liddell–Scott–Jones ('LSJ') *Greek–English Lexicon*, 9th edn. (Oxford University Press, 1940).

12 For changing views of medicine, but always respectful ones, in the Aristotelian writings see D. Gracia Guillén, 'The Structure of Medical Knowledge in Aristotle's Philosophy', *Sudhoffs Archiv, Zeitschrift für Wissenschaftsgeschichte*, 58 (1978), 1–36.

13 See W. Burkert, 'Aristoteles im Theater: Zur Datierung des 3. Buchs der *Rhetorik* und der *Poetik*', *Museum Helveticum*, 33 (1975), 67–72, for an ingenious and persuasive effort to date both works to the years before 335 (and *Politics* VII to before 347) on the basis of actors' and playwrights' datable careers.

14 Namely at 1111a9–10 in *Nicomachean Ethics* III, 1 (on Aeschylus' alleged disclosure of mystical secrets); at 1311b32–34 in *Politics* V, 8 (on Euripides' brutal reaction to a remark about his bad breath!); and at 1385a10–13 in *Rhetoric* II, 7 (on Antiphon the poet's boldness before his execution at Syracuse), at 1416a15–17 and 26–35 in III, 15 (respectively on eighty-year-old Sophocles' reply to an insinuation about his pathetic trembling and on Euripides' clever defense against a charge of impiety), and at 1419a26–30 in III, 18 (a conversation between Peisander and, probably, the *poet* Sophocles [rather than an orator-politician of the same name] about the antidemocratic Council of Four Hundred of 411BC).

On Aristotle's general interest in biographical material, especially, the author maintains, concerning the earliest poets, see G. Huxley, 'Aristotle's Interest in Biography', *Greek, Roman and Byzantine Studies*, 15 (1974), 203–13.

15 All in *Rhetoric*: misquotation in I, 15 (1375b2), a mystifying statement about Haemon in III, 16 (1417b16–20), and the false attribution in III, 9 (1409b9–10).

16 T. J. Saunders, who 'revised and re-presented' Aristotle, *The Politics*, trans. T. A. Sinclair (Harmondsworth and New York: Penguin, 1981), p. 56.

17 No exact count is possible since (among other reasons) it is not always clear that

a few words in iambic or other meter that Aristotle may be quoting are in fact quoted, and since, even where quotation is certain, we must frequently 'identify' its source as Anon. (and sometimes remain unsure whether this was a comic or a tragic poet – or a non-dramatic lyric writer). Nevertheless rough numbers may be interesting. Among the three treatises this paper surveys I find in *Nicomachean Ethics* eight clear allusions to and/or quotations from Euripides, two from Sophocles, four from other namable tragedians; in *Politics* five from Euripides, a single one from Sophocles, and another one from a named writer (Theodectes); and in *Rhetoric* nineteen from Euripides, a dozen from Sophocles, fourteen from definite others. The total scores are thus Euripides 32, Sophocles 15, ascertainable others 19.

18 For a typical comment see Gauthier and Jolif, *RE*, 2:1, p. 425.

19 For a reconstruction of the Euripidean *Oedipus*, controvertible though some of the lesser details and its tentative dating may be, see T. B. L. Webster, *The Tragedies of Euripides* (London: Methuen, 1967), pp. 238 and 241–6.

20 It is noteworthy that at Euripides *Phoenicians* 478, pleading for his 'turn' as king, Polyneices uses the phrase ἀνὰ μέρος to urge peaceful alternation with his brother Eteocles, especially since in *Nicomachean Ethics* IX, 6 (1167a32–4) Aristotle uses the same episode of the same play to illustrate the sort of political discord that he will take up in his forthcoming political work.

21 The only exceptions are II, 23 and III, 3, 9, and 10, where, although quotations from dramatic verse (mainly tragedy) are plentiful, those from orators' prose are even more so.

22 Not every scholar is convinced that Aristotle's purpose in producing the *Poetics* *was* essentially moral, for example N. Gulley, 'Aristotle on the Purposes of Literature' (inaugural lecture at St David's College, Lampeter), in J. Barnes, M. Schofield, and R. Sorabji, eds., *Articles on Aristotle*, vol. 4: *Psychology and Aesthetics* (London: Duckworth, 1969), pp. 166–76, arguing that tragedy has a moral value, but not the highest, and, of all sorts of imaginative art, 'Aristotle sees that their regulative function *can* be socially and politically important' (p. 175, my emphasis). I am convinced Aristotle would say not 'can' but 'must'. The matter can hardly be argued through here, however. Suffice it to record my agreement with I. Smithson, 'The Moral View of Aristotle's *Poetics*', *Journal of the History of Ideas*, 44 (1983), 3–17, who contends that the treatise combines essential moral argument with esthetics; see also the first of the two articles by Gould cited in n. 2 above (though Gould believes that Aristotle, 'who did not have a poetic atom in his body' [p. 70], was badly mistaken about the nature and effect of the art he offered to moralize). Instead of the trilogy of C. L. Johnstone ('An Aristotelian Trilogy: Ethics, Rhetoric, Politics and the Search for Truth', *Philosophy and Rhetoric* 13 [1980], 1–24), therefore, I find a tetralogy.

Faith, Reason and the Prophets' dialogue in the Coventry Pageant of the Shearmen and Taylors*

PAMELA M. KING

In its retrievable form, the Coventry cycle appears to have been the most ambitious of all the great cycles. It was seen by Queen Elizabeth I and other visitors from London throughout the late Middle Ages, and, quite possibly, the Herod of the Shearmen and Taylor's play was the inspiration for Hamlet's advice to the players. It is, therefore, unfortunate that only two play texts of true Coventry plays survive from the original cycle of mysteries, *The Pageant of the Shearmen and Taylors* and *The Pageant of the Weavers*.[1] These two, and a remarkably complete set of records of production are sufficient to show how different the Coventry cycle was to those of York or Chester.[2] Nothing compares with the two surviving plays in terms of range and length. The Shearmen and Taylors' play deals with all the events from the Annunciation by Gabriel to Mary to the Massacre of the Innocents by Herod's troops, including in passing the visit of the shepherds, the Nativity itself and the coming of the Magi. The material is equivalent to that of five separate plays in the Chester cycle or eight in York. Surviving records suggest that Coventry had only ten plays as opposed to York's forty-seven.[3] Far from implying a less ambitious production, the surviving texts indicate a very different style of production.

For all its structural success as a performance text, the evidence is that the Shearmen and Taylors' play evolved over several generations of rewriting, as did the other long plays. The section referred to as 'the prophets' dialogue' is part of a final rewriting of the 1530s, thinly disguising the join between the two chief units of dramatic action. Metrical analysis of the whole play text[4] has led to the conclusion that the play probably consists of several archaeological layers with, for example, the Annunciation, a formal piece of stylized action without much potential for lively embellishment, being one of the older elements. It is safe to assume that the play was in fact, at a later stage in its development, two – the Shearmen appropriately, would have staged the story of the Annunciation, Nativity and shepherds, whereas the Taylors, able to produce sumptuously tawdry

* A draft of this paper was read at the *Themes in Drama* International Conference held at the University of London, Westfield College, in March 1988.

robes, would have been responsible for the part concerning Herod. The redactor of the present version, one Robert Croo, finished his manuscript referring to it as 'tys matter nevly correcte be Robart Croo'.[5] The Weavers' manuscript has a colophon which states, 'tys matter nevly translate be Robert Croo ...'.[6] Corrected or translated, what Croo was actually doing was bringing over or realigning what was already a paste-up of old material, and embellishing it by the addition of his own verse, characterized by its ponderously intricate metres.

Certain aspects of the resultant composite play with multiple locations of action give advantages over the usual, York-style sequential pattern. In particular, the problem of how to present the birth of Christ in front of an audience without causing theological or aesthetic offence is overcome and the audience is, in fact, cheated of the central event, as the play moves from stable, to shepherds in the fields then back to stable after the child has been born. In all other cycles the two simultaneous events, birth and angels' appearance to shepherds, have to be treated sequentially in separate plays. On the other hand, the long play apparently caused problems for its redactor when it came to welding the two major sections together, for he inserted the prophets' dialogue,[7] an apparently dull and static discussion of preceding events between two so-called prophets. At first glance it appears to represent no more than an uninspired attempt to paper over a crack. Robert Croo, poet's, limitations are nowhere more evident than here; but for Robert Croo, the odd-job man and dramatist I should like to spare a second thought.

The prologue of the play, delivered by Isaiah[8] and also newly written by Croo, requires to be considered along with the dialogue. Both elements, taken in their performance context, are designed for delivery at street level, initially to clear space and later to cover up the entry of Herod and his court and possibly the setting up of a second vehicle. Functionally necessary, they perform the same task as the diversions of circus clowns while the lions' cages are being erected. Isaiah's first speech is an elaborate prologue delivered by an Old Testament figure most famous for his prophesy of the birth of Christ (Isaiah 7:14). If for the sake of argument one assumes that Coventry had some Old Testament plays, this prologue effectively bridges the gap from the last of these to the Nativity, thereby smoothing over another join. The established tradition of liturgical Latin drama was to precede the Nativity with a non-dramatic *Processus Prophetorum*, a solution borrowed by the compiler of the N-Town plays. The Chester cycle favours a single episode in this position, a play about Balaam and Balaak (Numbers 22:23–30) focusing on prophesy but with the more dramatic diversion of a miraculously speaking donkey. Thereafter there are seven non-dramatic prophesies. The Towneley cycle includes a play of only four prophets, including the Sibyll from Vergil's fifth *Eclogue*. So Isaiah in the Shearmen and Taylors' pageant appears to fulfil an established linking function. But Isaiah here is only a dramatized historical figure in part; he is also partly a non-dramatic prologue, priest or teacher. His speech is part visionary revelation,

> ... *Ecce virgo consepeet,* –
>   Loo, where a reymede schall ryse!
> Be-holde, a mayde schall conseyve a childe ...   (lines 22–4)

part commentary,

> Now be myrre eyuere mon
> For this dede bryffly in Isaraell schalbe done,
> And before the Fathur in trone,
> That schall glade vs all.   (lines 33–6)

The prophets' link passage has much in common with this role. They seem simply to describe what the audience has just seen happen, to present in dialogue a retelling of the story of the Nativity, which unbalances the dramatic action and destroys both atmosphere and illusion.

So who are these prophets? They do not predict, so they are not in the narrowest received sense prophets at all. The term has, however, a more complex semantic range than is conventionally granted. In Christian history, although the predictive qualities dominate, the prophet can also simply be a paradigm, and his oracular properties merge to some degree with the exemplary. The predicting role is mentioned as secondary in *The Oxford English Dictionary*, the prime meaning being given as: 'One who speaks for God or for any deity, as the inspired revealer or interpreter of his will; one who is held or (more loosely) who claims to have this function; an inspired or quasi-inspired teacher.' This specific function, especially the last element, is crucial to understanding what Croo is doing in dramatic terms with this section of the play. These are no mysterious visionaries; they serve to explain precisely, to interpret, the significance of the preceding revealed but apparently miraculous event, the Incarnation.

> II PROFETA. A wondur-full marvell
>   How thatt ma be,
>   And far dothe exsell
>   All owre capasete:
>   How thatt the Trenete,
>   Of soo hy regallete,
>   Schuld jonyd be
>   Vnto owre mortallete!
>
> I PROFETA. Of his one grett marce,
>   As ye shall se the exposyssion,
>   Throgh whose vmanyte
>   All Adamis progene
>   Reydemyd schalbe owt of perdyssion.   (lines 360–72)

The key lies in the word 'exposyssion'. The Chester cycle includes a non-dramatic character, called the Expositor, whose appearances are interspersed chiefly among figurally significant Old Testament episodes, to expound hidden meaning to the audience. This is the chief apparent function of the dialogue in the Shearmen and Taylors' play. Croo has not given the Expositor's job to a single speaker, but has framed it as a dramatic dialogue, a dialectic investigation of the revealed truth which has preceded.

What has just been presented to the audience as revelation is now subjected to the rigours of reason:

Syth man did offend,
Who schuld amend
   But the seyd mon and no nothur?
For the wyche cawse he
Incarnate wold be
   And lyve in mesere asse manis one brothur   (lines 373–8)

The entire substance of this little section of school-matter turns out to be an object lesson in the age-old debate between fideistic theology and the methods of Aristotelian logic. This debate has a long and complex history in the western Middle Ages. The argument goes back to St Paul:

Beware lest any man spoil you through philosophy and vain deceit after the tradition of men, after the rudiments of the world, and not after Christ.
(Colossians 2:8)

... it pleased God by the foolishness of preaching to save them that believe.
For the Jews require a sign, and the Greeks seek after wisdom:
But we preach Christ crucified, unto the Jews a stumbling block, and unto the Greeks foolishness ...   (1 Corinthians 1:21–3)

St Augustine made an influential statement of the primacy of faith over reason, as he argues in the *Confessions*[9] that man should never try to move from reason to faith, but from faith to reason, that revealed truth was the starting point for rational knowledge. Amongst his followers St Anselm of Canterbury[10] in the eleventh century subjected Christian revelation to the methods of philosophy, proving the Incarnation of Christ in his *Cur Deus Homo*. Anselm also coined the epithet which characterizes the rational fideist argument: *neque enim quaero intelligere ut credam, sed credo ut intelligum* ('For I do not seek to understand in order to believe, but I believe in order to understand'). He refused to submit holy scripture to dialectics, but saw faith as a given point from which to start. But conversely he took a stand against those who refused to submit their faith to dialectics, seeing no objection to striving to understand rationally what he believed. Not to probe belief by rational enquiry was for St Anselm a form of spiritual negligence. His principles are similar to those suggested by Prophet I, who reproves Prophet II for apparently doubting what he has seen, but suggests that doubt be constructively employed as the basis for rational exploration. Prophet II, on the other hand, is a pure fideist:

II PROFETA. Syr, vnto the Deyite,
  I beleve parfettle,
    Onpossibull to be there ys nothyng;
  How be yt this warke
  Vnto me ys darke
    In the opperacion or wyrkyng.

Peter Abelard,[11] whose writings actually predate the acquisition of Aristotle's *Metaphysics*, wrote in his *Sic et Non* as early as the 1120s, a logical speculation founded upon grammar, that doctrine could be confirmed by subjecting it to dialectic: 'by doubting we arrive at questions; by questioning we grasp the truth . . .' Or, in the words of the 'prophets',

II PROFETA. Yet dowtis oftymis hathe derevacion.
  II PROFETA. Thatt ys be the meynes of comenecacion
  Of trawthis to haue a dev probacion
    Be the same dowts reysoning.   (lines 388–91),

which translates, 'Yet doubts are often productive.' 'That occurs when the truth is communicated, being given appropriate examination by means of applying reason to the same doubts.' For Abelard faith was there to be *found* by reason, whereas for the orthodox Augustinians faith might be supported only by logic. The thirteenth century saw increasing polarization of theologians and philosophers, as certain philosophers in the University of Paris asserted the primacy of Aristotelian reason over theology.

Rationalism gained ground thereafter for two principle reasons. The first was the assimilation of Aristotle's *Metaphysics* and *Ethics* into logic. Thus, as logic was part of the *trivium* the foundation of the masters' degree, and theology was a higher degree, students came to theology already infected by a more extensive and scientific Aristotelian methodology.[12] Secondly there was the assimilation of the writings of the Spanish Arabian philosopher Averroës (d.1198).[13] To Averroës, Aristotle was the source of absolute truth. He argued that the power of the Koran to raise the barbarian to civilization derived from the fact that the majority of common people were incapable of pure philosophy, but needed to have their imagination fired by revelation. Divine revelation was, therefore, simply a way in which the Creator rendered truth accessible to those of lower intelligence. Above them are those who need dialectical justifications of the probability of their faith, that is theologians, but higher still are those who are unable to accept anything which cannot be rationally proved. They, the highest human minds, are the philosophers. Averroës produced what is, in the present context, a very interesting justification for the existence of prophets as those divinely inspired to know just what quantity of truth can be taken in by a given audience and how to catch the ear of that audience. Theology was, therefore, for Averroës at any rate, merely a popular approach to pure philosophy: *Aristotelis doctrina est summa veritas, quoniam ejus intellectus fuit finis humani intellectus. Quare bene dicitur, quod fuit creatus et datus nobis divina providentia, ut sciremus quidquid potest sciri.* These views presented problems in Moslem Spain and worse ones in a university run by the ecclesiastical authorities. The proponents could not maintain openly that Aristotle possessed ultimate truth. Many were forced into a position of blind fideism in their theology simultaneously with philosophical scepticism. What was considered much more dangerous was that there were those, notably Siger of Brabant and Boethius of Dacia, who, when their writings were examined closely, revealed a fundamental lack of belief.[14] This may seem strange to those used to seeing the Latin Middle Ages as a period without atheists. So serious was the influence of these Latin Averroists, pure philosophers, held to be, that the bishop of Paris was moved in 1270 and 1277 to list hundreds of propositions borrowed from Averroës and to condemn them. What they have in common is that they challenge the status of divine revelation as pure truth.[15]

The fideist backlash found its most eloquent proponent in St Bernard of Clairvaux, who asserted that there was little value in the profane sciences.[16] The way to truth was, for him, Christ; the method by degrees: first humility, then compassion, third the fervour of contemplation. The pure fideists ran into the problem that it is difficult to condemn dialectics without employing them. Yet the target was frequently the unreliability of dialectics, good servant but bad master as they could be used by the clever practitioner to prove anything. St Bernard's chief target was Abelard.

St Thomas Aquinas attempted to demonstrate that theology and philosophy were not incompatible or rival disciplines, but effectively simbiotic. Faith implies the assent of the intellect to that which cannot be proved. An act of faith cannot be proved by rational evidence, as if it can be it no longer requires that faith by definition:[17] 'it is impossible that one and the same thing should be believed and seen by the same person ...' In other words observation deletes the necessity of belief. In history, however, man can see that some things were revealed which could have been obtained by natural reason, but that was because all men were not philosophers. The Incarnation, the Trinity and the Redemption, however, had to be articles of faith properly, as they surpass human reason. Yet, although reason could not prove these things to be true, it could not prove them false either. In other words no harm can come from subjecting articles of faith to reason, for, if the conclusions of the two conflict this means simply that there is something wrong with your philosophy.

The later history of scholasticism was fraught with schism as to, for instance, which truths and how many were beyond the reach of rational understanding, but such nuances are well beyond the scope of the prophets' dialogue in the Coventry play. What we have, in *The Pageant of the Shearmen and Taylors*, it seems, are two 'prophets', in the sense of teachers, who are party to revelations of the deity, but who are also theologians, and dabblers in logic. Although Prophet II initially asserts a stance of pure fideism, he quickly moves to adopt the role of pupil, or questioner in the ensuing debate (lines 395–427), for example:

> II PROFETA. Yett can I nott aspy be noo wysse
> How thys chylde borne schuldbe with-owt naturis prejudyse.

> I PROFETA. Nay, no prejvdyse vnto nature I dare well sey;
> For the kyng of nature may
> Hawe all at his one wyll.   (lines 406–10)

After line 427, there is a further gear change into prophesy in the more normally understood sense of prediction and revelation, preparing for the next enacted piece of Christian mystery, for example:

> I PROFETA. Nothur in hallis nor yett in bowris
> Born wold he not be,
> Nother in castellis nor yet in towris
> That semly were to se;

> But att hys Fathurs wyll,
> The profeci to full-fyll,
> Be-twyxt an ox and an as
> Jesus, this kyng, borne he was.
> Heyvin he bryng us tyll!   (lines 455–63)

Not only does dialectic, therefore, supply a dramatic means of exposition: the approach mimics the favoured scholastic method which was the staple of medieval education. Dialectic was a means by which reason could be employed to establish truth, the well-worn debate was about the degree to which it could be applied to, or was appropriate to, revealed truth.

In the midst of the play illusion is shattered as the audience is wrenched from the essentially emotional world of enacted revelation, the star, the ox and the ass, back to the classroom. This can be seen as an insensitive breaking of 'mood' of the play which has to be re-established, or it can be seen as calculated for didactic purpose. Unity of emotional engagement is quite alien to this play's process. Even the elements of the play which consist of enactment rather than commentary conform to two contrastive styles of presentation. The Annunciation and Nativity are remote, miraculous and ceremonial, presented as living icons, but there are also burlesque scenes involving Joseph and the shepherds which serve to shatter that icon and merge the world of the play with the world of the everyday. The central debate offers a paradigm for the very methodology of didactic drama which is to engage its audience through direct revelatory experience, then to disengage them sufficiently to extract the lesson which that experience offers. Certainly the major figures from the history of medieval thought whom I have introduced were remote to the 1530s, but they are also mainstream and their ideas had the status of conventional wisdom. There is nothing to suggest that Croo entertained other than well-worn schoolroom notions of such ideas, or that he grasped, or saw fit to promulgate, the finer points of the argument.

If Croo does not have anything startling to offer in the venerable debate on faith and reason, the inclusion of such material in the play does, perhaps, shed a little more light on the intriguing figure of Robert Croo. No play, not even a crafts-guild play, is performed most efficiently by a co-operative of amateurs. The performance of all the individual tasks requires a decision-making process, which demands some indication of who acted as director/producer/stage manager. Both Glynne Wickham[18] and Reg Ingram[19] have identified men who were heavily involved in Coventry's pageant organization without necessarily either being a member of the guild concerned or of a craft directly related to the job they are employed to perform. These are the quasi-professionals whose names emerge from the records, the pageant masters of whom Croo was one. In the world of the crafts guilds where everything was organized by committees, if the form of the drama was to develop there had to be some unifying initiative, for reasons of efficiency and for aesthetic considerations. To identify these 'pageant masters', however, is not to define them or the extent to which their duties were in any sense regularized. Their origins, talents and involvements seem to have been entirely *ad hoc*.

The first was Thomas Colclow, a skinner employed by the Smiths from 1450, who seems to have had a flair for theatrical oreganization. His appointment carried an honorarium. Another name which appears later on in the records is that of James Hewet, leader of the waits. Although we do not have evidence that he had a controlling involvement such as Colclow's the scattered occurrences of his name suggest an eclectic interest and a roving brief concerning chiefly professional musical services. In the same category we may place the Thomas Linacers who held in his custody on his death in 1567 all the 'pageant vestures' of the Cappers which had to be inventoried and handed on to another 'wardrobe master'. Robert Croo presents the most interesting case of sustained extraordinary individual involvement. He gained unprecedented control of more than one pageant. And his role as named redactor of texts is unique. His particular involvement with the Drapers' Domesday play in the 1550s and beyond provides the most interesting commentary on areas of pageant organization beyond the spoken text. The now missing play as redacted by Croo appears to have had built into it a changed focus – Croo moved the Drapers from 'actors' theatre' into 'directors' theatre', casting himself as director.

The Drapers effects are well-known – the jobs of keeping of the windlass and hellmouth, clearly both mechanical operations requiring the operation of pulleys, went together at 16d; 16d also was paid for opening and shutting doors and windows on the pageant, probably as part of some transformation scene. There are also annual payments for setting fire to three worlds, which were replaced annually by Croo himself, and for tending the barrel of the earthquake. A production with this evident focus on effects is impossible to conceive of as being produced by a guild-actors' co-operative. Croo clearly wrote himself a job.[20] He was not contracted for a lump sum, but was paid in individual sums for his various scenic contributions and script redactions. He could do everything from making a hat for a pharisee to preparing a script, and he also played God for the Drapers, for which he received 3s.4d. In 1563 God was paid for his 'welke', which is a problematic entry, probably meaning 'welkin'. Perhaps Croo used the part of God in this play as a visible vantage point from which to direct operations, so that on his command in dual role as deity and artistic director the welkin, that is the display of heavenly pyrotechnics signifying the end of the world could take place. If we add to that his evident familiarity with schoolroom grammar and logic, one may be led to speculate that Robert Croo was one of the substantial army of schoolmasters who wrote and directed plays not only for the Chapel Royal and the boys of Pauls, but throughout the country in the early sixteenth century.

NOTES

1 The manuscript of *The Pageant of the Shearmen and Taylors* was lost in a fire at the end of the last century, but the text is preserved in Thomas Sharp, *A Dissertation on the Pageants or Dramatic Mysteries anciently performed at Coventry* (Coventry, 1825), republished with a new foreword by A. C. Cawley (Wakefield: E. P. Publishing, 1973), 83–124. The manuscript of *The Weavers' Pageant* is Coventry City Record Office Acquisition 11/2. Both plays are edited in, Hardin Craig, *Two Coventry Corpus Christi Plays*, Early English Text Society, e.s. 87 (1902; 2nd edn., 1957).

2 R. W. Ingram, *Coventry*, Records of Early English Drama (University of Toronto Press, 1981).

3 Hardin Craig, *Two Coventry Plays*, pp. xxv–xxix.

4 Ibid., p. xxiv.

5 Ibid., p. 31.

6 Ibid., p. 70.

7 Ibid., pp. 12–16 (lines 332–474).

8 Ibid., pp. 1–2 (lines 1–46).

9 Etienne Gilson, *Reason and Revelation in the Middle Ages* (New York and London: Charles Scribner's Sons, 1950), p. 11.

10 Ibid.

11 Sheila Delany, *Chaucer's 'House of Fame': The Poetics of Skeptical Fideism* (University of Chicago Press, 1972), quoting L. M. de Rijk ed., *Petrus Abelardus, Dialectica* (Assen, 1956).

12 John F. Wippel, 'The Condemnations of 1270 and 1277 at Paris', *The Journal of Medieval and Renaissance Studies*, 7 (1977), 2, 169–201, 172.

13 Gilson, *Reason and Revelation*, chapter 2 passim.

14 Ibid., 52–680; Wippel, 'Condemnations', p. 174.

15 Ibid., passim.

16 Gilson, *Reason and Revelation*, p. 11.

17 Ibid., p. 74; F. Sartiaux, *La foi et la raison dans le moyen age occidental* (Paris: Editions Ernest Leroux, 1924), pp. 16–18.

18 Glynne Wickham, *Early English Stages 1300–1660*, I *1300–1576* (London: Routledge and Kegan Paul, 1980), p. 299.

19 Reginald W. Ingram, ' "Pleyng geire accustumed belongyng & necessarie"; guild records and pageant production at Coventry', *Records of Early English Drama: Proceedings of the First Colloquium*, ed. Joanna Dutka (University of Toronto Press, 1979), pp. 60–92, 76–7.

20 Ingram, *Coventry*, p. 225 (l. 10), p. 476 (l. 1), p. 221 (l. 10), p. 237 (l. 20), p. 221 (l. 28), p. 217 (l. 31), p. 237 (l. 23).

Shakespearian self-knowledge:
the synthesizing imagination and the
limits of reason*

WILLIAM R. MORSE

Given the centrality of selfhood and identity to Shakespearian drama, post-structuralist theory's powerful deconstruction of the enunciating subject, the 'I' of Western discourse, must speak immediately and powerfully to our understanding of the plays. But paradoxically the effect of this deconstruction has redounded to Shakespeare's credit: we discover that, writing at the founding moment of our own intellectual epoch, he is there before us in his prescient insight into the implications of the sea-change from analogical to modern analytical discourse. Alive as he is to the presence of both a decaying traditional discourse of analogy and the incipient order of 'a discursive class ... determined as true, objective, and the permanent manifestation of universal common sense, [one that] marks a denial, an occultation, of the acknowledgement that the human view of the world is necessarily a "perspectival" one',[1] Shakespeare produces a canon remarkably sensitive to the blind spots and real dangers, both personal and cultural, of the new discourse.

With his own neoplatonic commitment to the human condition of immersion in life and world that produces perspective, to the materiality of language, and above all to metaphor as the basis of language rather than merely its ornament, Shakespeare proves to be himself something of a deconstructionist, and the key to this stance is his understanding of the cognitive functions of the imagination. Shakespeare's work reveals, both through the failure of discursive reason in the great tragedies and the invocation of imagination in the comedies, tragedies, and romances, an ongoing and progressively more pointed critique of the limits of this reason in the intellectual life of the individual. For Shakespeare, the world of human rationality encompasses *a* world, not *the* world, for it stands in inevitable distinction from the material reality of human existence. Whether he symbolizes the world of discursive reason by the city of Athens, the prison of Denmark, the court of Henry IV, or the house of Gloucester from which Lear is exiled, that world is always one of concepts, narrower

* A draft of this paper was read at the *Themes in Drama* International Conference held at the University of California, Riverside, in February 1988.

than, and standing at one remove from, the world those concepts purport to
embody.

In Shakespeare's plays, the true reality encloses the conceptual one, and
whether that reality appears as forest or moor, sea or island, the imagination is the vehicle that takes us to that reality and helps us to understand
what we encounter while there, as well as how the two worlds coexist,
interact, and ultimately interpenetrate. Shakespeare associates his 'green
world' at times with feelings, at times with belief and faith, and always with
nature and human nature; through the course of the plays we see, coming
progressively more clearly into focus, a vision of the healthy individual, and
the healthy society, as one aware of its manifold worlds and the place of
each in the life of that individual, that society.

Traditionally, this integrative function of the psyche had been assigned
by religious belief to the higher Understanding, Aquinas' *ratio superior*, but
of course as Shakespeare writes the tradition is in decay. The modern
concept of 'individuality' itself arises only when this breakdown eliminates
socially generated identity as a basis of selfhood. Its failure suggests, in that
historical moment before a new discourse asserts itself, the *constructed* nature
of human reality, and Shakespeare himself participates in this questioning
of the traditional verities in his exploration of the constructedness of
European cultural reality. But he interrogates even more acutely the failure
of the rising essentialist ideology to address the human need for belief as the
absolute ground for any subsequent act of comprehension: the plays ponder
the human need for belief, and they come to understand belief as that
mirror or glass that we 'hold up to nature' in order to reify the flux and
protean mutability of reality, impressing on it an order and shapeliness
susceptible of comprehension. The godhead one worships constitutes the
ideal of the self by which that self is defined, measured, and most fully
empowered, and neglect of this truth results in a failure at the heart of
individuating selfhood. Characters such as Claudius, Iago, and Edmund
embody this debased denial of human potential in their bestial lack of
higher human values. Articulated at the inaugural moment of a new
discourse for which the individual as enunciating subject constitutes the
central authority, Shakespeare's vision animates a thoroughgoing critique
of the ideology of rationality that has remained relevant throughout the
subsequent development of rationalist discourse.

Up to a point Shakespeare's critique of discursive reason directly
parallels traditional Scholastic teaching – the new rationalists of
Shakespeare's plays empower Aquinas' '*ratio inferior*' or discursive reason at
the expense of that more comprehensive '*ratio superior*' by which the
individual was intuitively to understand metaphysical reality and thus give
a meaningful context to the work of the lower faculty. His vision of the

imagination, however, radically subverts Scholastic tradition in the sense that he recognizes in the constitutive power of the traditional 'higher' reason the synthesizing aspect of the imagination itself, this constitutive power both explaining the imagination's mediating role between reason and the passions and validating art's reliance upon the imagination.

Shakespeare perceives that the new rationalist ideology fatally divorces the individual from much of his own nature, instituting a pervasive alienation that can never be reconciled within a conceptual world empowering itself by a forgetting of its own roots in material reality, that is, desire, and the body.[2] While the rationalist claims to focus the individual's energies more productively on the material world, on 'knowing' reality by objectifying it in the cause of Bacon's 'advancement of learning', this can come only at the price of disengaging intellect from the subjective self; the rationalist gives no thought – is incapable, within the new discourse of 'reason', of giving thought – to the alienated nature of the conceptual world he so energetically analyzes.

Observed from such a perspective, the tragedies, in particular, can be read as dramas of rationality run mad; as various characters blindly elevate the reason to preeminence, the individual is alienated from the reality of both world and self, and that person capable of resisting or overcoming this alienation through an act of imaginative belief, even at the cost of life itself, becomes the tragic hero. Hamlet, Lear, and Antony and Cleopatra illustrate the issue most clearly, while Othello, Macbeth, and Coriolanus evoke more ambiguous responses precisely because of their own more complex involvement in the fallen world of reason.

A discussion of *Hamlet* will serve to begin to illustrate these points. But rather than begin with the physical action of the play (that is, the act of revenge, long delayed and finally accomplished, by which Shakespeare's *Hamlet* fulfills its debt to its sources and genre), I will grant the play its own priorities and consider first the anterior issue of the play's *demands* for action. We must always attend to Mack's crucial perception that 'Hamlet's world is preeminently in the interrogative mood',[3] so privileging either particular assertions of the value of action or our own cultural preference for it constitute an unwarranted assumption: all 'action' in *Hamlet* is problematic. Mack's observation on the interrogative draws our attention to a persistent, resonant question on the lips of all the major characters: 'what's the matter?'[4] Already a dead metaphor to the ears of Polonius or Claudius when they use it, its recurrent presence nevertheless plays constantly against Hamlet's own question, 'what is a man?' and thereby defines the play's central preoccupation. To face human nature, as it is reflected in Hamlet, is to ask, with Barnardo, 'who's there?' If the physical act of revenge that so burdens Hamlet stands at the heart of the play, for

Shakespeare this act takes on its largest significance as it forces the protagonist to investigate and finally to answer this question of the true 'matter' of human nature.

Because the essential 'thought' of the playwright here seems to be a question, the structure of the play naturally takes the shape of a debate on that question: the dramatic conflict between the major characters defines two conflicting positions on this question 'what is the matter?' or 'what is a man?' The thought of the dramatist, then, finds its fullest articulation, not in Hamlet's pursuit of revenge, but in Hamlet's pursuit of an answer to his question, and this will prove to be the *praxis* of the play.

But the 'matter' of the play is complex: if human nature, especially as seen in Hamlet's nature, is the play's central preoccupation, one other motif of 'the matter' is prominent, and crucial, and that is the matter that is the raw material of art and artifice. The 'matter' of Polonius' conjectures on Hamlet's madness, the 'matter' that Hamlet reads, the 'matter' of Pyrrhus' revenge, the 'matter' of the Mousetrap, the 'matter' of Hamlet and Gertrude's talk, the 'matter' of Claudius' plotting with Laertes, the 'matter' of Osric's embassy, and, most troubling perhaps of all, the 'illness about the heart' that Hamlet ultimately dismisses as 'no matter' – Shakespeare constantly conflates within the action of the play the two senses of his own matter, that is, the theme of the play and the raw material of his art. And the two gradually coalesce, for to Shakespeare human nature is in its essence aesthetic, and humanity's most natural activity lies in the shaping of a sense of self within the larger shaping of one's sense of the world.

Shakespeare's repetition of the central question points to a clear structural antithesis in the play: Hamlet reflects constantly upon his own nature and the nature of the world he inhabits, while the denizens of Claudius' Elsinore think about such things very little if at all. The hero sets himself to answer the question 'what is a man?' against the backdrop of a society that never asks this question – because it takes for granted a particular answer to it. Such a perspective suggests that 'the matter' of the play is not simply human nature generally, but more specifically the nature of that consciousness that distinguishes the species.

Shakespeare, as is his wont, conceives of this situation metaphorically: Denmark's predicament is figured as a fall into consciousness. Claudius poisons his brother in the garden, and the fatal act exiles Denmark from the edenic realm of the elder Hamlet, inaugurating a diminished, fallen human existence aptly reflected in the dark atmosphere of the court. The figure of fallen humanity seems to express for Shakespeare the painfully reduced human consciousness associated with the new rationality of his day. Committed to a calculating rationality closely analogous to the traditional *ratio inferior*, Claudian Denmark stands fundamentally exiled from the ground of primal reality by its own essentialist conceptualizing. The court

mind, like the new rationalism, comprehends the world of concepts that it
has manufactured in order to objectify the world, without appreciating the
gap between conceptuality and the reality it would ostensibly represent.

Hamlet asks his question in the context of a world that assumes man to be
the rational animal. Claudius' regicide has been an act of calculation and
'policy', and that act overthrows a world traditionally based on 'custom'
and 'antiquity', a world whose basis was moral. The values associated
throughout the play with Hamlet Senior locate his earlier Elsinore within a
larger frame, a spiritual reality, that governs and regulates the social
community itself. Claudius' usurpation, then, is profoundly revolutionary
and institutes a new society founded upon a new basis. Where Hamlet
Senior governed according to tradition and accepted precedent, Claudius
elevates the common reason to unilateral government of himself and his
state. The play, in other words, presents an experiment on the question of
whether man is indeed 'the rational animal' as the backdrop to Hamlet's
intense questioning of human nature.

The action of the play implicitly characterizes the limitations of
Claudius' view. In such a corrupt world, devoid of any grounding ideals,
every self is its own agent, and the intellectual power of each devotes itself to
self-interest. That such 'reason' fallaciously comprehends its own nature
becomes clear as the reason of each of the various characters panders in its
own way to the 'rude will' it claims to control. Even Hamlet himself is sunk
in this new state; his own hatching of plots in this dungeon of Denmark, a
world of night and dark interiors, is no accident, for the new ideology of
rationality has reduced Elsinore to the materialist universal machine,
devoid of spiritual light. Though Shakespeare's vision predates Hobbes's, it
lacks nothing in stark intensity; the alienation of this world is all too familiar
to a twentieth-century audience.

Over against these transient, scurrying human plots stands the irresolute
world of Hamlet's delay, and his madness. They cannot be separated –
Hamlet's adoption of his 'antic disposition' is simultaneous with his turn to
delay, the disposition accompanies the delay, and its absence upon his
return coincides with the play's resolution. But in the strictest sense
'madness' describes, not an inherent condition, but rather the hero's
alienation from the community of values and norms represented by
Claudius' Denmark: to say that Hamlet is 'mad' is to recognize that he
perceives a different reality than does his community. Thus the oft-repeated
question 'Is Hamlet "really" mad?' can be put more fruitfully as 'In what
sense is Hamlet mad?' For his 'madness' grows to at least a relative
coherence when seen from the perspective, not of Denmark's court, but
rather of rebellion from that world. 'Hamlet's madness thus becomes a test
of the authenticity of his culture', as one critic puts it,[5] and stands in an
essentially critical relation to the dominant language as well as the

dominant ethos of the court. Those commentators who simply accept Hamlet's 'madness', and then go on to censure his 'failure to act', are adopting the Claudian imperial standard when they do so – Claudius of course acts regularly, and consistently, within a world ordered and 'purposed' by rational coordinates.

But human purposes themselves are a crucial issue in the play. What is the basis of that fracture of purposes and ends of which the Player King speaks? Standing at the very center of this self-reflexive play about acting – a player playing a player who plays the role of king in the play-within-a-play – the king recognizes that

> ... what we do determine, oft we break.
> Purpose is but the slave to memory,
> Of violent birth, but poor validity,
> ...
> What to ourselves in passion we propose,
> The passion ending, doth the purpose lose.

And he ends his commentary with the comment that

> Our wills and fates do so contrary run
> That our devices still are overthrown,
> Our thoughts are ours, their ends none of our own.
>
> (III, ii, 187–213)[6]

Although *Hamlet* criticism has traditionally focused almost exclusively on the hero's 'purposes' as 'of violent birth, but poor validity', the Player's comments extend far beyond Hamlet himself. Both of Elsinore's mighty opposites (as well as their inferiors) are actively engaged in proposing purposes to themselves, and Hamlet is equally active in meditating on 'the purpose of acting', Pyrrhus' 'black purpose', Claudius' 'founding' purposes – 'my crown, mine own ambition, and my queen' (III, iii, 55) – and his own, because this is the business of consciousness in a rationally-conceived, that is a causal, world frame.

So again with the Player King's words we see the question of simple action – the connective betwen purpose and end – yawn open, this space becoming, under the force of these concluding couplets, a veritable chasm. The Player King's words are of course appropriate to concentric audiences, and represent a comprehensive commentary on the entire range of purposes that constitute life in the prison of Denmark: our 'thoughts' and 'ends' diverge *because* 'our wills and fates do so contrary run'. Shakespeare will make the distinction more clear in act v, scene i, where the clowns distinguish between the man's going to the water to drown himself and the drowning itself. Because in Claudius' Denmark reason panders the will, and will is proximate in its goals (never ultimate), Claudius cannot purpose action toward his true end, his final fate: death.

It is often remarked that 'in conscience' Hamlet cannot seek death by committing the suicide that some presume to be contemplated in the central soliloquy. But his encounter with the unknowability of that 'undiscovered country' more strictly formulates the impossibility of consciousness (the second Renaissance meaning of 'conscience') positing death as its end or purpose. 'Dread ... puzzles the will' precisely because reason cannot grasp the abstraction except as a negation; consciousness 'doth make cowards of us all' precisely because 'thought ... sicklies o'er ... the native hue of resolution' when faced with the boundary of its conceptual field. Action can be willed only within these boundaries, and reason's boundary is death. We discover as we view the play through the mirror of the Player's vision a fundamental misalignment in Denmark between proximate purposes and ultimate ends. Claudius, Gertrude, Polonius, Laertes, Rosencrantz and Guildenstern, even Ophelia – none of these characters act with regard to that true and final end of death, our common 'fate'. Only Hamlet, riven by doubt and confusion as he is, defers action under the suspicion of this blind spot.[7]

From the first in *Hamlet* the question of death shows a tendency to grow from the specific towards the general, and the retributive death of Claudius is intimately entwined with the death of the hero himself, not only in Shakespeare's mind but in Hamlet's. The tableau of the final catastrophe – Hamlet and Claudius both dead, and indeed surrounded by death – only fulfills what has been a constant motif of the play, for the Ghost's indictment is not simply of Claudius, but of fallen nature generally, and thus places Hamlet in the quintessential Western quandary of alienation from the material. While the intellect conceptualizes human nature as dichotomous and thus distinguishes itself from the body by an act of self-exile and alienation, death must inevitably reassert that lower realm's ultimate reality. Reason must dismiss the physical body, even if one day that body's death will conquer reason. The Ghost demands that Hamlet reject fallen human nature even as the Prince discovers that nature in himself: he must 'taint not [his] mind' while ridding his world of that nature that has 'fallen off'. But how can he be true to the command when he is already 'tainted'? The serpent has struck, the world is fallen, the voice of 'revenge' is a voice from another realm, a realm that Hamlet can never know. Hamlet lives, not in his father's orchard, but in an 'unweeded garden'.

This conflation of death and death thrusts itself forward repeatedly in acts II and III. In the Player's speech at the end of act II, are we to relate Hamlet to Pyrrhus' filial piety, or his murderous visage, 'horribly trick'd ... [in] total gules' (II, ii, 457)? Hamlet stuns us with the casual comment that Lucianus in *The Murder of Gonzago* is *nephew* to the king. With the hero's murder of Polonius our false dichotomizing must cease: though his continuing conscience/consciousness marks him as anything but 'indifferent', both he and the audience henceforth are fully aware that he, just as his antagonists, is a 'child of the earth', and the graveyard scene's function is to explore the now truly universal implications of this through the singular experience of the hero.

Shakespeare thus emphatically presses at every turn the question of the reason and its boundaries. Hamlet's early exclamation against his mother, that 'a beast that wants discourse of reason would have mourn'd longer' (I, ii, 150–1), presents it as a paradox: how can a human, blessed with 'discourse of reason', forget even more quickly than a beast? By act IV, scene iv, as Hamlet ponders Fortinbras' army, the idea is less paradoxical:

> What is a man,
> If his chief good and market of his time
> Be but to sleep and feed? a beast, no more.
> Sure He that made us with such large discourse,
> Looking before and after, gave us not
> That capability and godlike reason
> To fust in us unus'd.   (IV, iv, 33–8)

The scholastic echoes of this speech make clear that the calculation of Elsinore is a mere parody of that true, 'godlike' reason of the complete consciousness marking human potentiality in the earlier tradition, for the integrative functions of consciousness responsible for unifying memory, experience, thought, and expectation into a significant whole – that is, for articulating meaning – have been completely dismissed. Though Hamlet focuses on his own failure to act against Claudius, none but Hamlet has fully experienced his human potential for 'looking before and after'. Hamlet's sense of man's capability dwarfs Claudius', and emphasizes the distance between man's broadest faculties – his 'godlike reason' – and that *ratio inferior* of narrow cunning by which Claudius and Polonius seek politicly to advance their interests.

Hamlet thus stands in the archetypal human position of having to constitute for himself, against the backdrop and enmity of a meaningless environment, a human, that is to say coherent and meaningful, world, and he eventually does so by accepting his persistent urge to transcend the rational boundaries of his position via the feigning disposition, the urge to play, with its necessary freeing of the imaginative faculty. Whereas the adoption of the 'antic disposition' early in the play is originally an act of calculation, Hamlet's intense confrontation with the artistic set-pieces of the middle acts gradually transforms his understanding of the role of play by providing him with a distanced 'mirror' of the reality of Elsinore. For if 'looking before and after' is Hamlet's ideal, it is also the nature of art, and the crucial speech of the Player King, to which I must now return, enacts it.

As, simultaneously, a character speaking within his own dramatic cosmos and a voice of some author speaking artfully, the Player King articulates two distinct realities. As a 'King' – a man – the Player asserts the absolute disjunction of purpose and end, will and fate, for all men. But as a character shaped into art by his author's hand, his larger reality is quite other: the very assertion 'that our devices still are overthrown' is itself drawn into a perfectly framed whole as the Player moves 'orderly to end where I begun' (iii, ii, 210). Art, unlike reason, does not forget, and within the world of the artistic creation the character speaks lines that do indeed 'look before and after', beyond *The Murder of Gonzago*, throwing an entirely new light on Hamlet's earlier thoughts on play. For the first time since the Ghost left the stage we see enacted a real relationship of purpose and end, even as we hear the Player deny our ability rationally to effect such a union.

Moreover, the Player King's reflections intimately relate him to Pyrrhus' in the earlier artistic inset. For like the Player King, the Pyrrhus of this narrative is both a man and a character of art, and Shakespeare draws attention to his dual nature by 'painting' him a 'neutral' to his duality: though as a man his 'will' drives him on to his revenge, his poet's 'matter' demands the inactivity of a tableaux. This inactivity is so out of character that we dwell upon its 'seeming', and this seeming is precisely echoed in the second inset, where the words of the Player King resolve his human awareness of the divergence of 'will' and 'fate' into the artifactual reality of his own artistic 'end'.

We should hardly be surprised to find these two artistic insets bracketing Hamlet's own famous advice to the players. Most obviously a lecture to the players on the virtues of showing decorum in their art, and thus a Renaissance commonplace, the speech resonates against the matter of the two insets, and thus against Hamlet's practice of *his* 'art'. Hamlet's predicament is analogous to that of the two characters, and thus Shakespeare forces us to ask whether, and in what ways, Hamlet applies his own advice: how has he and how ought he, 'suit the action to the word, the word to the action'?

Moreover, still caught up in the role of dramatist himself here in act iii, Hamlet cannot yet recognize the implications of his poetic principles. His recognition of the problem of the 'matter' in question will finally be reified in the metaphor, not of the dramatist, the creator of plots, but of the actor and the 'matter' of acting itself, a matter beyond the actor's own control and shaped design. 'It is not the contents of a play (the subject matter) but the theatrical mode itself that finally serves "to hold the mirror up to nature." '[8] As he recognizes the limits of his rational control of events, the play metaphor will finally force him to imagine some extrapersonal shaper of events, and to project unto the cosmos the directing of his action.

This is exactly what happens in the shipboard incident, but the important point about this 'epiphany', as it has frequently been conceived, is that it actually includes two distinct, though intimately connected, revelations. Hamlet's perception of that 'divinity' that he now assumes will 'shape his ends', stems from his immediate confrontation with his own death: 'where I found . . . an exact command . . . that, . . . no leisure bated, . . . my head should be strook off' (v, ii, 18–25). The monosyllabic terror of that line conveys the breakdown of all Hamlet's intellectual constructions; free finally and irrevocably from the delusions and perversity of the world of Elsinore, Hamlet is momentarily stripped of all the contextual density that constitutes the world for the individual: he is stripped bare as Lear will be, and stands before death as 'the thing itself, unaccommodated man'.

In response to this revelation he undergoes a second – or, more accurately, he imaginatively creates a second. His own plots overwhelmed by a rush of apparently fortuitous events, Hamlet frames a pattern of these events, and then projects the pattern onto 'a providence' and 'a divinity that shapes our ends, / Rough-hew them how we will' (v, ii, 10–11). The revelation is seen by many Christian commentators on Shakespeare as a clear indication of his new religious affiliation, but, strictly speaking, nothing in the play authorizes such a reading. Shakespeare himself is preoccupied with this distinctly different question of the process by which Hamlet himself *creates*, rather than simply *discovers*, his final belief. Hamlet does not merely turn to a preconceived godhead. He formulates for himself, in the light of all his experience, a deity in his own image that can nevertheless account for the larger world of mutability whose presence now fills his consciousness. Acutely aware of the failure of his own project to shape the world of Elsinore to his desires, he spontaneously predicates a divinity 'like' his own conception of the shaping hand, but extra-personal. As Pyrrhus' will was stymied for one moment by the 'matter' of his author, and as the Player King recognized 'our fate's none of our own', so now Hamlet accepts the submission of *his* matter, both his human nature and his social role of revenger, to his own 'heavenly maker'.

In act v we see a Hamlet who much more adequately embodies his own highest standards. His 'smoothness' even 'in the very torrent, tempest . . . and whirlwind of his passion' (iii, ii, 5–7) flows precisely from the 'temperance' of his now calm mind. His passions now generally 'suit the action to the word, the word to the action' (lines 17–18), whether parodically matching Osric's verbosity with absolute nonsense or seriously requiting deadly treachery with deadly revenge. This ultimate congruence of his advice with the largest issues of the play finally fulfills all the expectation it aroused, for we now can see that 'the purpose of playing' is nothing less than the purpose of life, 'whose end, both at the first and now, was and is, to hold as 'twere the mirror up to nature' (iii, ii, 21–35). In a dark world full of journeymen who have in their pride erected an image not 'made well', Hamlet stands apart as one who has finally learned to 'imitate' properly.

However, where Hamlet in his ignorance learnedly espoused in act III, scene ii the mirror of Ciceronian *mimesis*[9] – an artistic imitation like the Mousetrap that would objectify the virtues and sins it reflected – he now sees a profounder truth, for the mirror revealed in act V is not mimetic but Pauline, reflecting not 'nature' as it appears in daily intercourse, the human nature of Elsinore, but rather that larger, truer nature that for Paul is explicitly God and for Hamlet is the metaphoric, metamorphic imagination[10] that echoes, in human nature, nature's own mutability in all of its various rhythms. In Paul's Christian formulation

> we all beholde as in a mirrour the glorie of the Lord with open face, and are changed into the same image, from glorie to glorie, as by the Spirit of the Lord.
>   (2 Cor. 3:18)

The Pauline mirror, in other words, is an ideal that reflects upon both human virtue and scorn according to the *disparity* between the individual and its reflection – 'darkly', as Paul elsewhere describes the reflection.

In *Hamlet*, I believe, the 'mirror' is not Christ, but rather Hamlet's own imaginative ideal; Shakespeare's interest in Hamlet's belief is not strictly theological, but metaphysical in a broader sense, and psychological, and we might thus say that Shakespeare 'secularizes belief'.[11] The early Hamlet, for all his nobility and idealism, can find no firm point upon which to ground his judgement, because he is confined within a solipsistic world of reason elevated to absolute rule. Only the establishment of some extra-rational, fixed absolute of valuation can ever transcend the absolute meaninglessness of such a world. Having irrevocably lost that earlier world of custom on which his father's realm was founded, Hamlet's only recourse is to create a new world of meaning, that is to say, a new standard or ideal, and this he does in the last act.

This new standard is a product of his integrative imagination. The divinity's characterization is entirely metaphorical, a metamorphosis into a world principle of that which Hamlet finds most fundamental and real in human nature. Immersed in a world of plot and counterplot, of chronicle, report and 'forg'd process', Hamlet naturally resolves his doubt by the replication of his own previous ideal at a cosmic level, fashioning an understanding of the wholeness of reality out of those elements of his own reality that suggest the possibility of wholeness. As Shakespeare has Hamlet articulate his situation after his revelation, he has been 'learned' (i.e. 'taught') that our attempts at control and direction only 'rough-hew' the matter; the 'divinity' finally 'shapes' them, only the divinity *can* finally shape them. For Shakespeare, Hamlet's god is like man (and not *vice versa*) in being a maker, because man's essential nature is that of the maker.

Hamlet's newfound understanding of relation to his (and I stress the possessive) providence makes possible a fundamental reconciliation between those fragmented selves that have made him so complex and confusing a character, especially his public self (reified by his name or reputation), and his personal, felt sense of self.[12] Throughout the last scene our attention focuses, after the agonies his self-division has cost him, on Hamlet's finally achieved integrity. As Ralph Berry recently noted, the final scene, though short, is sufficient: 'a man's life's no more than to say "one"' (v, ii, 74). Unable to enact such a unity earlier in the play, Hamlet is here reconciled to his humanity, its limits, and its prerequisites, and that 'union' that Claudius pledges to the victor Hamlet has rightfully earned. Now we can see why, earlier, the murder of Claudius would not have served: it would have been either an act of reason and calculation or one of passion, not one of the whole man, and thus it would only have furthered his alienation, driving deeper the wedge between self and self-conception. If his action was to be the adequate emblem of the whole self it could only occur once that self was united.

The final scene clearly reveals how central the metaphoric imagination is to Hamlet's final achievement. Hamlet's imaginative enactment of the 'metaphor' actually creates the resolution to the action. If the 'actor' has been an inadequate analogy for the Prince because it expresses to him only one aspect of his self – the calculating player of chameleon public roles – then the 'role' of the fencer unites his whole self: public self, imaged in style, proficiency and strategy, is absorbed into the instinctual passion of competitive confrontation. Hamlet's perception of 'acting' and 'play' has now been fused with his perception of action in life, and with this fusion he is 'ready' to enact that scene that will express his self, if only for a moment, in its true fullness. To speak of the 'tenor' and 'vehicle' of metaphor here, the reality and the image, misses Shakespeare's complex reality: tenor and vehicle coalesce and Hamlet's world reveals itself as metaphoric in its deepest nature. The metamorphic imagination has solved Hamlet's dilemma by imagining a frame for his 'story' capable of instilling meaning in that story by 'shaping an end' to it, and only by his end do we know him.

NOTES

1 Timothy Reiss, *The Discourse of Modernism* (Ithaca: Cornell University Press, 1982), p. 37. In dissecting this rise of a new 'discursive class' Reiss follows Foucault's notion of 'epistemic rupture'; his analysis of the development of the new discourse, which he labels the 'analytico-referential', out of the older one, and its gradual 'occultation' of patterning as a basis for discourse, provides the single most thoroughly articulated analysis of the origins of modern discourse, and the tensions at work in Elizabethan–Jacobean culture.

2 Francis Barker, in *The Tremulous Private Body* (London: Methuen, 1984), addresses *Hamlet* within the context of his discussion of the emergence of the new

discursive class in just these terms, this 'metaphysic of [the body's] ... erasure': speaking of the spectacular violence of Jacobean drama, he comments that 'the deadly subjectivity of the modern is already beginning to emerge and to round vindictively on the most prevalent emblem [i.e., the body] of the discursive order it supersedes' (p. 25).

3 Maynard Mack, 'The World of *Hamlet*', *Yale Review*, 41 (1952), 504.

4 I focus on the aesthetic dimensions of the 'matter' of the play at the expense of other lines of development of this crucial concept; Margaret Ferguson, for instance, pursues the hero's interest in using the idiom as a vehicle for illustrating the metaphorical dimension, the 'play', of all language. Nevertheless, her emphasis on the 'materiality' of language suggests a connection to aesthetic issues in the play. See '*Hamlet*: Letters and Spirits', in *Shakespeare and The Question of Theory*, ed. Patricia Parker and Geoffrey Hartman (New York: Methuen, 1985), pp. 294ff.

5 Anthony B. Dawson, *Indirections: Shakespeare and the Art of Illusion* (Toronto: University of Toronto Press, 1978), p. 50.

6 All references are to the text of *The Riverside Shakespeare*, ed. G. Blakemore Evans (Boston: Houghton Mifflin, 1974).

7 James L. Calderwood, in *To Be and Not To Be* (New York: Columbia University Press, 1983) remarks of the famous soliloquy that 'the indeterminance of death ... blur[s] his distinction between To Be and Not To Be' (p. 99); it is precisely this indeterminance that lies beyond the realm of rationality, and thus separates Hamlet's self-awareness from that of the other characters.

8 Alvin B. Kernan, *The Playwright as Magician* (New Haven: Yale University Press, 1979), p. 106.

9 My discussion of *mimesis* here is particularly indebted to Howard Felperin's chapter on *Hamlet* in *Shakespearian Representation* (Princeton University Press, 1977), esp. pp. 45–6.

10 The phrase was coined by Marjorie B. Garber, *Dream in Shakespeare* (New Haven: Yale University Press, 1974).

11 Both the term itself and the idea that Shakespeare has been influenced by the Christian as well as the classical conception of *mimesis* were suggested to me by my colleague Helen Whall.

12 On this point see Calderwood, *To Be and Not To Be*, Part I.

Shakespeare's problem comedies: an Hegelian approach to genre*

SHAWN WATSON

Interpretation is often a matter of haggling over the emotional value of language, imagery, incident, plot, character, which are the real goods of a text: the critic prices and catalogues each item and tallies the sum like a bookkeeper. In drama, that total is often expressed as genre, and plays are rated according to comic or tragic standards. Unhappily, especially in rich and complex plays, genre is paper money, worth the whole world of a work if we have confidence in it and know what concrete values back it up, but worthless otherwise, or even worse than worthless: counterfeit and capable of deceiving. Nowhere else does generic value seem so arbitrarily assigned or so bankrupt of precision as in later Shakespearian comedy, where the conventional counters of both tragedy and comedy – pleasure and regret, promises of life and threats of death, farcical moments and sombre moments, wonderful characters and repulsive characters – are so admixed that ideas of genre seem incapable of governing the variety or drawing a total. The problems of the problem comedies are often, it seems to me, generic problems. Critics cannot bargain their way into reasonable inter-pretations because comic values are largely speculative and comic standards generally imprecise. No *persona*, no incident, no resolution, no moral tone is by and of itself exclusively comic, and it seems that no simple appeal to form or affect or intention will uncover a proper definition of comedy. Genre seems to me to require subtler tactics, and it is to philosophers, not critics, that we must turn for those – to Schopenhauer or to Hegel.

But the trouble with philosophers is that comedy is only a part of their business. For Schopenhauer, the grim force of reason, the Idea, is a harsh 'governess' against whom the individual Will revolts in an almost spiteful impulse toward an impossible freedom. Comedy, by virtue of its association with that Will, is exhilarating, but unkind, and bitter, and hopeless in Schopenhauer's scheme – things which it never is in Shakespeare's plays. By postulating a happier conflict, a flux that bespeaks a unity, Hegel makes

* A draft of this paper was read at the *Themes in Drama* International Conference held at the University of California, Riverside, in February 1988.

comedy joyous rather than rebellious, a sign of the expansiveness rather
than the recalcitrance of experience. In comedy – or rather, the comic
dialectic moment – the mind, self-satisfied and self-assured, finds release
from fear and escape from threat; it sees the world as genial and responds
with geniality. Hegel's metaphor for this kind of being is the fruit that
moves toward the hand that would pluck it:[1] he specifies a magical
synchronization of subject and object that transcends an action. In comedy,
the universe turns in concert, achieves a harmony. I see exactly that sort of
poise in Isabella's turn toward her Duke and in his to her; it marks the
pardon Bertram begs of Helena; it is the kind of equilibrium which Troilus
reaches when he embraces silence and Prospero reaches when he eschews
black magic. Hegel names the feelings and even offers an experiential
pattern that explains their presence at given moments. But he does not
explain how writers enforce those patterns, how they construct a play to
control an audience, or what concrete norms must govern a play in order to
make it reassuring. His description of comic experience is supple enough to
fit these problem plays, but the existential principles need to be expressed
as critical terms before the problem of genre is addressed.

I think those terms must concern the relationship between objectivity
and subjectivity. In discussing the 'truth of self-certainty', Hegel describes
the relationship as a process:

> The simple substance of life, therefore, is the diremption of itself into shapes
> and forms, and at the same time the dissolution of these substantial differences;
> and the resolution of this diremption is just as much a process of diremption, of
> articulating. Thus both sides of the entire movement which were before
> distinguished – namely, the *setting up of individual forms* lying apart and
> undisturbed in the universal medium of independent existence, and the *process*
> of life – collapse into one another. The latter is just as much a formation of
> individual shapes, as it is a way of cancelling a shape assumed; and the former,
> the setting up of individual forms, is as much a cancelling as an articulation of
> them. The fluent, continuous element is itself only the abstraction of the
> essential reality, or it is actual only as a definite shape or form; and that it
> articulates itself is once more a breaking up of articulated form, or a dissolution
> of it. The *entire* circuit of this activity constitutes Life. It is neither what is
> expressed to begin with, the immediate continuity and concrete solidarity of its
> essential nature; nor the stable, subsisting form, the discrete individual which
> exists on its own account; nor the bare process of this form, nor again is it the
> simple combination of all these moments. It is none of these; it is the *whole*
> which develops itself, resolves its own development, and in this movement
> simply preserves itself.[2]

Hegel speaks of the 'articulation' of 'individual forms' – their objectification
– and the 'process of life' – subjective experience, the conscious self not
separated from the medium which nourishes it. A play must freeze some
moment of the dialectical equilibrium: art stops Life. When the comic
moment occurs,

the pretentious claims of the universal abstract nature are shown up and discovered in the actual self; it is seen to be caught and held in a concrete reality, and lets the mask drop, just when it wants to be something genuine. The self, appearing here in its significance as something actual, plays with the mask which it once puts on, in order to be its own person; but it breaks away from this seeming and pretence just as quickly again, and comes out in its nakedness and commonness, which it shows not to be distinct from the proper self, the actor, nor again from the onlooker.[3]

Subjective and objective modes of being are, however, elusive enough in a metaphysical discourse; in a literary one, they tend to evaporate altogether. More concrete equivalents would be more useful, and I think Aristotle can supply them. He identifies *action* and *character* as separate ingredients of drama. Action – that which, even if its significance is ambiguous, is representative and defining – is the analogue of Hegel's objectivity. Out of an infinity of possible motions, an action is a single choice that denies all others. Action is irrevocable; what is done may be corrected but cannot be (perceptually) undone. Action creates history, necessity, even fate. Action is what creates actuality out of potentiality.

And the Aristotlean version of Hegel's subjectivity is character, from which action arises and which is made manifest by that action. Character is nature, essence, potential, and it is incapable of complete, final or perfectly objective representation: it is simply conscious (but not self-conscious) self, indefinite and inexpressible. This subjectivity is what triumphs in Hegel's comic moment. Put in more conventional literary terms, a comic play is one in which character attempts to objectify itself through action and, failing, rejoices to find self-consciousness (the newly-wise or newly-reformed state) able to master all difficulties (a mastery which implies 'the return of everythng universal into certainty of self, a certainty which, in consequence, is this complete loss of fear of everything strange and alien, and complete loss of substantial reality on the part of that which is alien and external'[4]). The 'form of essentiality' – dramatic action – is 'dissolved' by 'self-consciousness' – by the posited existence and unexpressed action of dramatic character. The comic writer, therefore, must follow a generic prescription for the relationship of action and character. He must write plays in which that action comprises patently false information about character or proves incompetent or insufficient to express character. Comic action allows comic character to remain subjective by proving its inexpressibility. Comedy, and the pleasure, solace, reassurance and geniality derived from it, depend upon the spectacle of belied action.

The question, then, is how a dramatist shows action counterfeit. In Shakespeare, and probably in all fine comedy, the answer is by showing recognizably aberrant action, action that is not simply witless or ridiculous or purposeless or contradictory, but that is self-disguising and therefore incredible. The simplest sort of self-disguising action is farce, or rather, the simplest controls for illuminating the disguise are farcical, since farce, in *Measure for Measure*, is an incredibly sophisticated affair.

Farce? In a play that is often grim and threatening enough to be a passable tragi-comedy? I think so, but the trick is to separate the sinner from the sin – a fairly standard moral rule and one urged by great authority, but difficult in this play because the sinners generally pronounce their sins themselves, and do it with a certain amount of pride. But I think we must yield to Shakespeare's authority and allow the play to be comic. To measure Isabella by her responses to her difficulties, Angelo by his responses to temptation, Claudio by his despair or Vincentio by his intellectualizing is to forget that the play is a comedy and to accept action as sincere testimony to character. In this play, it isn't; the joke, scene by scene, is that the characters are always more than they do. Isabella acts gently with Lucio, rationally with Angelo, and viciously with her poor harried brother; the speeches she makes are so obviously ill-tuned to the situations she makes them in that we are forced to conclude that her character is far deeper than the single dimensions that her actions express in linear order. They disguise rather than clarify her nature. Similarly, Vincentio is magisterial with his counselors and stoic with his priest and clumsy with the folk he rules; like Isabella, he is too many things to be anything at all if we rely on his actions for information about his character. Both use words to paint what they would, for various and not very admirable reasons, be; both are attempting to renounce their essential selves. By denying passion they make themselves comic, and the thwarting of their verbal ruses is the comic action of the play.

That action converts tragic material to comic by giving it the proper generic context. Certainly Claudio's 'ravening rats' speech sounds full of tragedy and despair and existential anguish, but that *sounding* is exactly what makes it funny. His confession shows poor estimation of human nature, and a certain narrowness to boot. How unhappy ought he to be for having made love to a lovely lady who deserves both love and him – and who is on-stage for handy reference during this self-damning speech, just in case the audience might be tempted to take Claudio at his own unflattering word. Transgression is, after all, not damnation; some of us may escape whipping, after all, unless we succumb to self-flagellation, which Claudio seems capable of. Action is, after all, not character, and his confusion of the two makes Claudio's gravest speeches his silliest. Vincentio's most serious speech, his 'absolute for death' sermon, is evidence that he's also infected with the impulse to flog himself; in context of his posited mercifulness, the speech is flap and fluff, seriously intended, to be sure, but impossible to take seriously. Isabella's repeated rages are balanced against her robes, her crucifix, her loveliness. Angelo's sudden vile passion, threatening as it might be, isn't: he overestimates an action and underestimates – or momentarily forgets, stock-fish that he is – his character. He considers himself wicked, but then everyone in this play who has the slightest claim to virtue does that; they panic, embroil themselves in subtle plots, run headlong into the brick walls of one another's stubbornness, and the result is farce.

The walls, of course, are metaphorical, and the puppets that are entangled in each other's strings are incarnations of aspects of larger and finer characters rather than the wispy stereotypes that people most farces, but *Measure for Measure* is farce just the same. It is even a kind of psychological slapstick, and it depends upon the same indestructibility of presence that broad farce does. Cartoon *personae* survive brutal beatings; Feydeau characters survive accidents and abuses both physical and emotional, but trudge on, unscathed, to a sparkling conclusion which reveals, almost by miracle, almost with a puff of a magician's camouflaging smoke, a thoroughgoing immortality of character. Nobody changes in farce – and nobody changes in *Measure for Measure*. What happens is that the blinding veils of action have been removed from character, and the whole crew returns to themselves. Despite purposeful objectification, despite will, despite their best efforts to be something else, the characters finally become what, by nature, they were all along. They endure and are unsullied by what they've done. *Measure for Measure* ends with its characters resigning themselves to *being* in place of *seeming*, and that constitutes the comic triumph of the self.

This suggests that, in dramatic comedy, essence (or character) is incorruptible. In the comic world nothing save surface admits of change. Intricate convolutions of plot, whether they are created by mistaken identity, physical disguise, misguided steps in a sly or awkward dance serve to establish, by their very transitoriness and ineffectuality, the permanence of subjective existence. Actions threaten and threats evaporate; Shakespeare and Charlie Chaplin knew the same tricks for making them do so. In *Measure for Measure* and in simple farce, action is the foiled objectivity whose dissolution Hegel says we applaud, enjoy, and assume we share.

One caution: for the characters in *Measure for Measure* and in most farces, things turn out as they should, but that *should* is not the sign of comic resolution: Macbeth and Othello and Hamlet, given their play history, seem to have ended as they should have. Genre works on the principle of *must*, not *ought*, and that is why comedy can encompass satire as well as farce. Satire is another method of using self-disguising action, and so it fulfills the generic specifications of comedy. *Measure for Measure* returns its characters to themselves after separating silly behaviour from very pretty nature, and thus the sweet sentimentality of its weddings-all-around ending; *Troilus and Cressida*, on the other hand, is kind to neither action nor character – both are debased and so the tone of the play is baleful. It is nevertheless comic because it proposes the same enigmatic subjectivity of character and the same impotence of action to suggest the enigma as does *Measure for Measure*. The play is censorious and reassuring at the same time.

The satire of *Troilus and Cressida* is aimed at language; bad language creates an objective surface underneath which character follows an inscrutable and unruffled path. Troilus is obsessed with rhetoric and uses it to seduce a lady; Ulysses is obsessed with rhetoric and uses it to seduce a prince; Thersites and Pandarus are obsessed with words, though they can barely handle syntax, let alone rhetoric, and manage to seduce good sense in general. Each *persona* tries to pass off language as sincere expression of genuine emotion, as substance, and each receives a comic, though bitter, come-uppance for his pains. The lies they tell are palpable, stupid, gross, and they make, comically, not an *ort* of difference in the outcome of the play. Action exposes faults but does not express character. As in Jonsonian satire, in *Troilus and Cressida* humours, perversions, manipulations are finally rendered harmless and painless because they are objective targets that draw affection away from subjective characters. Essence is not disturbed because it is, in satire, nearly perfectly disguised.

Troilus' 'what is Cressid?' speech is typical of the play's comedy: it breaks down under the weight of its own artifice. The language self-destructs; Troilus has mocked himself. That would be pathetic and forgivable were he, like the characters in *Measure for Measure*, simply taking himself too seriously, but his vice is worse: he is not taking the world seriously enough. Arrogantly, he assumes that in objectifying himself he can recreate the world according to the demands of his nature. He is never wise enough to be frightened of the alien and the external; he insults independent forms and they prove their substance by resisting his definitions. He loses the lover his actions have gained him because her character is something that he takes no account of. Ulysses' infamous 'degree' speech makes him Troilus' brother. He works his will in fine flowing metaphor, but the tail end of his eloquence trips him up: Shakespeare has him end with just enough of a show of ire over Achilles' mockery that the audience can distinguish the seeming and the being, the false objectivity and the shadowy character imperfectly glimpsed beneath it. Achilles and Hector, of course, eventually become the prime movers of the play; Ulysses and Troilus, despite their best efforts, cannot prevent themselves from the frustrating deflation of being minor actors.

Cressida, though, is the comic masterpiece of the play. She turns from pretty poetry to randy prose without any effort at all, just as she turns from one lover to another without having been touched by either. Her character is so far uninvolved in the play that no style can express it nor relationship affect it. We see of her only a series of dressing gowns, disguises, complacent objectivities; like Troilus, she can never control the objective world – she never learns to use her character. She settles for ineffectuality and for actions; she survives her poor choices, and that makes her comic. Neither her betrayals of herself nor Troilus' misplaced faith in himself amounts to powerful or positive being; neither Troilus' sugary language nor Thersites' dill can make Cressida or Achilles or Ajax any different than they are. That is the comedy of the play and the source of the one-dimensionality of satiric figures. Subjectivity endures all impulses to objectify it, in satire as well as farce, but in satire, the self seeks to compel not itself but others to be objective, which means that satire's prime concern is tyranny. The characters in Jonsonian comedy are victimized – made objects – by Face and Subtle, by Volpone and Mosca by the same proces; these manipulators, too, demean and reduce themselves in that making. In *The Alchemist* and *Volpone* as well as in *Troilus and Cressida*, language is the medium of objectification, and it always proves insufficient to the task. Action in a satire need not restore or create wisdom in a character, because comedy is a function of the ineffectuality of action, not of the quality of a character. Troilus foreswears bad language, Face and Subtle save themselves from a plan that has misfired; Volpone and Mosca are punished for their schemes, which have fallen to pieces, but not for their vices, which remain, as part of character, unchanged. All these figures outlive their failures to enact themselves and so are comic figures. The plays they appear in do not allow them to be consumed in their actions, as tragic characters are; thus satire, even when it is cruel, is comic, since an audience never fears for the existence of the figures it watches. Existence – character – never finds a place on the stage; it remains invulnerable while its actions are ridiculed. This invulnerability (or absence) prevents fear, as Hegel says comedy must, and fear is just what Shakespeare and Jonson avoid producing in their satire. Manners change; men don't. Satire depends on Hegel's dichotomy, for it displays action it would modify against an essence which it takes as given.

In farce, action is contradictory; in satire, it is evasive or abusive; in romance, it is simply peripheral. *All's Well That Ends Well* is perfect romance because it perfectly obeys the generic rules of comedy. In fact, it is almost a play about comedy. Helena's task, a wonderfully comic one, is to make her character sufficiently known to her unwilling beloved through the insufficient mode of action. She courts Bertram and becomes objective and a threat to him in doing so. Each is alien and recalcitrant to the apprehension of the other; his refusal of her is a perfect emblem of Hegel's independent form lying isolate and dead and removed from the process of life. Her wooing and winning of him is an emblem of the incorporation of the world into the certainty of self that happens at the comic moment. Throughout most of the play, Helena's purpose is to dissolve Bertram.

But how can the inexpressible character, the dissolving agent, be expressed? Helena's actions are a wonderful and puzzling mixture of right and wrong, laudable and not. She can cure her king but finds that act incapable of curing Bertram's loathing. What she would force by her actions she can move only through her nature; the task of seduction, for her as much as for Troilus, is objective enactment of will and therefore bound, by comic convention, to fail. What never fails in romance is love, which, in Shakespeare, is a sort of invisible exhalation of essence or of nature. Shakespeare's comic lovers always love without proof or cause: they sense one another's characters by means of a special faculty that figures more ordinary don't possess. Their affection is motivated by nothing or by very little except an unexpressed virtue that manifests itself largely in the ability to love. Comic characters love the essence, not the object, which is why comic love is so superhumanly sweet – and why *All's Well*, though its plot seems arbitrary and its heroine seems sometimes selfish or even tyrannical, is such a funny play.

Helena simply exercises the comic figure's prerogative to be more than her relentless courtship makes her out to be. As an indication of how much more, the audience has the testimony of a chorus of aristocratic characters, who praise at every opportunity her unseen virtue, and the testimony of her love. Between them, those witnesses are great authority and should be enough to establish Helena's character despite the peculiarity of her actions. What seems most bothersome about the play, though, is not Helena's ambiguity but Bertram's downright deceitfulness. He lies, evades, schemes, clear to the very end of the last act, and his conversion to love is more miraculous than we are used to finding in Shakespeare, whom we require psychological realism from. Comedy, though, is anti-realistic insofar as it is anti-objective; when it denies the validity of action it sets up the possibility of denying logic and rejecting logical motivation. The comedy of *All's Well* depends on the exaggeration of that denial – in fact, on the delightful destruction of motive altogether.

The last scene of the play is not a botch but a masterpiece; Bertram's magic conversion is actually Hegel's self's reaffirmation of its independence of history and circumstance, which are that self's objectifications in time. The play's resolution defies both memory and reason, and that defiance is the source of our pleasure. Helena and Bertram have both been, as comic characters must be, shadows rather than selves; their actions have hidden them from one another and disguised them in front of the audience. The disguise is discarded on both sides; when Bertram recognizes his wife's nature instead of her actions, he apprehends her worth and drops to his knees: Helena has proven to *be* more than he thought she could *do*. She appears, serene, mysterious, quiet (for the first time in the play), and quite pregnant, which makes her a double enigma. She is the source and container of her self and her child's self; essence is the 'receptacle of all contraries',[5] and what better image of essence could there be than such miraculous motherhood as Helena's? The impossible has been made possible in Helena, and the impossible is made actual at the end of her play. Bertram capitulates to the awesomeness of it all; he yields to a comic view of the world; he joins the subjective universe. What prompts him to do that is not what he has discovered, but a new understanding of what can't be discovered – of character.

He asks for explanation, but what kind will he get? One that's guaranteed to prove the utter dependence of event on character, for the actions of the play have been incredible, arbitrary, manufactured, and governed by what nature deserves rather than by what action has won. Of course the ending of *All's Well* is unlikely; action has been subservient to character, and when that happens, motives are never articulated, except love, which, like the comically-disposed self, takes all the world calmly and confidently to itself. Bertram is the fruit that has come to Helena's hand.

All's Well is an emblem, all told, of the comic dialectic that Hegel describes, and *The Tempest* is the next stage in the movement Hegel describes toward divine knowledge. Prospero goes through the countermotions that Hegel postulates in *Phenomenology of Mind* and stops at nothing short of Revealed Religion. *The Tempest* is not comic but supracomic. Prospero spends his time in the play accomplishing a little revenge that has nothing to do with his nature – which, in fact, runs counter to it and which is rejected in the course of the play. The joke is that Prospero undergoes a steady process of religious conversion that is only accidentally related to, and certainly not motivated or defined by, his political or artistic machinations. The play seems confounding and ill-ordered and threatening on its surface, and it is; what is clarifying and certain and reassuring is the allegory of enlightenment that takes place behind that surface.

Prospero has two major speeches in the play and a third at its end; together they form a dialectical pattern. The 'rounded by a sleep' speech is occasioned by a recognition of mortality and the finite scope of human nature – by the awareness of the objective universal. Prospero objectifies himself in this speech, which is fearfully poignant because it is profoundly tragic. It is exactly the kind of awareness that marks Hegel's tragic moment. In the presence of summoned goddesses, Prospero thinks on Caliban: the contradiction of the divine and the bestial suggests a human nature that, in trying to be both, is neither, that is crushed by the weight of alien principles. At this point, Prospero's self is dissolved in the solemn objectivity of the world, not it in him. The counterbalance to this perception is Prospero's drowning of his book – his foreswearing of individual manipulation for a faithful, orthodox, and comic reliance on the concord he hopes for between himself and the world. He calls upon divine motion to replace his magic, and the friendly universe obliges. This is comic percep-

tion and comic experience in which the self seems to encompass, blissfully,
everything that is. Prospero goes from feeling at odds with the world, an
objective creation himself, to feeling that his will and the world's are one
and the same.

The process, though, is not complete. The comic moment is, after all,
one-sided; it must subsume conflict, opposition and objectivity before it
becomes, in turn, revelation. This combination Prospero signals when, very
startlingly, he acknowledges Caliban as his own. All things are a unity to
divine wisdom, and it is out of such wisdom that Prospero speaks when he
answers Miranda's enthusiasm for the 'brave new world' with, ' 'Tis new to
thee.' The world is beautiful and new to the creature who experiences it
comically, subjectively, with delight and self-assurance. Prospero's answer
implies, of course, knowledge more complete than hers – a wisdom higher
than comic self-certainty – but the remark is kind and hopeful rather than
chastising or resigned. The final measure of that kindness is the grace with
which Prospero turns to his audience in his epilogue and ends the play with
the Christian formula for mixing self and other and for approaching Grace
through Charity. The epilogue of *The Tempest* is a restatement of the
Athanasian Creed, spoken by a figure whose conversion, if less obvious
than Bertram's, is more profound. If a play can be said to demonstrate how
an Hegelian approach to genre works, it is this play, which seems almost to
be a dramatic allegory of the phenomenology of mind. Its protagonist first
apprehends tragic objectivity (the slight meaning of his own and others'
actions), next manages to remake and restore the world to a subjective self,
and finally succeeds in experiencing the Hegelian and paradoxical unity of
'diremption' and 'articulation', of the circuitry of cancellation and assumption of shape and form, of the 'activity' that 'constitutes Life'.

The types of comedy, from farce to allegory, seem to me equally indebted,
not to a form or subject, but to a perspective which informs and colors and
shapes all forms and subjects the genre treats. In all those types, what an
audience sees is that behavior, history, memory, objective manifestation of
character in action are incapable of expressing or defining essence, human
nature: they are ephemeral, and when they are, they can never harm or
exhaust that nature. Comic vitality depends upon that inexhaustability,
that endurance, that changelessness, and the genre of comedy is marked
and governed by the purposeful setting up of objective action against a
background of subjective character. In the comic moment, the subjective
must always triumph, and as it does, comedy stamps the visage of the self on
the metal of experience. In that moment we take the measure and know the
value of the genre.

NOTES

1 G. W. F. Hegel, *The Phenomenology of Mind*, trans. J. B. Baillie (London: George Allen & Unwin Ltd, 1949), pp. 384–5.
2 Hegel, pp. 223–4.
3 Hegel, p. 745.
4 Hegel, pp. 748–9.
5 Paphnutius, a character in the play of the same name by Hroswitha, uses this phrase.

Self-undoing paradox, scepticism, and Lear's abdication*

WILLIAM O. SCOTT

One aspect of the role of philosophy in drama is that dramatic characters often express philosophical ideas. Another is that philosophy requires a close questioning of positions and of their formulation and the process of inquiry is frequently dramatized. Dramatic action can also put beliefs and resolutions to a test. All of these possibilities – which implicate the textbook dramatic elements of dialogue, characterization, and action – can provoke retractions, re-thinkings, a process of almost unending search. As a philosophical model for these conditions I propose the liar paradox, and my main dramatic example will be *King Lear*. Moreover, without actually entailing such a result, this paradox has some affinity with scepticism in philosophy, which is also relevant to Shakespeare's play.

The liar paradox – a sentence such as 'This very sentence is false' – is a paradox in being self-referential; because it is a self-conflicting instance of itself, it seems to be false if true, and true if false. It has a long philosophical history, and it has continued to raise problems for set theory and metamathematics, with the famous twentieth-century names including Russell and Gödel.[1] In drama an analogue to such problematic self-reference would be problematic metadrama, an allusion to the play as play that would somehow be at odds with itself: thus the actor playing Macbeth implies that an actor's words (even those very ones he is saying) are full of sound and fury, signifying nothing.[2] Less radically, the circumstances or identity of a dramatic character might undercut or modify his or her words, whether purposely or through dramatic irony. A deliberate allusion by the speaker to his own circumstances so as to undermine his words does seem evident in the historical form of the liar paradox, in which Epimenides of Crete says that all Cretans are liars. Here is the comment on that paradox in a logic text which Shakespeare evidently knew:

> This is called a liyng argument, for what soeuer ye shal saie, ye must nedes saie amisse. Epimenides a man borne in Crete, saied that the people borne in Crete, were liars, saied he true, or no? If ye saie that he saied truth, I maie well saie,

* A draft of this paper was read at the *Themes in Drama* International Conference held at the University of California, Riverside, in February 1988: its writing was aided by a University of Kansas research grant.

that cannot be well saied: for if the people in Crete be liers, then lied Epimenides, and so his saiyng cannot bee true, because he was a manne there borne, and one of Crete, and saied thei were liers. Again, if ye iudge that the people there, been no liers, then Epimenides saied trueth, euen when he saied, the people of Crete are liers, because he himself was a man of Crete.[3]

Epimenides' point depends on our quasi-dramatic recognition that he wants us to see an incongruity between what he says and who he is. Naturally we react to him and his speech as shifty, and our judgment reflects on problems of language and self-reference in general.

In turn one could say that theatrical performance is broadly similar in its very nature to the liar paradox. Umberto Eco makes that comparison and considers that the mere presence of an actor on stage implies the assertion, 'I am acting'; thus 'By this implicit statement the actor tells the truth since he announces that *from that moment on* he will lie.'[4] This situation is not quite a paradox if the distinction between true moments and the ensuing false moments can be held; but it often does not hold, as in the many performances where the aim is precisely to demolish the boundaries between the performance and its context. The lie may be announced by nothing other than a lying show with which we the audience already play at collusion.

Dramatic characters may play these paradoxical games with each other, just as actors do with an audience. In Amiri Baraka's *Dutchman*, Lula toys with Clay:

Clay. You act like you're on television already.
Lula. That's because I'm an actress.
Clay. I thought so.
Lula. Well, you're wrong. I'm no actress. I told you I always lie. I'm nothing, honey, and don't you ever forget it...
Clay. You sure you're not an actress? All that self-aggrandizement.
Lula. Well, I told you I wasn't an actress... but I also told you I lie all the time. Draw your own conclusions.[5]

How much an actress Lula is will appear only at the close and in a far-from-playful fashion. Indeed the title of the play, a subject of much speculation, might well imply a metadramatic allusion to dutchman as the scene-builder's tape that covers the joins, like papering over the cracks: the action of the play strikes the set and strips the tape to reveal the fissures in society and between and within individuals. The games of the characters thus become a hint of the savage game in the whole play.

In *King Lear* some of these paradoxical functions belong to the Fool. His commentary, though directed mainly at others, depends much for its complex effect on his acknowledged position as Fool who applies that label to himself and others. The would-be wise persons, as he shows, prove their folly and thereby undercut their own speech; and so (except for his crafty self-deprecating irony) does the self-confessed professional fool. The actor who first played this role, Robert Armin, must have excelled at this sport before he ever came to act for Shakespeare's company; his *Quips upon Questions* (1600), a collection of caustic rhymes which seems in part to reflect his earlier playhouse experience, has some one-upmanship jokes where the quipping character puts the label of fool (or other disparagements) on a previous satiric commentator or on the audience.[6] He describes the role of stage Fool as a sort of self-mutilation, but for a financial reward which in turn makes fools of the audience:

> He playes the Wise man then, and not the Foole,
> That wisely for his lyuing so can do:
> So doth the Carpenter with his sharpe toole,
> Cut his owne finger oft, yet liues by't to.
>> He is a foole to cut his limbe say I,
>> But not so, with his toole to liue thereby.
> ... For he shalle haue what thou that time hast spent,
>> Playing the foole, thy folly to content.

> (B4v, quotations reversed)

The Fool has his fun out of making these reversals explicit, and so, doubtless, does the audience; in paying to be called fool it both contents and confirms its own folly. The cycle of enjoyment takes yet another turn in the Fool's overt reference to it; thus there is an action like self-disclosing paradox about the exchange.

In *King Lear* the Fool, whatever the ambiguities of his position, harangues Lear on his foolish treatment of his daughters and shows how his misfortunes result from it:

> Fathers that wear rags
>> Do make their children blind,
> But fathers that bear bags
>> Shall see their children kind.
> Fortune, that arrant whore,
> Ne'er turns the key to th' poor.

> (II, iv, 47–52)[7]

Perhaps we concur too easily in this prudential judgment; for it makes a cynical assumption that one can buy love which repeats Lear's first error in his demands from his daughters. The Fool's advice, then, parodies that mistake; and as a parodistic mistake it must deprecate itself, like a paradox. But it is also a further statement of misguided consequences, for Lear's erring attept at prudence has only made him more vulnerable. Thus the parody, reversing its role, simultaneously gains authority as a lesson from the Fool to Lear.

In other ways too, the Fool shows prudence to be both an appealing and a treacherous guide, as in this admonition to Kent about his loyalty to Lear:

> We'll set thee to school to an ant, to teach thee there's no laboring i' th' winter.
> All that follow their noses are led by their eyes but blind men, and there's not a

nose among twenty but can smell him that's stinking. Let go thy hold when a
great wheel runs down a hill, lest it break thy neck with following; but the great
one that goes upward, let him draw thee after. When a wise man gives thee
better counsel, give me mine again. I would have none but knaves follow it,
since a fool gives it.

> That sir which serves and seeks for gain,
> 　And follows but for form,
> Will pack when it begins to rain,
> 　And leave thee in the storm.
> But I will tarry; the fool will stay,
> 　And let the wise man fly.
> The knave turns fool that runs away;
> 　The fool no knave, perdy.

(lines 66–83)

The Fool's moves are at least doubly paradoxical and self-mutilating.
Should one let go the wheel, as he first seems to advise? He unsays his self-
protective counsel, invoking the conventional lack of authority in a Fool's
discourse; but the unsaying is itself a saying of his ironic intent, by which
that authority would still hold.[8] Again, in the rhyme which follows, he
reclaims authority in that the label of 'fool' belongs really to the self-serving
knave who is morally unwise. The paradoxical self-underminings explore
the dilemma of fool or knave in Kent's situation, as they could not do so
effectively were it not for the precarious status of a fool's advice. The
dilemmas of the helpless follower are also those of Cordelia confronted with
a demand to which no reply is adequate,[9] of Kent protesting in that same
early scene, and of Gloucester risking his safety for the mad king.

Here is another downhill career of the great wheel, Gloucester's blinding
for his fidelity to Lear; though himself a follower, Gloucester is also a wheel
whose fall could break his loyal son Edgar. In turn a consequence of both
falls is also in some ways an emblem of them, Gloucester's attempt to
plunge off Dover cliff.[10] The ironies and duplicities of that emblem begin to
hint at the paradoxes of the whole play. At the outset, the supposed
approach of Edgar and Gloucester to the cliff is ambiguously presented:
Edgar's description of it to beguile Gloucester's imagination is exactly what
one would expect if they were 'really' nearing it on Shakespeare's bare,
unillusory stage.[11] Thus the visible lie seems at first none other than the lie
that Eco attributes to all playing. But Edgar patently deceives Gloucester
that he has fallen and that a devil tempted him to it, with the stated
motivation that 'Why I do trifle thus with his despair / Is done to cure it'
(IV, vi, 33–4). This fakery must undercut for us Edgar's authority as a
moralist, inviting as it does our paradoxical qualification. And to imagine
Shakespeare himself making such a trifle of his whole play is to recognize
how far the play is from this didactic trick. Yet what is the total effect of
dramatic illusion except such a contrivance, translated to a metadramatic

level and in this case wrested from one character's control and deprived of moralization and optimism?[12]

There are discrepancies between Gloucester's leap and Lear's sufferings, and sometimes between Lear's thoughts and the facts, which we ought to notice for their ironic self-undoings of tidy parallel meanings. Though both Lear and Gloucester fall forward on their own in abdication or would-be suicide, other characters are ready to tell them what the fall means, albeit with paradoxical self-deprecations that undermine claims to meaning. Both Kent and the Fool want Lear to know the mistakes which have brought on his woes, and they must therefore share some responsibility for his ensuing madness.[13] Yet the Fool's parables, because they are self-evident in their contrived messages but also carry their own obviously-ironic dismissal as a fool's satire, sustain a paradoxical doubt of the process by which a fallible interpreter finds meaning in events. Edgar too, in his guise as poor Tom the lunatic, contributes to Lear's mistakings and perhaps thereby his madness; though the innocence of his intent excuses him, it is far from validating his words. It is actually Lear's choice to read in Tom's plight his own: 'Has his daughters brought him to this pass? / Couldst thou save nothing? Wouldst thou give 'em all?' (III, iv, 62–3). But Edgar's tale of being possessed and maddened by the foul fiend for his past sins finds an accidental match in Lear's desire to find avenging gods in the storm; thus, perhaps, we are to see a hint of falsity in both characters' mental patterns. The paradoxical disruption of closure in form and meaning between the two stories is well expressed in this statement by Ann Thompson: 'it is remarkable in this play how Shakespeare constantly disrupts the apparent simplicity of the parallel plots by having his characters ignore the similarities the audience can see and suggest others which we know to be false.'[14] Lear is also deluded by Edgar's disguise; the 'poor, bare, forked animal' is not, at least in the way that Lear thinks, 'the thing itself' or 'unaccommodated man' (lines 105–6).[15] The content of that vision is qualified, though not quite denied, by the dubious means of achieving it. For us, then, the set-builder's dutchman is ripped from the scene to reveal (with paradoxically guilty openness) the nature of its contrivance.

It is important in another sense that Lear takes the initiative in his own misfortunes: not only does he choose the initial mistake, he continually, from the moment he rushes out into the storm, wills to expose himself to hardship. There is a pertinent fiction that he chose the results of his error in the error itself: the Fool often talks this way, and, once having begun to suffer, Lear seems determined to make his words come true:

> Take physic, pomp;
> Expose thyself to feel what wretches feel,
> That thou mayst shake the superflux to them,
> And show the heavens more just.(III, iv, 33–6)

His new-found sense of justice and compassion reverses his arguments to his daughters that he needed more than the little that was still left to him; at the same time, though, it continues the action of giving and abdication that he had begun without knowing its end.

This reversal and continued search has its counterpart in another kind of 'paradox' (rhetorical rather than philosophical) popular in Shakespeare's time, the one that reverses common opinion, especially to value an opposite quality or condition over the one that is usually thought best. A list of these inversions (some of them, at least, from a collection by his contemporary Anthony Munday that Shakespeare seems to have used) that would apply to Lear, Gloucester, or Kent would include acceptance of poverty, blindness, folly, loss of goods, banishment, speedy death, hard lodging, and imprisonment.[16] As presented in the English works, the motive for these reversals of opinion is not *jeu d'esprit* so much as consolation for worldly disadvantages or losses; thus the declamation 'That a man ought not to be greeued, though he be despoiled of his goods and honours' is offered 'For him that hath lost his worldly Honours and Preferments' (p. 53). Though the tone claims to be serious (unlike the ironies of the paradoxical encomium such as Erasmus' *Praise of Folly*),[17] the movement of substitution and reversal is strong, even if limited to the replacement, itself conventional, of worldly values by otherworldly ones. Lear's distinction is to press on beyond even these newly-conventional values of suffering and of knowledge through suffering, as if to show that the searches and reversals paradoxically undermine themselves.[18] Perhaps what drives him can only be hinted; he gives such a hint, and exposes the dilemma of inevitable suffering, in his contrast between the ordinary storm (bad enough for the Fool and Kent) and his inner tempest:

> Thou think'st 'tis much that this contentious storm
> Invades us to the skin. So 'tis to thee,
> But where the greater malady is fix'd,
> The lesser is scarce felt. Thou'dst shun a bear,
> But if thy flight lay toward the roaring sea,
> Thou'dst meet the bear i' th' mouth. When the mind's free,
> The body's delicate. The tempest in my mind
> Doth from my senses take all feeling else
> Save what beats there.

(III, iv, 6–14)

In declaring this unknown, he undoes the experience that the other characters and the audience can share with him and forces us to contemplate a scarcely-imaginable paradoxical excess. In a different sense from Dover cliff, the tempest staged by the dialogue is not 'real', is patently belied by a claimed inner reality. Yet that claim is ironically undercut too by Edgar's guise that presents Lear with a false vision.

There is a different kind of match to the movement of Lear's experience in the mock prophecy with which the Fool takes his leave of the play:

> When priests are more in word than matter;
> When brewers mar their malt with water;
> When nobles are their tailors' tutors;
> No heretics burn'd, but wenches' suitors;
> Then shall the realm of Albion
> Come to great confusion.
> When every case in law is right;
> No squire in debt, nor no poor knight;
> When slanders do not live in tongues;
> Nor cutpurses come not to throngs;
> When usurers tell their gold i' th' field,
> And bawds and whores do churches build;
> Then comes the time, who lives to see 't,
> That going shall be us'd with feet.
> This prophecy Merlin shall make, for I live before his time.
>
> (III, ii, 81–96)

This is an ironic futurism, delicately poised between the milennium and a doomsday which is now. The mingling of literal description of present corruption with an ironic prediction of its distant remedy is to be found in other satiric prophecies, such as the 'Prognostication' in Nicholas Breton's *Pasquil's Passe, and passeth not* (1600), where there are alike predictions of the world's end when (as now) 'children teach their parents how to speake, / And seruants learne their masters to command' (stanza 1) and when (as never) 'euery child his father knowes, / And euery man will loue his wife' (stanza 13).[19] Likewise the Fool's prophecy, which is akin to inspired folly and madness, is fittingly wild in its irony and at war with itself.[20] Its essence is at once the necessity and impossibility of its fulfilment; such a world can hardly last, yet Merlin will foretell the same, and so could we in our latter days. The prediction has always already been shown, as surely as feet are used for walking, to be false and yet true. In its social censure, especially its reversal from jeremiad to utopia which is a condemnation either way, it resembles Lear's coming judgment that 'None does offend' in that all are at fault.[21] And this judgment, as will be seen, is another of Lear's self-undoings that surpasses itself.

Although the model for these suggestions about *King Lear* has been primarily a logical relationship of conflict in self-reference, some attitudes toward matters of belief have been taking shape. These can be identified as a philosophy, or at least a philosophical tendency, that was available in Shakespeare's time if not widely held in its strict form. The liar paradox figures in Sextus Empiricus' explanation of the way that Pyrrhonian scepticism avoids dogmatism even about its own basic principle of doubt:

> even in the act of enunciating the Sceptic formulae concerning things non-evident – such as the formula 'No more (one thing than another)' or the formula 'I determine nothing', or any of the others which we shall presently

mention, – he does not dogmatize. For whereas the dogmatizer posits the things about which he is said to be dogmatizing as really existent, the Sceptic does not posit these formulae in any absolute sense; for he conceives that, just as the formula 'All things are false' asserts the falsity of itself as well as of everything else, as does the formula 'Nothing is true', so also the formula 'No more' asserts that itself, like all the rest, is 'No more (this than that)', and thus cancels itself along with the rest. And of the other formulae we say the same. If then, while the dogmatizer posits the matter of his dogma as substantial truth, the Sceptic enunciates his formulae so that they are virtually cancelled by themselves, he should not be said to dogmatize in his enunciation of them. And, most important of all, in his enunciation of these formulae he states what appears to himself and announces his own impression in an undogmatic way, without making any positive assertion regarding the external realities.[22]

Yet the outcome, in the Renaissance at least, need by no means be this negative, for scepticism was often a prelude to fideism.[23] The ease with which the sentiment turns inside out is appropriate not only to the processes considered thus far in Shakespeare's play but to the variety of critical conclusions about its ultimate purport.[24]

There are more revolutions in judgment and in withdrawal of judgment. Lear's most radical one, in the great act IV, scene vi, follows Gloucester's attempt at suicide and Edgar's staging of a providence to induce him to 'bear / Affliction till it do cry out itself / "Enough, enough," and die' (IV, vi, 75–7). Though Lear's achievement of a kind of fortitude is conspicuously not dependent on an illusory providence such as Edgar had contrived, it bears its causes for our scepticism also. Lear continues to mistake the Gloucester–Edgar–Edmund story in extreme ways. He is unattractively severe, though not altogether unjust, in calling Gloucester 'blind Cupid' and 'Goneril with a white beard'. On the other hand, Lear's intended meaning is too lenient when he declares that 'Gloucester's bastard son / Was kinder to his father than my daughters / Got 'tween the lawful sheets' (lines 114–16). Knowing what we know, we may find the competition almost even; but the irony that even in its wild error the assessment might be accurate for Lear's daughters must shake our confidence. Lear's condemnation of female lechery, 'Down from the waist they are Centaurs, / Though women all above' (lines 124–5), seems to fit better with what he does not know, the intrigues of Goneril and Regan for Edmund, than what he does.[25] But while it is a direct reading of others' experience, it is also an oblique one of his own: his vision is of a corruption of filial love which he helped to nurture, and now its consequences embitter his imagination (as he knows) and thereby poison his judgments. Though he would claim still to be a king, able both to make a subject quake and to pardon him (and both powers are important to Lear though counter to fact), he knows himself weakened by the flaws of humanity: the hand that Gloucester would kiss in love and feudal devotion 'smells of mortality' (line 133).

His next observation of 'how this world goes' is cynical indeed:

Lear.   Thou hast seen a farmer's dog bark at a beggar?
Gloucester. Ay, sir.
Lear. And the creature run from the cur? There thou mightst behold the great
    image of authority; a dog's obey'd in office.
  Thou rascal beadle, hold thy bloody hand!
  Why dost thou lash that whore? Strip thy own back;
  Thou hotly lusts to use her in that kind
  For which thou whipp'st her. The usurer hangs the cozener.
  Through tatter'd clothes small vices do appear;
  Robes and furr'd gowns hide all. Plate sin with gold,
  And the strong lance of justice hurtless breaks;
  Arm it in rags, a pigmy's straw does pierce it.
  None does offend, none, I say, none! I'll able 'em.
  Take that of me, my friend, who have the power
  To seal th' accuser's lips. Get thee glass eyes,
  And, like a scurvy politician, seem
  To see the things thou dost not.

                                                    (lines 154–72)

Lear turns meanings inside-out like a chev'ril glove: none offends because all offend, and because none is in a position to censure.[26] His indictment of society is by no means merely of corrupt judges but generally, as he says, of the 'image of authority'. But the dubious verdict expressed in 'I'll able 'em' is not at all either an exoneration or an outpouring of compassion; it is none other than an exercise of that very authority he has just nullified. The savagery of his social vision undoes itself in paradox: not only can he only know how power should be used by losing it, he must illegitimize even the power of correction in the process of correcting. If he does indeed still 'have the power / To seal th' accuser's lips', that is far from either justice or a mercy properly consequent on justice. When he preaches to Gloucester on patience, that 'When we are born, we cry that we are come / To this great stage of fools' (lines 182–3), he can fittingly rely on nothing stronger than a radically simplified, manifestly fictitious analogy. There is paradoxical aptness in the words about 'this great stage': they disparage their speaker (among others on stage), they direct (in the pointed, here-and-now word 'this') a fictitious audience response of infantile bawling, and they suggest that a tragedy of patience is the dramatic form that matches birth and indeed all life.[27]

In his reunion with Cordelia Lear's mind is still awry and its processes, even now, incomplete:

Lear. Be your tears wet? Yes, faith. I pray weep not.
  If you have poison for me, I will drink it.
  I know you do not love me; for your sisters
  Have, as I do remember, done me wrong.
  You have some cause, they have not.
Cordelia.   No cause, no cause.

                                                    (IV, vii, 73–7)

He mistakes the motive of Cordelia's tears and wants to atone for them. He is still trying to fit punishments with misdeeds,[28] as if in faint recollection of his hopes for the storm. Not so much has changed, after all, since his first attempt to attach rewards to professions of love; this is merely its obverse. But this guilt-ridden figure of authority, now reduced to the simply human, gives moral authority to Cordelia, and, in forgiving by a kind of abdication, she applies the only corrective.

The best that remains for Lear, especially after the loss in battle, is a retreat to private life with Cordelia, though we already suspect from Edmund's machinations that such a hope is vain.

> Come, let's away to prison.
> We two alone will sing like birds i' th' cage.
> When thou dost ask me blessing, I'll kneel down,
> And ask of thee forgiveness. So we'll live,
> And pray, and sing, and tell old tales, and laugh
> At gilded butterflies, and hear poor rogues
> Talk of court news; and we'll talk with them too –
> Who loses and who wins; who's in, who's out –
> And take upon 's the mystery of things,
> As if we were God's spies; and we'll wear out,
> In a wall'd prison, packs and sects of great ones,
> That ebb and flow by th' moon.
>
>   (v, iii, 8–19)

There is a fiction in Lear's own mind too in his thought to outlast metaphorically the packs and sects of great ones;[29] he talks as if somehow abdication is a moral preservative. His fictionalizing has gone further toward a sceptical quietism: gone is the condemnation, the savage clemency, even the outright rejection of authority that would have had no dealings whatever with court news. This is a qualified detachment that will hear and talk so that it may laugh. But even this tranquility too is a dependent and passing state, as Lear knows when he bears Cordelia in his arms and howls.

Despite the unlooked-for and almost unbearable chances that befall, the cruel reversals in the play justify themselves as a necessary sequence of undoings. The process of Lear's experience begins with literal abdication, is stimulated by both the Fool's satire and Lear's own madness (forms of perception or mimesis assertively outside the social norms),[30] and passes beyond even pity and social activism in his dream of seclusion in prison. There is in the play a frank avowal of fiction or artifice, in the manner of the liar paradox, and it carries Lear to the far side of authority of any kind (traditional society's, his own, or even Cordelia's), and past any experience that the saddened bystanders – 'we that are young' – can formulate. The play, in driving itself paradoxically beyond itself, is sceptically humble before paradox.

NOTES

1 Useful readings include two collections by Robert L. Martin: *The Paradox of The Liar* (New Haven: Yale University Press, 1970) and *Recent Essays on Truth and the Liar Paradox* (Oxford: Clarendon Press, 1984). Gödel's work and the liar paradox are considered in relation to self-knowledge and the human sciences in Joel C. Weinsheimer, *Gadamer's Hermeneutics* (New Haven: Yale University Press, 1985), pp. 45–59.

2 I have discussed this and other paradoxical features of the play in 'Macbeth's – And Our – Self-Equivocations', *Shakespeare Quarterly*, 37 (1986), 160–74.

3 Thomas Wilson, *The Rule of Reason* (1553), ed. Richard S. Sprague (Northridge, Calif.: San Fernando Valley State College, 1972), p. 216. I have given evidence of Shakespeare's use of Wilson, and discussed the paradox in some plays, in the article on *Macbeth* and also in 'The Paradox of Timon's Self-Cursing', *Shakespeare Quarterly*, 35 (1984), 290–304, and 'The Speculative Eye: Problematic Self-Knowledge in *Julius Caesar*', *Shakespeare Survey 40* (Cambridge University Press, 1987), pp. 77–89.

4 'Semiotics of Theatrical Performance', *The Drama Review*, 21 (March 1977), 115.

5 *Dutchman and The Slave* (New York: William Morrow, 1964), pp. 19, 27. In *The Slave*, a character contemplates the notions of protective lying and of a 'meta-language' to clarify differences in meaning between individuals. Baraka's social views and dramatic style soon took a quite different turn.

6 *Quips upon Questions* (London, 1600): e.g. 'Two Fooles well met', 'Who wins most?' and 'Who is happy?' The features of this work, and the extent of its playhouse connections, are discussed by Charles S. Felver, *Robert Armin, Shakespeare's Fool* (Kent, Ohio: Kent State University, 1961), pp. 25–31, 79–80, and M. C. Bradbrook, *Shakespeare the Craftsman* (London: Chatto & Windus, 1969), pp. 52–7.

7 Quotations are from *Complete Works*, ed. David Bevington, 3rd edn. (Glenview, Ill.: Scott, Foresman, 1980). The passages quoted all appear in the Folio text.

8 The passage is discussed by Enid Welsford, *The Fool* (New York: Anchor Books, 1961), pp. 257–9.

9 Timothy J. Reiss, *Tragedy and Truth* (New Haven: Yale University Press, 1980), pp. 192–3. His work is based on the thought of Michel Foucault. James L. Calderwood makes an apt metadramatic comparison of Cordelia's position to Shakespeare's in *Shakespeare and the Denial of Death* (Amherst: University of Massachusetts Press, 1987), pp. 144–5.

10 Harry Levin, 'The Heights and the Depths: A Scene from "King Lear"' in *More Talking of Shakespeare*, ed. John Garrett (London: Longmans, 1959), pp. 87–103; Alvin B. Kernan, *The Playwright as Magician* (New Haven: Yale University Press, 1979), pp. 124–5.

11 Robert Egan, *Drama within Drama* (New York: Columbia University Press, 1975), pp. 21–3; Derek Peat, '"And That's True Too": "King Lear" and the Tension of Uncertainty' in *Aspects of King Lear*, ed. Kenneth Muir and Stanley Wells (Cambridge University Press, 1982), pp. 47–8; Jonathan Goldberg,

'Dover Cliff and the Conditions of Representation: *King Lear* 4:6 in Perspective', *Poetics Today*, 5 (1984), 537–47.

12 These metadramatic implications are explored effectively, under the metaphor of abdication, by Calderwood, *Shakespeare and the Denial of Death*, pp. 146–62. But in the context of the liar paradox I do not share his reluctance to accept, in a positive sense, that 'the entire play is a fraud' (p. 161). In these matters I have profited from discussion with Professor Edwin M. Eigner of the University of California, Riverside.

13 Robert Hillis Goldsmith, *Wise Fools in Shakespeare* (Liverpool University Press, 1958), pp. 64–5; Rosalie L. Colie, *Paradoxia Epidemica* (rpt. Hamden, Conn.: Archon Books, 1976), pp. 467–8.

14 'Who Sees Double in the Double Plot?' in *Shakespearian Tragedy*, ed. David Palmer and Malcolm Bradbury (London: Edward Arnold, 1984), p. 62 (Stratford-upon-Avon Studies 20).

15 Michael Hays, 'Reason's Rhetoric: *King Lear* and the Social Uses of Irony', *Boundary 2*, 7 (Winter 1979), 108; Colin N. Manlove, *The Gap in Shakespeare* (London: Vision, 1981), p. 118.

16 The first five are from *The Defense of Contraries*, trans. Anthony Munday (London, 1593); the others, from *The Treasurie of Auncient and Moderne Times*, trans. Thomas Milles (London, 1613); Munday's collection, and directly or indirectly Milles's, derive from Charles Estienne's *Paradoxes* (Paris, 1553), an adaptation of Ortensio Lando's *Paradossi* (Venice, 1543). Shakespeare's probable use of Munday and Milles's possible derivation from lost translations by Munday are discussed by Brian Vickers, '"King Lear" and Renaissance Paradoxes', *Modern Language Review*, 63 (1968), 305–14. See also Warner G. Rice, 'The *Paradossi* of Ortensio Lando', *University of Michigan Publications. Essays and Studies in English and Comparative Literature*, 8 (1932), 59–74. Rice notes the relevance of the paradox on bastardy (not extant in Munday) to Edmund. Two additions are possible: on speedy death, Edgar's words in v, iii, 188f.; on freedom from debts in imprisonment (or, in Shakespeare's version, in death), the Jailer in *Cymbeline*, v, iv, 157f.

17 These are discussed by Henry Knight Miller, 'The Paradoxical Encomium, with Special Reference to its Vogue in England, 1600–1800', *Modern Philology*, 53 (1956), 145–78. The consolatory notion mentioned above appears also in Estienne.

18 Reversal of hierarchical oppositions (as in these rhetorical paradoxes though by a more sophisticated process) is a feature of contemporary deconstructive criticism. See Jonathan Culler, *On Deconstruction* (Ithaca: Cornell University Press, 1982), pp. 85–6, 150–1, 181–7.

19 Breton, *Pasquil's Passe, and passeth not* (London, 1600), pp. 29, 32. A few examples of such prophecies are listed by F. P. Wilson, *Shakespearian and Other Studies* (Oxford: Clarendon Press, 1969), p. 253. However, Shakespeare was in fact most probably influenced by two prophecies quoted in George Puttenham's *The Arte of English Poesie*: see Gary Taylor, '*King Lear*: The Date and Authorship of the Folio Version' in *The Division of the Kingdoms*, ed. Gary Taylor and Michael Warren (Oxford: Clarendon Press, 1983), pp. 382–5.

20 The kinship with madness is discussed by Joseph Wittreich, *Image of that Horror* (San Marino, Calif.: Huntington Library, 1984), pp. 48–9. Festive wildness

and parody in the prophecy are evoked by Malcolm Evans, *Signifying Nothing* (Athens: University of Georgia, 1986), pp. 229–30; see also John Kerrigan, 'Revision, Adaptation, and the Fool in *King Lear*' in *The Division of the Kingdoms*, ed. Taylor and Warren, p. 226.

21 Taylor, 'King Lear', p. 384.

22 *Outlines of Pyrrhonism*, I, 14–15, trans. R. G. Bury, in *Sextus Empiricus* (London: Heinemann, 1933), vol. I, p. 11. On Sextus' influence, see Richard H. Popkin, *The History of Scepticism from Erasmus to Spinoza* (Berkeley: University of California Press, 1979); Charles B. Schmitt, *Cicero Scepticus* (The Hague: Martinus Nijhoff, 1972); Victoria Kahn, *Rhetoric, Prudence, and Skepticism in the Renaissance* (Ithaca: Cornell University Press, 1985). Graham Bradshaw makes a distinction between dogmatic and radical scepticism which bears on *King Lear* and which could be historically established: *Shakespeare's Scepticism* (Brighton: Harvester Press, 1987), p. 39.

23 See the references in Kahn, *Rhetoric*, p. 204n38, and the quotations (possible sources of Shakespeare) in my article on *Julius Caesar* cited in note 3.

24 Examples of the range of opinion would include John F. Danby, *Shakespeare's Doctrine of Nature: A Study of King Lear* (London: Faber and Faber, 1949); William R. Elton, *King Lear and the Gods* (San Marino: Huntington Library, 1966); and Jonathan Dollimore, *Radical Tragedy* (University of Chicago Press, 1984).

25 Thompson, 'Who Sees Double?', pp. 66–7.

26 L. C. Knights, '*King Lear* as Metaphor', in *Myth and Symbol*, ed. Bernice Slote (Lincoln: University of Nebraska Press, 1963), pp. 35–6. Stanley Cavell makes an ironic comparison with Edmund: *Must We Mean What We Say?* (New York: Scribner, 1969), pp. 304–5.

27 Despite the attention that his title gives to these words, Robert B. Heilman limits his comment on them to the idea that 'fumbling humanity deserves pity' and to a suggestive allusion to the Fool or 'man of insight' among the other fools on stage – *This Great Stage* (Baton Rouge: Louisiana State University Press, 1948), pp. 212–13.

28 Knights, '*King Lear* as Metaphor', p. 36.

29 The metaphorical element, though not the rest, is argued by J. K. Walton, 'Lear's Last Speech' in *Aspects of King Lear*, ed. Muir and Wells, p. 70.

30 Michel Foucault, *Madness and Civilization*, trans. Richard Howard (New York: Pantheon Books, 1965). Dollimore also alludes to such an idea (p. 195). In a movement complementary to Lear's, Edgar the moralist passes through a series of experiences, each of which seems at the time to be the worst but is later exceeded. His retelling of one of these, Gloucester's death, seems to effect Edmund's repentance but, by delaying and distracting, also contributes to Cordelia's death (Calderwood, *Shakespeare and the Denial of Death*, pp. 165–6).

'His legs bestrid the ocean' as a 'form of life'*

BRIAN CHEADLE

The critic of Shakespeare might seem most at hazard when, in an apparently frantic zest for originality, he cries with Cleopatra, 'Give me mine angle' (II, v, 10) and yokes together the most unlikely opposites: *Antony and Cleopatra* and Barbara Pym, say. And yet even this is not so foolish if one recalls Jane wondering why Prudence has fallen in love with such a colourless young man:

> But of course ... that was why women were so wonderful; it was their love and imagination that transformed these unremarkable beings.[1]

This directs our attention to Cleopatra's description of her 'Emperor Antony' after his death. More obliquely, I would bring together *Antony and Cleopatra* and Wittgenstein, in the hope of seeing Cleopatra's retrospect in a different light:

> His legs bestrid the ocean, his rear'd arm
> Crested the world: his voice was propertied
> As all the tuned spheres, and that to friends:
> But when he meant to quail, and shake the orb,
> He was as rattling thunder. For his bounty,
> There was no winter in 't: an autumn 'twas
> That grew the more by reaping: his delights
> Were dolphin-like, they show'd his back above
> The element they lived in: in his livery
> Walked crowns and crownets: realms and islands were
> As plates dropp'd from his pocket.
>
> (v, ii, 82ff.)

Janet Adelman encapsulates the traditional approaches to this speech by asking with almost embarrassing bluntness: 'And what of Cleopatra's vision of her emperor Antony? Is this the vision of the play or her own particular brand of delusion?'[2] Those critics who opt for delusion treat the speech in effect as an empirical proposition, to be tested by asking 'Does the evidence of Antony's behaviour in the play back up this view of him?' And

* A draft of this paper was read at the *Themes in Drama* International Conference held at the University of London, Westfield College, in March 1988.

of course it does not, for the case against Antony is overwhelming.[3] What is most worth remarking in the record, given Antony's reputation for magnanimity, is the high incidence of betrayal (of Cleopatra no less than of Octavia and Caesar, to mention only the most notable examples) and of mean-spiritedness, as in the indication to Caesar that he can do as he wishes with Antony's bondsman Hipparchus in return for the whipping of Thidias. Antony's is a career appropriately capped with the two final demeaning vignettes in which with a sort of 'slow-motion clumsiness'[4] he first pitifully bungles his suicide attempt, and then achieves a final 'exaltation' in love in the ludicrous form of being winched laboriously aloft the monument by Cleopatra and her handmaidens. Even his last words of advice to Cleopatra – that she should trust only Proculeius – reveal his utter lack of judgment.

On the other hand, those, like Adelman herself, who do not see Cleopatra as deluded in her 'dream' of Antony but find in it the 'vision of the play' argue that the force of the poetry, here and elsewhere, is such as to establish a transcendent or imaginative value in the love.[5] René Weiss is the most recent in a line of critics who have focused specifically on Cleopatra's vision of Antony, arguing that, like Sir Philip Sidney whose claim it is that only the poets deliver a golden world, 'Cleopatra pleads against a rational objector for an imagination that can create independently of nature and beyond its scope.'[6] Perhaps we should not be surprised in a post-Wallace-Stevens age to find Cleopatra so frequently cast as a sort of 'Comedian as the Letter C', her imagination hanging on 'silentious porpoises', intent on creating a 'mythology of self / Blotched out beyond unblotching', and seeking 'seraphic proclamations of the pure' (lines 13, 20–1, 558). But the enlisting of Sidney as a witness is inconclusive, for one can bring more pertinent contemporary witnesses to bear who are closer to the Jacobean spirit, Sir Francis Bacon for example in *The Great Instauration*:

> All depends on keeping the eye fixed steadily upon the facts of nature and so receiving their images simply as they are. For God forbid that we should give out a dream of our own imagination for a pattern of the world.[7]

Significantly, however, both of these radically divergent kinds of response to Cleopatra's 'dream' of Antony assume that what is at issue is a claim to truth. Among those who see Cleopatra as deluded, Shaw is the most blunt with home truths in summing up what are for him the facts of the matter by categorizing Antony as a 'soldier broken down by debauchery';[8] for Adelman, at the other end of the spectrum, it is still the case that 'the poetic language makes its claim as cognitive statement; and our emotion will depend partly on our judgment of the truth of the statement'. But if Shaw's view is Shavianly onesided, what sort of truth is there in a claim such as Adelman's that 'the lovers are larger than human, that their union is somehow cosmic like that of their great prototypes [Mars and Venus], the

union of male and female, war and love, strife and friendship'?[9] In the face
of such telling shuffles as Adelman's 'depend partly' and 'somehow cosmic'
one can only answer 'Gentle madam, no' (v, i, 94).

A quite different kind of approach to Cleopatra's evocation of her
Emperor Antony would see the speech simply in psychological terms as an
understandable and poignant example of the compensatory reflex,
honoured in the elegiac tradition, whereby the act of mourning seeks fitting
expression of grief, and strives to accommodate the fact of loss by indulging
in an idealized memory. ('This was a man' says Hamlet, and 'Who would
not sing for Lycidas, *who hath not left his peer . . .*' writes Milton). Dolabella,
who is audience to the speech, certainly attests to its power as an expresson
of grief:

> I do feel
> By the rebound of yours, a grief that smites
> My very heart at root
>
> (v, ii, 103–5)

and his very presence adds to the consolatory force of the gesture,
encouraging it, as it were, towards the gratifications of the mode of
spectacle so habitual to the lovers. One might remember too that in
'interposing a little ease' in this way Cleopatra is instructed by Antony
himself, for almost his last urging was that she should

> Please your thoughts
> In feeding them with those my former fortunes.
>
> (IV, xv, 52–3)

Clearly Cleopatra's speech *is* elegiac in this compensatory way, but to say
no more is to give only a partial account of it, one that goes no further than
Dolabella's sympathetic but literal-minded denial when Cleopatra asks
him 'Think you there was, or might be, such a man?' (v, ii, 93) – an
outsider's response which we can hardly take as normative.

A more intricate variation of this psychological approach relates the
speech to the gratifications of the audience. Thus Laurence Lerner argues
that Antony's irresponsibility has been so palpable that while he is alive we
can identify with him and with his love only if we feel guilt at the same time;
but when he is dead and the need to punish him has been symbolically
fulfilled we are free to satisfy our instinctual gratifications through the
sublimated images of reaping and of showing our virile backs in dolphin-
like leaping – and free too to indulge with Cleopatra our wish to believe in
an illicit love which does not end by causing pain and suffering.[10] This is an
intriguing argument, and it usefully stresses the strong charge of erotic
energy in the imagery; but it is reductive in its account of the sort of interest
we have in watching or reading the play. Moreover, like the placing of the
speech in the elegiac tradition it leans on the rather condescending
supposition that the characters or the audience are being gratified by

dallying with a consoling surmise that candid judgment must admit to be 'false'.

It would thus seem that regardless of one's stance, be it sceptical, affirmative or psychological, the problem of whether the speech offers true judgment or delusion cannot be avoided. In this preoccupation with judgment critics are only following the cue given by the characters of the play itself, for every footsoldier and messenger with a walk-on part seems to spend his few moments on stage contradicting the nearest eunuch or attendant on the subject of how to judge Antony or what to think of Cleopatra. 'The nobleness of life' and 'strumpet's fool' (i, i, 36, 13) cry the characters vending their views, and the critics echo them.

Much of the most astute criticism of the play has argued that it is Shakespeare's intention to make the whole question of judgment problematic and to leave us with the chastened sense of the paradox and ambivalence of a world in which all things, 'lackeying the varying tide' (i, iv, 46), rot themselves with motion.[11] Certainly it seems true that sentence by sentence, and scene by scene, the play deconstructs itself with such avidity that Shakespeare might almost have learned to follow in the footsteps of the university wits at Yale.

But what if 'His legs bestrid the ocean ...' is, in its immediate and essential effect, not an attempt to make a 'true' judgment of Antony, not a paradoxical presentation of an ambivalent world; nor a speech offering consolation in the form of transcendent or imaginative 'truth', or of emotional gratification? I want to suggest a more inward way of taking the speech, seeing it as pivotal in the dramatic structure, and finding it as much forward-looking as retrospective in presenting Cleopatra's attempt to re-establish grounds for action after Antony's death.

The speech (and the play) needs first to be set in the broad context of Shakespeare's developing exploration of love as the human experience which pre-eminently provokes the problematics of certainty and scepticism. The idealizing Petrarchan and Neoplatonic tradition, dominant in the Renaissance, grounded love in an unquestioning belief in the beauty, firmness and perfection of the beloved, making it, for the lover, something certain beyond doubt. Thus the well-known Renaissance poet Hamlet writes to Ophelia:

> Doubt that the stars are fire,
> Doubt that the sun doth move,
> Doubt truth to be a liar,
> But never doubt I love.

> (ii, ii, 115f.)

More sophisticated Renaissance love poetry sees the extension of this devotional tradition into the realistic contexts of mutual and even married love. Thus in Donne's 'Valediction: forbidding mourning', the famous compass image is used, in its final turn, to 'prove' the lover's absolute commitment: 'Thy firmness makes my circle just', makes the bedrock affirmation that the beloved is the sole centre of value in the lover's world, the only thing that gives or could give direction and purpose to his actions. Similarly, at the end of Shakespeare's sonnet 109 the protesting lover is also wrought to make an ultimate commitment; though in declaring that the young man is the only thing that gives his life value he draws not on an audaciously centred metaphysical conceit but on the centuries old emblem of love, the image of the rose:

> For nothing this wide universe I call,
> Save thou my Rose, in it thou art my all.

Nevertheless, as Shakespeare's continuing sonnet sequence shows, the lover who has staked his all on the firmness of the beloved is in an extremely vulnerable position, for 'ever-fixed' marks (sonnet 116) are all too prone to waver. Shakespeare's Troilus tries to love on an absolutist basis, investing everything in Cressida; but when his own eyes show her being false to him with Diomed his whole system of belief crumbles and he can only cry in dismay:

> This is, and is not, Cressid!
>
> (v, ii, 146)

Moreover, as *Othello* and *Hamlet* in the Nunnery scene show, love is vulnerable not only to the waverings of the beloved but also to fatal misconceptions on the part of the lover.

Not surprisingly, it is 'the autotoxic exaltation' that is the most vulnerable to 'the irony of diminution'.[12] From Chaucer's Arcite feeling that his face in the mirror is 'al in another kynde' (*The Knight's Tale*, 1401) to the distractions of Don Quixote, romantic love is presented as the great estranger, but it is Shakespeare who pushes this insight furthest and gives it its sharpest edge: his most intense explorations of passionate love seem driven relentlessly towards the discovery of chaos and nothingness, towards the lover's appalled apprehension that this 'wide universe', 'this firmament the earth', is nothing.

Shakespeare takes his exploration of love a decisive stage further in *King Lear* in his stress on self-sufficient mutuality in the presentation of the *filial* love between Lear and Cordelia. After father and daughter have found each other they are consigned to prison by Edmund, but Lear feels that the new security of their mutual love will be sufficient to itself:

> We two alone will sing like birds i' th' cage
>
> (v, iii, 9)

This proves only one more vaunt. Lear and Cordelia are sundered, Edmund's remission arrives too late, and the senseless and almost gratuitous death of the daughter whom he has come to recognize as the sole source of value in his world is more than Lear can bear. He dies with the most terrible of all assaults on any residual certainties:

> Why should a dog, a horse, a rat, have life
> And thou no breath at all?
>
> (v, iii, 306–7)

Antony and Cleopatra builds on Shakespeare's earlier precedents then in two respects: it brings Antony (like Troilus, Othello and Hamlet) to the experience of a world-dissolving scepticism after Cleopatra has deserted him at Actium, and it faces Cleopatra (like Lear) with the problem of continuing in a meaningful way after the death of the one whose love has been all.

It is a commonplace that the love of Antony and Cleopatra is particularly characterized by the stress on expansive mutuality, and that the imagery used in the play to affirm mutuality continuously invokes breadth and enlargement, even to the finding out of 'new heaven, new earth' (i, i, 17). The idea that lovers can together enjoy a more intense vitality and an expansion of being is familiar from Donne's 'The Good-morrow' and 'The Canonisation' where love constitutes itself an 'everywhere'; and in what might seem virtually the same terms, Antony in embracing Cleopatra, declares 'here is my space' (i, i, 34). Nevertheless, Antony's claim is radically unlike Donne's in that his love seeks not exclusion from the world in 'one little room' but opportunities to display itself to the world. It is not merely the need to project the love dramatically on a stage that gives the love of Antony and Cleopatra this quality of spectacular hyperbole: rather it would seem that the love seeks and needs a validation in the world's envy of it as an extravagant show.

Paradoxically, the confident assumption of amplitude, in investing the love of these seasoned veterans with what John Bayley has described as a 'sublime simplicity',[13] also gives it an uncanny resilience. There is, however, more than a tinge of defiance, and even apprehension of annulment, in the claim to share a love which is oblivious to limit. This threshold intimation emerges poignantly in Cleopatra's anguished 'My oblivion is a very Antony' (i, iii, 90) when he leaves her for Octavia: she is made oblivious to all else but Antony's absence, and this absence of Antony has the force of an infinite obliteration. Antony himself undergoes an experience matching Cleopatra's intuition of 'oblivion' and very similar to that of Troilus. This occurs at the nadir of the play when, after Cleopatra has yielded her fleet to Caesar, his hopes are in ruins and he feels himself 'beguil'd ... to the very heart of loss' (iv, xii, 29). Antony's experience is more moving than that of Troilus because he has up to this point shown so much more emotional flexibility and resilience; but now, in his fury, he drives Cleopatra from him and is overtaken by a sense of total dissolution.

It is as though, all along, the barely detectable ground bass of 'Here is my space' has been Othello's 'Perdition catch my soul, / But I do love thee, and when I love thee not, / Chaos is come again' (III, iii, 91f.).

Having set *Antony and Cleopatra* in this context, I want first simply to place Antony's experience of dissolution and recovery in relation to Wittgenstein's arguments concerning certainty and doubt in his late work *On Certainty*; and I will use this discussion as an introduction to his notion of 'forms of life' which I will then bring to bear on Cleopatra's 'His legs bestrid the ocean' speech.

It is the peculiar interest and uniqueness of *On Certainty* that in resisting G. E. Moore's 'foundationist' attempts to find firm grounds for our knowledge of basic empirical propositions, it yet manages to avoid a retreat into complete scepticism.[14] In his search for bedrock propositions Moore, looking back to the famous early arguments of Descartes in the *Meditations*, makes assertions such as, 'I know that I have two hands' or 'I know that the earth existed for a long time before my birth.' In a long and intricate inquisition of this sort of claim, Wittgenstein disallows it on a number of grounds, pointing out, for example, that in order to say that such empirical propositions are 'true', and not just expressions of subjective conviction, one would have to be able to satisfy oneself that one was right, and this one could not do by an act of verification, for 'my having two hands is not less certain before I have looked at them than afterwards' (*OC*, 245). Wittgenstein thus insists on 'the groundlessness of our believing' (*OC*, 166). But at the same time he tries to set a limit to scepticism by arguing that there *are* limits to doubt. The continuing thrust of his assault on the foundationist position is the insistence that it is wrong to think that we can build belief on single propositions. This is, after all, something alien to the ordinary processes of believing; for when we believe, 'what we believe is not a single proposition, it is a whole system of propositions ... in which consequences and premises give one another *mutual* support' (*OC*, 141–2). Here Wittgenstein encapsulates his idea in one of his memorable images: 'Light dawns gradually over the whole'. Two further images extend this central idea that though we can *know* nothing for certain our very capacity to function is dependent on our taking for granted a whole system of propositions that in effect 'stand fast' for us:

> I do not explicitly learn the propositions that stand fast for me. I can *discover* them subsequently like the axis around which a body rotates. This axis is not fixed in the sense that anything holds it fast, but the movement around it determines its immobility.   (*OC*, 152)

The second image is even more paradoxical in presenting the notion of standing fast, for Wittgenstein argues that within our whole system of ungrounded and ungroundable belief, 'one might almost say that these foundation walls are carried by the whole house' (*OC*, 248). He goes on to insist then that 'My *life* consists in my being content to accept many things' (*OC*, 344). Accordingly, it *is* impossible to doubt that I have two hands, but only in so far as 'so far I have no system at all within which this doubt might exist' (*OC*, 247). It is only in this sense then that I can say 'I have arrived at the rock bottom of my convictions' (*OC*, 248).

Thus Wittgenstein rejects foundationist approaches to knowledge while retaining some sympathy for Moore's position. We can know nothing for certain, and yet we behave as though a whole range of 'framework facts' could be taken as certain – in the manner of a 'direct taking-hold [which] corresponds to a *sureness*, not to a knowing' (*OC*, 511). These 'ordinary certainties' are the 'hinges' (*OC*, 341) of our thoughts and actions; they hold as long as our sense of normality holds.[15]

Moreover, they are inextricably involved in the whole vast range of ways of coping with daily life which Wittgenstein calls 'the entire system of our language-games' (*OC*, 411). These language-games are 'agreed upon activities which establish ... a possibility of sense';[16] and like ordinary certainties they too are beyond question:

> You must bear in mind that the language-game is so to say something unpredictable. I mean: it is not based on grounds.
> It is not reasonable (or unreasonable).
> It is there – like our life.
>
> (*OC*, 559)

It is important to realize that Wittgenstein conceives of language-games essentially as *activities* (they comprehend such diverse actions as giving orders and obeying them, making up a story and reading it, even solving a problem in practical arithmetic);[17] and as such they are taken up in various ways into those established patterns of action *shared* by members of a group, which Wittgenstein calls 'forms of life'. These, then, are the various practices or systems of practices which are so unquestionably the basis of all that we do that they seem to 'hold fast'. No less than the framework facts upon which they are built, forms of life are 'what has to be accepted, the given' (*PI*, II, 226). With the consistency of a refrain Wittgenstein insists that to call a language a form of life 'means I want to conceive it as something that lies beyond being justified or unjustified' (*OC*, 359).

There is something touchingly frank about this last acknowledgement, as though it were admitting the human need to crave a '*comfortable* certainty' (*OC*, 357). But the implications of this position are that the possibility of sudden 'bewilderment' (*OC*, 355) remains always open. As Kenny nicely puts it, 'Wittgenstein does not think the sceptic can be answered, only silenced.'[18] And indeed Wittgenstein allows that *any* certainty may be upset: 'But might it not be possible for something to happen that threw me entirely off the rails?' (*OC*, 517), he asks, conceiving an irruption that would break down the whole frame of my sense of normality.

This is precisely what happens to the lover who has centred his life on his love and whose certainty in his love is thrown into radical doubt; and the more he has tried to make the love the sole or central ground of his actions the more devastating the experience is. Such a person finds himself suddenly abandoned in a position where he has no meaningful set of practices, no form of life, within which to go on. Thus Troilus, betrayed in his love, is left capable only of a suicidal rage, a wild and flailing urge to destroy, which is directed as much towards himself as against the Greeks; and Othello, faced with the final evidence of the handkerchief, loses all power over his speech and even over his very physical being, falling into an animal-like fit.

When Antony finds himself abandoned by Cleopatra and drives her from his sight, his sense of total dissolution is communicated through the famous passage describing the shifting movement of the evening clouds, black vesper's pageants. The passage concludes:

> That which is now a horse, even with a thought
> The rack dislimns, and makes it indistinct
> As water is in water.

(IV, xiv, 9–11)

Milan Kundera has appositely remarked of the drowned Ophelia that 'Water is the element that kills those who have drowned in their own selves, in their love, in their emotions, in their madness, in their reflections and maelstroms',[19] and Antony here has an intuition of a comparable deathly dissolution. Wittgenstein says 'The existence of the earth is ... part of the whole *picture* which forms the starting-point of belief' (*OC*, 209), but the logic works the other way as well: when certainty goes, the whole picture crumbles. The defeated Antony is thus in the insupportable position of a man who has no limit to his doubt; and his life seems so insubstantial that he feels he cannot even 'hold [the] visible shape' (IV, xiv, 14) of his own body. His is the despair of the man who can no longer say with any sureness, 'I know that these are my hands.'

But when he is told that Cleopatra has died with his name on her lips he rises above the weight of weary emptiness and finds an extraordinary access of energy:

> Where souls do couch on flowers, we'll hand in hand,
> And with our sprightly port make the ghosts gaze:
> Dido, and her Aeneas, shall want troops,
> And all the haunt be ours.

(IV, xiv, 51)

In that 'hand in hand' Antony's language reclaims all the lost innocence of their mutuality in love; and the witty play in 'sprightly' indicates that his old confidence has overtaken him at a bound. Once more he can imagine their love as a kinetic spectacle, as though he were again '*discover*[ing] ... the axis around which [his] body rotates' (*OC*, 152). He is not consciously correcting a false judgment of Cleopatra; rather, the recovery has the force and instantaneousness of what Wittgenstein calls an 'awakening' (*OC*, 643).

But what then is the status of the assertion Antony is making? In terms of the play's dramatic economy it is clear that the lines are not offered as any sort of 'truth' to which we as hearers are asked to assent. This is apparent from the fact that Shakespeare takes great care to bracket Antony's recovery for the audience, in that we are aware that Cleopatra is *not* dead. Far from being able to surrender to the 'poetry' of his words, we are curiously detached from Antony because of our knowledge of the deception that is being wrought on him. We are stirred by the energy of the regained commitment and yet sharply aware of 'the groundlessness of [Antony's] believing' (*OC*, 166). The poetic locus of this apprehension is the word 'haunt', which in the very audacity of its attempt to make the ghostly world intimate and particular yet connotes a spectral insubstantiality.

Nevertheless, we are aware that, in Wittgenstein's terms, Antony is once again taking possession of the ability to act in a way that seems meaningful, resuming the 'form of life' which he and Cleopatra had *shared* in the hyperbolic acting out and speaking out of love as a gaze-enthralling spectacle. Once more Antony has a frame within which to go forward, even though it be only to death; and the foundation-walls are again 'carried by the whole house' (*OC*, 248). Moments later, with the deception unveiled for which he never blames her, even when she is too fearful to open the monument to receive him, Antony is hauled up ineptly by the women. In the grieving presence of Cleopatra, filled with magnanimous concern for *her* safety, he has 'no system at all within which ... doubt might exist' (*OC*, 247). One might say that Shakespeare, following his historical sources in allowing Antony to die in Cleopatra's arms, is content to present him as in a sense lucky in his bungled death – which is one reason for the peculiar pathos which attends it. Antony has been rescued from his intuition of the ungroundedness of being by a fortunate set of chances: he believes the messenger, he bungles his suicide, and after the disclosure of the deception he survives long enough to be physically reunited with Cleopatra. It is left for his opposite, Prospero, the reflective man par excellence, the figure in Shakespeare who most stands for hard truths, to endure the full consequences of a similar intuition of the groundlessness of being in the courageous aloneness of self-knowledge after the dissolution of the masque he has arranged for Miranda and Ferdinand.[20]

With Cleopatra, however, things are very different, for Antony is dead. On Antony's death Cleopatra had experienced a sense of a world dissolving comparable to his in the 'the rack dislimns' speech, expressed in her case in images of withering, falling and levelling, and epitomized in her cry 'the

odds is gone' (IV, xv, 64–6). Her fuller testing of 'oblivion' is symbolically
enacted in her fainting (line 68). But though the shock of grief often initially
has this sort of effect, she does have the knowledge that Antony loved her to
the last. When persuaded that Cleopatra had died with his name on her lips
Antony, in his recovery, felt that life was now empty but *not* purposeless:

> I will o'ertake thee, Cleopatra, and
> Weep for my pardon. So it must be, for now
> All length is torture: since the torch is out,
> Lie down and stray no farther.
>
> (IV, xiv, 44–7)

Significantly, after the first shock of Antony's death, Cleopatra uses the
identical form of words to express a new-found sense of resolution:

> Look,
> Our lamp is spent, it's out ...
> Ah, women, women! come, we have no friend
> But resolution, and the briefest end.
>
> (IV, xv, 84–5, 90–1)

She puts off thoughts of suicide only until Antony has been buried, and
when next we meet her this intention has taken a slightly more positive
colouring. Her wry reflection, 'My desolation does begin to make / A better
life' (v, ii, 1–2), seems to be the result of a growing attempt to convince
herself of Caesar's 'paltriness': at the same time, this reference to Caesar is
the first hint that she has begun shrewdly to assess her prospects as far as he
is concerned. Once Gallus has surprised and captured her, her determination to 'ruin' her 'mortal house' (v, ii, 51) takes on a new desperation, for,
significantly in one whose power has fed on spectacle, what her imagination
cannot bear is the thought of being a spectacle of another kind:

> Know, sir, that I
> Will not wait pinion'd at your master's court,
> Nor once be chastis'd with the sober eye
> Of dull Octavia. Shall they hoist me up,
> And show me to the shouting varletry
> Of censuring Rome?
>
> (v, ii, 52–7)

The conversation with Dolabella, who is guarding her while Proculeius
goes to report the successful capture of the Queen to Caesar, provides a
moment of reflective quiet, marking the crucial change in her status. In her
dream of Antony, Cleopatra once again adopts the hyperbolic language
that marked the expansive affirmations of their love. One might say, in a
fairly loose way, that no less than Antony just before his death she is once
again participating in the 'form of life' that they had shared, by summoning
up a vision of Antony in the enlarged images of public spectacle. But it is
time to give Wittgenstein's term greater definition, and in so doing to

reopen the question of whether, or in what way, her speech is concerned with judgment.

Wittgenstein says that when people 'agree in the *language* they use,

> That is not agreement in opinions but in forms of life.   (*PI*, I, 241)

But he goes on much more interestingly to add that

> If language is to be a means of communication there must be agreement not only in definitions but also (queer as this may sound) in judgments. (PI, I, 242)

The account that I have so far given of Wittgenstein's notion of 'forms of life' might have suggested that there is something flatly behaviourist about his position (the agreed-upon forms of our language determine the forms of our actions). The reason why this is anything but the case is apparent in his stress not only on the notion of 'agreement', but also on that of 'judgment'. All the accumulated conventions, processes, 'rules' and 'definitions' which make up language provide the grounds for agreement. That is to say that there is attunement in the criteria on which agreement can be based; and it is precisely this agreement in the language one uses that constitutes a form of life. This is why language can be spoken of as a game, a set of formed and agreed activities which are operative in our coming to terms with experience. But the course of a game is never predictable, and it is in this respect that the notion of *judgment* adds a further dimension to the process of communication. Judgment is operative in deciding how some new experience matches up to the criteria and can be considered as counting under them; and it is equally involved in deciding that one will take a public stance as it were in 'proclaiming' on it on a particular occasion.[21] This is the level of inwardness at which we make judgments about the new and then offer them to others for sharing. Language is thus not simply what we do, but the activity of *discovering* what we do, discovering what we can agree on.

To decide how the process of judgment is working in the dream of Antony it is necessary to bear in mind that its context is Cleopatra's sense of her imminent meeting with Caesar and her need to know where she stands vis-a-vis him. Caesar, the play's man of destiny, is never far from the minds of the lovers; but this speech in particular is spoken in his shadow. One must not forget that Cleopatra, unlike Antony in his last moments, has two choices open to her – to follow Antony's example and take her own life, or to submit herself to Caesar's mercy as Antony had urged. Her need is thus not so much, as his was, to regain a belief but to balance two possibilities of proceeding. She has always been too unpredictably in love with life to want to die; which means that her choice, though it might seem inevitable to us in retrospect, and though she intuitively knows it to be so, is far from easy.

The speech is thus located within a context of decision, and what Cleopatra is implicitly doing in it is bringing together *two* figures for comparison. The first is that of Antony, set forth as he would have desired, in enlarged images of magnificence. But the second awareness lurking in the lines is that of Caesar, who is now 'lord of the whole world' (II, vii, 62), just about to become the first Emperor of Rome, and the one on whose bounty Cleopatra now solely depends. This dual presence is primarily established by the context; but it is activated too within the language of the speech by the challenging naming of Antony as 'Emperor', and subtly underlined by the intertextual echo, within the phrase 'His legs bestrid the ocean', of the earlier Caesar who was thought to 'bestride the narrow world / Like a Colossus' (*Julius Caesar*, I, ii, 134–5). The shadowing effect is continued in the way that 'an autumn 'twas / That grew the more by reaping' recalls Agrippa's comment on Cleopatra's affair with Caesar, 'he ploughed her, and she cropped' (II, ii, 228). It is this dual awareness, oriented more firmly after the dream has been recounted towards the 'boy' whom she is about to meet, that makes sense of the peculiar tenses in Cleopatra's subsequent remark to Dolabella, 'But if there *be*, or ever were one such / It's past the size of dreaming'. The dual awareness is also brought home to us by the very presence of Dolabella and by his incomprehension, for he inevitably sees her, as it were, through his master's Roman eyes.

In her vision of Antony, then, Cleopatra is musing backwards, but she is also musing forward. What is most intriguing is the implicit dynamic of the 'judgment' involved in musing backward. This is by no means a matter of simply assessing Antony in relation to his actions. Rather it can best be thought of as her discovering what 'agreement' there is between the language of enlargement as a form of life which she is using, and the relationship in which she now finds herself to the memory of Antony. Her first thoughts are of Antony's charismatic presence which she now lacks, the bodily potency of legs, arms and voice. Then, in dwelling successively on his 'rattling thunder' and his 'bounty' she is obliquely reliving his terrible anger towards her after the flight from battle that led directly to his death, and recalling the unchiding quickness of his forgiveness. This grateful memory of Antony's capacity for fruitful renewal releases a vigorous evocation of the expansive pleasures of their loving in the most powerful image of the whole speech, that of the leaping dolphins. This imagining is, in turn, so vivid that it gives her the confidence to return to, and triumphantly confirm, the opening premise of a matchless 'Emperor'.

If Cleopatra has been shrewd enough and woman enough to weigh the prospect of the new young Emperor with her dream of the Emperor Antony, the issue of her judgment has never really been in doubt. As is so often the case in ordinary experience, decision is arrived at not by saying explicitly 'I am finally going to make up my mind here by consciously balancing this against that'; rather, agreement with oneself that something can count within a form of life gives one the surety to go forward. It is by such largely subliminal judgments, inherent in the activities of language, that our decisions and our commitments are made. In her dream of Antony Cleopatra is thus participating in the fundamentally heuristic activity that constitutes a form of life, testing words and understanding in the effort to discover 'how to go on' (*PI*, I, 150–200).[22] She might in effect be saying with Wittgenstein, in the presence of what she takes to be a sceptical Roman:

> How do I know that my judgment will agree with someone else's? How do I know that this colour is blue? If I don't trust *myself* here, why should I trust anyone else's judgment? Is there a why? Must I not begin to trust somewhere? That is to say: somewhere I must begin with not doubting; and that is not, so to speak, hasty but excusable: it is part of judging.   (*OC*, 150)

What is at issue in the speech is not a claim to 'truth' in the sense that it provides a judgment upon Antony which we as audience must endorse or reject; rather the lines are a 'part of judging', the dramatic enactment of the process whereby Cleopatra accomplishes the extension of a 'form of life'.

Cleopatra's choice emerges explicitly only in her final setting of her dream of Antony as 'nature's piece' against fanciful 'shadows'; and there is a touching concessiveness in her final words to Dolabella after he has denied her vision: 'But if there be, or ever were one such, / It's past the size of dreaming'. One imagines a long stage pause after these words. It is as if she is saying:

> If I have exhausted the justifications I have reached bedrock, and my spade is turned. Then I am inclined to say: 'This is simply what I do.'   (*PI*, I, 217)

What angered Antony most in Caesar's growing ascendency was that he felt Caesar was always 'harping on what I am / Not what he knew I was' (III, xiii, 142–3): Cleopatra's bestowing of an emperorship upon the Antony that *was* is a way of making amends for all that she contributed towards his fall, and even, as it were, for his fall itself. This done, she is prepared to move forward to death not simply in a spirit of despairing revulsion at the thought of being 'shown / In Rome' (V, ii, 207–8), and of being made to submit to the falsification of her love in having herself to see

> Some squeaking Cleopatra boy my greatness
> I' the posture of a whore.
>
>   (V, ii, 219–20)

Rather, she can once again assume her robe and crown, and encounter death within a sustaining frame of remembered and projected largeness which alone affords her 'a certainty that knows no doubt' (*OC*, 360). For her 'the end is not an ungrounded presupposition: it is an ungrounded way of acting' (*OC*, 110). The memory of Antony, enshrined in the very language that they made their own, is all that Cleopatra has to release her into a 'noble act' (v, ii, 284). By comparison the 'form of life' which an equivocal parleying with Caesar offers is unrewarding, and the world she leaves behind 'is not worth leave-taking' (v, ii, 297).

It might be argued against my interpretation that after her dream of Antony, far from having positively committed herself to death, Cleopatra keeps open the possibility of coming to terms with Caesar, and remains committed to life in seeking to keep a part of her treasure. Significantly, however, the immediate issue of her dream of Antony is her asking Dolabella 'Know you what Caesar means to do with me?' (v, ii, 106), and his confirmation that Caesar intends to lead her in triumph. Once again Shakespeare achieves an extraordinary effect of dramatic bracketing, for though what follows Dolabella's disclosure is Cleopatra's kneeling before the Caesar whom she has never previously met, inscrutably declaring him 'my master and my lord' (v, ii, 115) and delivering him only as much of her treasure as she deems fit, what follows *that* meeting is the returning Dolabella's fuller disclosure of the details of Caesar's intentions. The effect of this bracketing of Cleopatra's meeting with Caesar is to convince the audience that the parleying with Caesar and the withholding of the treasure have a suspended status: the signal to the audience is that Cleopatra is buying time by convincing Caesar that she has no immediate intention of taking her life.

The virtue of the reading I have offered of the dream of Antony is that it makes both this speech and Cleopatra's final scenes more courageous and more desperate, more humanly desperate, than those which distance themselves from the lovers' 'autotoxic exaltations', discover some gratifying consolation, or simply rest in grief.

Stanley Cavell has produced a brilliant series of articles on Shakespeare written under the aegis of Wittgenstein. His preoccupation has been with a different aspect of the problem of scepticism, the attempt of the tragic protagonist to avoid what Cavell describes as the 'all but undeniable' impingement of the other, the burden of acknowledging

> that a loving daughter loves you, that your imagination has elicited the desire of a beautiful young woman, that however exceptional you may be you are a member of human society.[23]

Though one might well see Cleopatra's 'His legs bestrid the ocean' speech as her final acknowledgement that even beyond one's prime one can encounter a binding love, the dialectic of avoidance and acknowledgement is not as inward and harrowing in this play as in those Cavell has approached. The unique persistence of one tragic protagonist after the first catastrophe makes *Antony and Cleopatra* akin to a comedy which goes beyond the marriage dance; hence it has seemed more rewarding to focus on the mechanism of the going on.

Having given an account of the role of 'His legs bestrid the ocean' within the dramatic action, it remains to assess its status within the economy of the play as a whole. Wittgenstein says:

> One human being can be a complete enigma to another. We learn this when we come into a strange country with entirely strange traditions; and, what is more, even given a mastery of the country's language. We do not *understand* the people. (And not because of not knowing what they are saying to themselves.) We cannot find our feet with them.   (*PI*, II, 223)

Cavell points out that the literal translation of the German idiom in that final sentence is 'We cannot find ourselves in them',[24] which makes the sense of total incomprehension even more compelling. When Dolabella hears Cleopatra's 'proclamation', all he understands is her grief; and when in response to her prodding he denies her vision of Antony she counters sharply 'You lie up to the hearing of the gods.' There is an absolute gulf between the Roman 'truth' and the lovers' capacity for an enlarged experience, as the play reveals, from Philo's opening comment on his general's dotage to the vignette of fastidious Caesar marvelling at the knowledge that Antony drank the stale of horses.

But for all his incomprehension Dolabella is moved enough by Cleopatra to betray his master's intentions. This leads Arnold Stein to assert that Dolabella 'unwittingly testifies to an authenticity in the "dream" ';[25] but we need not take it so, even if we are not approaching the speech in Wittgenstein's terms. Cleopatra's vision of Antony has the same *defiantly* assertive quality, as though it were the apotheosis of all whistling to keep one's spirits up, that we have come to associate with the love poetry of the play; and it is laden with ironies. Antony's magnanimity is real, as Enobarbus discovers, and more attractive than the cold efficiency of Octavius; but Antony has indeed allowed 'realms and islands' to drop casually from his pocket. Again, though we have seen him 'thunder' in the play, the only recipient who really quailed was Thidias, and Antony's treatment of that poor unfortunate was his least magnanimous action. This peculiar undertow of irony in the speech is such as to make us aware of the gulf that there inevitably is between a man and how he would be seen, rather than to make us identify with the lovers and endorse the values they espouse. The mannered way in which Cleopatra's dream of Antony begins by structuring itself in terms of the conventional attributes of the Herculean hero,[26] the hyperbolic diction, and the effect of self-conscious spectacle, all help to keep us detached, even while we are intrigued and moved. In its extravagant claims the speech is poised a knife-edge away from the ridiculous, just as there is an inherent ridiculousness in the very notion of a passionate love affair between middle-aged veterans. It is significant that Cleopatra embarks on her eulogy by twice cutting across Dolabella's address to her, and the compulsive effect makes us sense how close she is to losing her grip, how terrible it is for her to fight down the sense that she is on the wrong side and a spectacle now only for pity or sardonic mockery. The fact that the speech is so extravagant and desperate, straining against our incredulity, makes it the more glorious and the more deeply human; but, with a fitting irony, it ensures that we too stand apart from it as from a prodigious spectacle. Thus it is that we are allowed room both to sympathize with Cleopatra's choice and yet, for example, to remain aware of the political bankruptcy of the particular martial and individualistic ideology which inspires its form of life (and for which Dollimore has suggested a pertinent contemporary context[27]).

Moreover, the play makes it apparent that the magnanimity of spirit which the lovers aspired to, and in part achieved, is far from being a self-sufficient value. The Steward in *Timon of Athens* says of his master Timon: 'Bounty, that makes gods, does still mar men' (IV, ii, 41), for the very good reason that no man can be a Hercules. Then too, measured in terms of man's deepest needs, magnanimity is a 'superfluity'. Though Lear is right to cry 'Allow not nature more than nature needs, / Man's life is cheap as beasts'' (II, iv, 267–8), in a terrible sense man's life is as cheap as that of 'a dog, a horse, a rat' (V, iii, 306), as Lear discovers when he has Cordelia dead in his arms. There are extremities beyond the reach of magnanimity. There are also virtues beyond magnanimity, as appears from the long catalogue of 'king-becoming graces' which Malcolm unfolds to Macduff:

As justice, verity, temp'rance, stableness,
Bounty, perseverance, mercy, lowliness,
Devotion, patience, courage, fortitude

(IV, iii, 92f.)

Given the richness of its poetry, it might seem strange to think of *Antony and Cleopatra* as a very bleak play, and yet to measure it against Malcolm's list is to realize how thin it is on virtues. And it is thin too in the sense it leaves us with of a heroic world that has passed for ever.[28] Caesar says wryly of Antony's death, thinking of the portents which marked the death of Julius,

The breaking of so great a thing should make
A greater crack

(V, i, 14–5)

and Maecenas shrewdly notes how Caesar's own self-regarding fears are touched by the intuition of largeness universally in decline.

Though Antony's passing might be thought to have mattered little, without the bounty, courage and fortitude of the lovers the world they leave behind is a paltry one indeed, shabby, compromised and well schooled in all 'the shifts of lowness' (III, xi, 63). Bradley was right to emphasize the sadness of the play's ending,[29] a sadness which leaves us thankful that we have at least been party to all the splendid energies of the lovers' language-game.

More broadly, however, it is a sadness related to that inherent in the ending of any play, though more 'intrinsicate' to this particular 'revel' than any other except perhaps *The Tempest*, a sadness that recognizes in drama the model of ungrounded being and makes us starkly aware that the moment a language ceases to be spoken, a form of life displayed, there is nothing that we can know for certain.

NOTES

1 Barbara Pym, *Jane and Prudence* (London: Cape, 1953; repr. 1979), p. 217.

2 Janet Adelman, *The Common Liar* (New Haven: Yale University Press, 1973), p. 78.

3 The following are some of the charges that could be brought. In the very first scene Antony allows himself to be manoeuvred by Cleopatra into dishonourably refusing to hear the messengers from Rome; he breaks the article of his oath to lend Caesar arms and aid when he needs them (II, ii); he shows a Roman capacity for the duplicities of policy and an unlovely concern that his reputation should not suffer 'ill report' when he seals his alliance with Caesar and Lepidus against Pompey (II, ii, 159f.); he betrays Cleopatra by making the marriage with Octavia for his peace (II, ii); on Pompey's galley he proves himself 'a child o' the time' along with the rest (II, vii, 99); he betrays Octavia and Caesar in going back to Cleopatra (III, vi); he shows poor judgment as a commander in resolving to fight by sea simply because he is dared to (III, vii) and then infatuatedly follows Cleopatra from the battle, deserting his followers (III, x); he foolishly imagines that Caesar might agree to meet him in single combat (III, xiii); he has Thidias whipped as Caesar's proxy when he finds him kissing Cleopatra's hand and he tells Caesar that he may do as he chooses in return to his enfranchised bondsman Hipparchus (III, xiii).

4 John Bayley, *Shakespeare and Tragedy* (London: Routledge and Kegan Paul, 1981), p. 127.

5 Wilson Knight is foremost among those who have argued that the love of Antony and Cleopatra 'translineates man to divine likeness', and Arnold Stein has urged the force of the 'unapologetic' lyric imagination in the lovers, asserting itself against brute fact. See G. Wilson Knight, 'The Transcendental Humanism of *Antony and Cleopatra*' in *The Imperial Theme* (London: Methuen, 1951), p. 217; and Arnold Stein, 'The Image of Antony: Lyric and Tragic Imagination', *Kenyon Review*, 21 (1959), 586–606.

6 René J. A. Weiss, 'Antony and Cleopatra: The Challenge of Fiction', *English*, 32:132 (1983), 1–14. See also Phyllis Rackin, 'Shakespeare's Boy Cleopatra, the Decorum of Nature, and the Golden World of Poetry', *PMLA*, 87 (1972).

7 Sir Francis Bacon, *The Great Instauration*, *The Works*, ed. James Spedding, R. L. Ellis and D. D. Mark (London: Longman, 1857–74), vol. 4, p. 32.

8 George Bernard Shaw, *Three Plays for Puritans* (London: Constable, 1931), p. xxx.

9 Adelman, *The Common Liar*, pp. 225 and 101.

10 Laurence Lerner, 'Psychoanalysis and Art' in *The Literary Imagination* (Brighton: Harvester Press, 1982).

11 See in particular Maynard Mack, '*Antony and Cleopatra*: The Stillness and the Dance' in *Shakespeare's Art*, ed. Milton Crane (Chicago: University of Chicago Press, 1972), who makes much of the presence of paradox and ambiguity in the play but finally settles for an affirmative view of the lovers; and John Danby, '*Antony and Cleopatra*: A Shakespearian Adjustment' in *Elizabethan and Jacobean Poets* (London: Faber and Faber, 1965), formerly *Poets on Fortunes's Hill* (1952), who stresses the quality of the 'dialectic' in the play – 'the deliquescent reality that expresses itself through the contraries' (p. 148).

12 The first phrase is Danby's, p. 145; the second that of A. P. Rossiter, 'Bruegel's Ambivalences: A Preliminary Survey', *The Cambridge Journal*, 2:3 (1948), 137.

13 Bayley, *Shakespeare and Tragedy*, p. 143.

14 The texts of Wittgenstein I draw on are *On Certainty* (Oxford: Basil Blackwell, 1969); and *Philosophical Investigations* (Oxford: Basil Blackwell, 1967). References are provided in parenthesis in the text, and all italics are Wittgenstein's.

15 I have borrowed the terms 'framework facts' and 'ordinary certainties' from Henry Le Roy Finch, *Wittgenstein: The Later Philosophy* (Atlantic Highlands: Humanities Press, 1977), p. 222 and chapter 13. On Wittgenstein's later philosophy I am also indebted to Anthony Kenny, *Wittgenstein* (London: Allen Lane, 1973); Thomas Morawetz, *Wittgenstein and Knowledge: The Importance of On Certainty* (Amherst: University of Massachusetts Press, 1978); and two works by Stanley Cavell, 'The Availability of Wittgenstein's Later Philosophy' in *Must We Mean What We Say?* (Cambridge University Press, 1976); and *The Claim of Reason* (Oxford: Clarendon Press, 1979).

16 Finch, *Wittgenstein*, p. 75.

17 The fullest list of language games provided by Wittgenstein is *PI*, 1, 23. On giving orders and obeying them see *PI*, 1, 1, 2, 8; and on making up a story and reading it *PI*, 1, 156–71.

18 Kenny, *Wittgenstein*, p. 218.

19 Milan Kundera, *Life is Elsewhere* (London: Faber and Faber, 1974), p. 290.

20 See Cavell, *Must We Mean What We Say?*, p. 52: 'Human speech and activity, sanity and community, rest upon nothing more, but nothing less, than this. It is a vision as simple as it is difficult, and as difficult as it is (and because it is) terrifying.'

21 Cavell, *The Claim of Reason*, pp. 31ff.

22 See Mary Ann Creadon, 'Wittgenstein's Forms of Life: Language and Literature as a Heuristic Tool', *Studies in Language*, 8:1 (1984), 35–43.

23 Stanley Cavell, 'Hamlet's Burden of Proof', *Hebrew Studies in Literature and the Arts*, 14 (1986), 1–17. See also in particular, 'The Avoidance of Love: A Reading of *King Lear*' in *Must We Mean What We Say?*. Since this paper was delivered in March 1988, Cavell's articles have been collected in *Disowning Knowledge: in Six Plays of Shakespeare* (Cambridge University Press, 1988).

24 Cavell, *Must We Mean What We Say?*, p. 67.

25 Stein, 'The Image of Antony', p. 598.

26 See Eugene M. Waith, *The Herculean Hero in Marlowe, Chapman, Shakespeare and Dryden* (New York: Columbia University Press, 1962).

27 Jonathan Dollimore, '*Antony and Cleopatra* (c.1607): Virtus under Erasure' in *Radical Tragedy* (Brighton: Harvester Press, 1984). The emphasis of my discussion has been such as to slight the social dimension of the play, but this does not mean that I underestimate its importance. It was an essential part of the Renaissance symbolics of power that the monarch rehearsed and consolidated his authority by becoming the object of the public gaze. Within this more general contemporary context of conspicuous display, an interesting gloss on the lovers' need, as their political power wanes, to make of love an ever more extravagant spectacle of power is provided by Clifford Geertz's remark ('Centers, Kings and Charisma' in *Culture and its Creators*, ed. Joseph Ben-David, University of Chicago Press, 1977), that it is 'the paradox of charisma [in its cultural dimension] that its most flamboyant expressions tend to appear among people at some distance from the center.'

28 See G. K. Hunter, 'The Last Tragic Heroes' in *Later Shakespeare*, ed. John Russell Brown and Bernard Harris, Stratford-upon-Avon Studies 8 (London: Arnold, 1966).

29 A. C. Bradley, '*Antony and Cleopatra*' in *Oxford Lectures on Poetry* (London: Macmillan, 1909; repr. 1965).

'A curious way of torturing': language and ideological transformation in *A King and No King*

DAVID LAIRD

There is widespread agreement that Beaumont and Fletcher's tragi-comedies stand aloof from the tensions and anxieties of the period, their brilliant theatricality washed clean of the dust and heat of social and political controversy. Critical attention fastens on distinctive features of language and action – a rich concoction of purple passages and melodram-atic situations – and the plays are customarily dismissed as emotional potboilers, highly charged verbal cartwheels exhausting themselves in a display of their own spinning brilliance. In the typical opinion of one influential critic, Beaumont and Fletcher treated their Jacobean audiences to an easy escape from a reality of despondency and anxiety.[1] Another critic is persuaded that their plays 'lack high seriousness of purpose and are morally shabby'.[2]

But the case is not quite so clear when we turn to the details of language and structure that mark particular texts. There is reason to believe that the dramatists were able to find within the resources of the tragicomic mode a freedom to explore political and social issues which, under strict censor-ship, were too controversial, too dangerous, to be dealt with in less subtle or ambiguous ways.

Margot Heinemann has recently reminded us that Jacobean censorship was almost exclusively a *political* censorship: 'The censor was scarcely concerned with questions of morality or good taste. At incest, adultery, rape, sexual invective and innuendo, or Rabelaisian sex-and-lavatory clowning he seems not to have turned a hair'.[3] *A King and No King* takes full theatrical advantage of subjects exempt from the censor's scrutiny. Indeed, some critics have credited the play with doing little else. They have located its distinctiveness in a firestorm of theatrical tricks meant to indulge the erotic fantasies and jaded tastes of Jacobean audiences:

> What member of [Jacobean] society . . . would not like to see his own licentious fantasies symbolically projected with such dramatic effectiveness? Not only

was it titillating, but it must have been rather a relief to be told that there was a world ... where technicalities existed which permitted one to lie with one's own sister or perhaps to gorge on such other exotic emotional confections as suited one's palate without having to pay with a moral illness that might last an eternity.[4]

Such ingenious attempts to determine the play's appeal mistake its final character and value. I hope to show that *A King and No King* is, among other things, a seriously philosophical drama: its obvious exploitation of sexuality and of violent, transgressive behavior is expressive of substantive political and ideological concerns. What is at issue here touches the deployment of sexual relations, incestuous passions, rape, or the threat of rape, in the larger design of the play. Sexuality and incest are used not exclusively to titillate or divert, but rather to offer instruction on a variety of issues and concerns that imperil the body politic, its institutions and practices, and, at the same time, to lift that instruction beyond the reach of political censorship. Sexual relations and the complications to which they give rise play a strategic role in exposing some familiar institutional formations involving both the discourse and the practice of kingship and manage to do so without getting into the serious trouble that a less veiled or artful criticism was sure to invite.[5]

The play addresses the problem of monarchical absolutism in ways both linguistic and ideological. It embarks on a necessarily guarded but insistent probing of attitudes and assumptions implicit in the language of power, or more precisely, in the glittering rhetoric of monarchical absolutism. It tracks the network of verbal relationships, distinctions, discriminations, and privileges in terms of which an absolutist rhetoric organizes and seeks to control the raw fortuity of things. The effect is not only to dissipate meanings and mysteries associated with kingship, but also to bring into question the language by which such meanings are projected, its very capacity to fathom a world of people and events, affairs of state no less than a state of affairs. The play dramatizes a monarch's attempt to bring things under the order of words, to make meanings determinate, univocal, and unambiguous, in a sense, to transcend the constraints according to which ordinary language must operate. Events disrupt imposed meanings and bring to light a tumbling multiplicity of things and significations. In the process, language is delivered from solopsistic or absolutist deployment, no longer an instrument of intimidation or mystification, restored finally to a social or discursive function and the rule of common usage. Linguistic analysis thus bears the burden of and, in some sense, the responsibility for a political and social criticism.

And it is, I think, significant that this maneuvering is informed by a linguistic skepticism with precedent in the non-dramatic literature of the period, in Hooker, for example, and in the works of other defenders of

English Common Law. It is a skepticism wary of abstractions, schooled in fundamental law and legal history, and unintimidated by pronouncements that rest upon absolutes and intangibles. In this aspect and in more openly ideological ones involving conflicting claims for monarchy and the law, the play builds a case against prerogative power and in support of a legally limited monarchy. Thus it situates itself firmly on the side of those in Parliament and elsewhere who found themselves and their institutions increasingly threatened and provoked by a monarch who, in defiance of custom and usage, held himself to be above the law, answerable to no one but God and his own conscience, who ruled by the word and whose word was the law, no longer subject to amendment or ratification.[6]

There are other threads to untie in the play's address to the language of power. Embedded in the absolutist rhetoric of the player-king are unmistakable echoes of the utterances of the then reigning sovereign on the nature of monarchy and the royal prerogative. *A King and No King* gains a special force and currency from a rhetoric inspired by exposure to what James I had declared about his high office in *The Trew Law of Free Monarchies*, in letters to his ministers, and in speeches to Parliament, most notably in one delivered in the spring of 1610, less than a year before the first performance of *A King and No King*.

It should perhaps be noted at the outset that I am not proposing a point-by-point representation or identification of historical personages or events. I do not, for example, suggest that Arbaces is fashioned so as to portray or replicate the then ruling sovereign. Rather I treat those more general, issue-related concerns that surface momentarily in what remains decidedly, resolutely, a make-believe or fictional world. This, of course, is something of a paradox. The extravagant theatricality which seems to bar reference to a world beyond the fictional one becomes, in fact, the necessary condition which makes such reference possible, divulging meanings, obliquely, cunningly, that would otherwise be prohibited in stage performances. Within a dramatic context distanced by the outlandish trappings of the tragicomic mode, there are moments of transparency open to the larger drama of Jacobean politics and culture. Such moments capture a reflection of issues and attitudes neither foreign to nor separate from those upon which the interpretation of contemporary social and political realities depends. As Jonathan Goldberg puts it, a king's role on the stage of history is played according to an historical or social text and a player-king may at times echo that text and still remain in character, sheltered by a fictional identity.[7]

And a distinctive fictional identity it certainly is. The player-king in question is the brilliant, young Arbaces, King of Iberia, who has not laid eyes upon his sister Panthea since childhood, having been out of the country many years at the wars. The play stages his victorious homecoming and reunion with his sister. He is immediately struck down by her beauty, overwhelmed by carnal desire and the wilderness of an incestuous passion that threatens to engulf him. Arbaces' struggle to maneuver in situations increasingly disruptive and self-deflating constitutes the central conflict of the play. Attention focuses upon the various strategies by means of which he tries to regain mastery and control. There is a further point to be made about the ordeal to which he is subjected. We discover well into the play that he is the victim of an elaborate hoax, planned and stage-managed by the chief minister of the kingdom, Gobrius, who all along knows that Arbaces is not Panthea's brother and that the incest-problem, with which Arbaces so furiously contends, is without substance. We learn that Gobrius' plotting is intended to expose the young king to what lies beyond his command and thus to curb his arrogance and pride. The deception and the fury it releases serve to demystify the great image of authority to which Arbaces fitfully aspires in both word and deed.

An examination of the various ways in which the play is linked to its historical setting will, I believe, persuade us that it addresses matters of public policy and offers a way of responding with some measure of what is required to understand them. The argument is worth pursuing in so far as it claims a unity of purpose for the play as a whole and, at the same time, seeks to situate the play within the larger social and political drama of the period, to claim, that is, that the play is more carefully crafted than usually supposed and more expressive of substantive issues and concerns.

THE ORDER OF WORDS

I begin with the scene in which the victorious Arbaces returns to his court after years of fighting on foreign soil. He flaunts his victory in battle, 'taking a prince prisoner in the heart of his own country in single combat' as witness to a god-like power: 'I could tell the world / How I have laid his kingdom desolate / With this sole arm propp'd by divinity' (I, i, 27–8, 126–8).[8] Mardonius, a blunt, plain-speaking companion in arms, is sickened by Arbaces' arrogance and by his extravagant boasts. Without him, he declares to Arbaces, 'you may talk, and be believ'd and grow, / And have your too self-glorius temper rock'd / Into a dead sleep ...' (IV, ii, 177–9).[9] The present danger lies in Arbaces' belief in his own invincibility: 'This combat has undone him. If he had been well beaten, he had been temperate. I shall never see him handsome again till he have a horseman's staff pok'd through his shoulders or an arm broke with a bullet' (IV, ii, 120–3). This idea of the wounding of the king carries through the play and is strongly supported by stage action and imagery. As the action progresses, Arbaces suffers a succession of disabling blows, inflicted not in war but in 'pelting, prattling peace' and by altogether unexpected adversaries. The first blow comes at the moment of his long-anticipated homecoming and reunion with his sister – certainly one the most remarkable, carefully articulated scenes of the play. Arbaces enters before the assembled court, bringing with him the prizes of his recent victory including the captured prince Tigranes, whom he intends to marry to his sister. Beginning in great formality, the scene takes an abrupt and unexpected turn when the king is unable to respond to his sister's elaborate speech of welcome. A defiant aside reveals the cause of his distress. Momentarily overcome by sudden passion for his sister, he tries to control the situation and the feelings it evokes by naming what he feels. He translates experience into the familiar idiom of the Petrarchan convention, the wound inflicted comes by way of Cupid's dart. What he rails against and tries to intimidate is a figure of speech:

> If thou beest love, begone,
> Or I will tear thee from my wounded flesh,
> Pull thy lov'd down away, and with a quill,
> By this right arm drawn from thy wanton wing,
> Write to thy laughing mother in thy blood
> That you are powers belied and all your darts
> Are to be blown away by men resolv'd
> Like dust. I know thou fear'st my words; away.

> (III, i, 83–90)

We are, of course, not persuaded by the king's blustering rhetoric, his tattletale threat to inscribe the news of love's defeat. Even the phrase, 'like dust', tends to attach itself to 'men resolv'd', and thus to underscore the ironic cast of the passage. When rhetorical intervention changes nothing, Arbaces shifts the mode of attack from one that moves at a level of literary abstraction to one that draws upon the full power and mystery of kingship. Refusing now to recognize his sister, he demands that she must be brought to him. When nothing happens, he reasons that she must be dead, a startling conclusion in view of what we know to be happening on the stage, but one to which Arbaces, at least, is prepared to reconcile himself in a display of manly fortitude: 'We all must.die, / And she hath taught us how' (III, i, 142–3). This extraordinary utterance, possessing the settled elegance and precision of epigram, serves only to measure the distance between the fiction Arbaces is determined to play out and what we perceive to be happening. For him, there remains only the quiet acceptance of the self-imposed, isolating fiction. But Gobrius, his chief minister, insists that Panthea lives and must be recognized. The king responds by threatening death to anyone 'that names / Or thinks her for my sister' (III, i, 158–9).

> She is no kin to me nor shall she be;
> If she were any, I create her none,
> And which of you can question this? My power
> Is like the sea, that is to be obey'd

And not disputed with. I have decreed her
As far from having part of blood with me,
As the nak'd Indians. Come and answer me,
He that is boldest now: is that my sister?

(III, i, 165–72)

Adam with a perfect knowledge imparted by God named the creatures in
Paradise. In a grotesque parody of that ritual in the Garden, Arbaces now
undertakes through the magic of his majesty to unname one, creating her
anew and of no kin to him. No one dares shout down this blasphemy and
even the bewildered Panthea asks only that by Arbaces' unquestioned word
she receive some name, 'else I shall live / Like sinful issues that are left in
streets / By their regardless mothers ...' (III, i, 183–6).

The scene elaborates the resources of an authoritarian, kin-dissolving
power. It stages the presumed enactment of a mystery from which those
around Arbaces derive their being and to which they must submit. Arbaces
confronts the disordering, unpredictable sweep of events by way of incan-
tation and ceremony. Initially, he retreats to a genre-typical artificiality
and, when that strategy fails, he invokes the power of kingship to transform
the world of subjects and of things. Behind each strategy is the notion that
an imagined, idealized order is somehow truer than actuality, and what
follows is a shamanistic performance in which the world as ordinarily
perceived and understood is called upon to yield to the king's word which is
both law and substance, an absolute authority from which there is no
appeal. Clearly the scene represents monarchical authority as it embarks
upon the linguistic conquest of reality and pits that authority against a
recalcitrant, everyday world of people and events. The outcome is fore-
shadowed in the king's lofty, inflated rhetoric. And, in the end, even he is
forced to acknowledge his defeat: 'Why should there be such music in a
voice / And sin for me to hear it? All the world / May take delight in this,
and 'tis damnation / For me to do so' (III, i, 187–90). It is the sensuous
property of words, not their representational content, their thingness, not
their meaning, that prevails. Unable to change or to accept the present state
of affairs, overcome by a deepening sense of bewilderment and loss, Arbaces
arrogates to himself a new role, that of a beleaguered, hapless victim. He
had earlier taken Tigranes prisoner 'in the heart of own country'; now it is
his turn to endure the shame of an enforced captivity.

Arbaces' performance throughout much of this scene is fashioned
according to a familiar pattern of divine-right monarchy; his bold pronouncements on the nature of kingly authority include the following claims:
(1) there is no legal limit to the exercise of kingly power, (2) subjects may
not question or dispute what the king may do, and (3) it lies within the
mystery of the king's power to make and unmake subjects, to intervene at

will in the lives of subjects by virtue of an absolute authority over them. These are, of course, extraordinary claims and they rehearse with remarkable precision those made by the Stuart monarchy. James had resolutely refused to permit the Commons to debate matters touching the royal prerogative and regularly issued imperious commands that the prerogative should not be called in question. In the spring of 1610, James declared to the Commons that as 'to dispute what God may do, is Blasphemie . . . So is it sedition in Subjects, to dispute what a King may do in the height of his power . . . I will not be content that my power be disputed upon: but I shall ever be willing to make the reason appeare of all my doings, and rule my actions according to my Lawes'.[10] With respect to the king's absolute sovereignty over his subjects, James made his position no less clear, declaring that:

> The State of *Monarchie* is the supremest thing upon earth: For Kings are not only *Gods* Lieutenants upon earth, and sit upon *Gods* throne, but even by God himself they are called *Gods* . . . Kings are justly called Gods, for that they exercise a manner or resemblance of Divine power upon earth: For if you wil consider the Attributes to God, you shall see how they agree in the person of a King. God hath the power to create, or destroy, make, or unmake at his pleasure, to give life, or send death, to judge all and to be not judged nor accomptable to none: To raise low things, and to make high things low at his pleasure, and to God are both soule and body due. And the like power have Kings: they make and unmake their subjects: they have power of raising, and casting down: of life, and of death: Judges over all their subjects, and in all causes, and yet accomptable to none but God onely.   (*Works*, pp. 307–8)

Willson remarks that on this occasion the king had talked for two hours and 'had offended many of his audience by his frequent and casual use of God and by his lofty exaltation of the royal prerogative' (p. 264). James's views were widely disseminated in the published text of the speech. The STC lists three editions, each bearing the date of 1609 on the title-page, the new year not beginning until 25 March according to the Julian calendar then used in England. Since those editions were official publications of the king's printer, Robert Barker, they were not subject to the prohibition of the Stationers' Company against printing more than 1500 copies from any one setting of type. And the number of extant copies further strengthens the probability of overprinting which, in turn, suggests that the speech was accessible to, read and discussed in, a segment of contemporary society broader than the one where such texts would normally be available. Thus, there is reason to suppose that the speech entered into the currency of political discourse beyond Whitehall, the issues it raised being as familiar to Beaumont and Fletcher's audiences as to a larger public not directly involved in parliamentary proceedings. James himself called attention to the speech in an appearance before Parliament on 21 May. He repeated a large part of it and then indicated that he had been at pains to have it printed. He told the Commons that he meant what he said, that he would not permit any challenge to his authority.

> I sent a message to will and require you to forbear to meddle touching prerogative and the privilege of a king. Now that I may ever be so far like myself, that my conclusion and actions may not vary, I must remember you that in my last speech I gave you warning that it is not lawful for you to dispute what a king may do.[11]

He further warned against any attempt to enact 'such laws as make shadows of kings and dukes of Venice ... You cannot so clip the wing of greatness' (*Proceedings*, vol. II, p. 103). The king's speech, wrote a contemporary,

> bred generally much discomfort; to see our monarchicall powre and regall prerogative strained so high and made so transcendent every way, that yf the practise shold follow the positions, we are not like to leave to our successors that freedome we receved from our forefathers, nor make account of any thing we have longer then they list that govern.[12]

To the evident distress of the Commons and with considerable embarrassment to his ministers, James regularly argued that all judicial authority began in the Crown and flowed thence 'in two great streams, the temporal jurisdiction of the Common Law courts, the spiritual to the courts of the Church' (Willson, p. 258). Since the king is 'above the law, as both the author and giver of strength thereto,' since laws passed by Parliament become statutes only upon the king's ratification, 'and if there bee anything that I dislike, they rase it out before', the king can limit the jurisdiction of any court, and, if it please him, set aside or amend its judgments, the king being the supreme interpreter of the law: 'Kings are properly Judges, and judgement properly belongs to them from God: for Kings sit in the Throne of God, and thence all Judgement is derived' (pp. 63, 302, 326). Or again, 'the King the supreme judge; inferior judges his shadows and ministers ... and the King may, if he please, sit and judge in Westminster Hall in any Court there, and call their Judgements in question... The King beinge the author of the Lawe is the interpreter of the Lawe'.[13] When judges of the Common Law courts reminded James that they had an oath of office to fulfill, he sharply rebuked them declaring that 'the King is their judge and it is his part to interpret their oaths, and not they, for in disobeying his commandment they deserved to be hanged' (*EHR*, vol. XVIII, pp. 672–3, Willson, p. 258). Such utterances were, of course, a direct challenge both to the Commons and to the Common Law tradition. The Commons retaliated by drawing up a petition of right, asserting the privilege of its members to engage in free debate. Attempts to compose the bitterness on both sides failed and in January 1611 the king dissolved his parliament. James's repeated and tactless claims to absolute supremacy, his stubborn refusal, against the courageous protests of his ministers, to qualify or mute those claims, had outraged the Commons. He had succeeded only in intensifying a conflict he could not afford and in focusing public attention upon the very issues he sought to suppress. When Beaumont and Fletcher's fictional king voices similar claims dressed out in rhetoric no less lofty and overbearing than that employed by James, the key to the play's larger, essentially satiric, purpose is ready-at-hand.

The route Arbaces travels leads from the ceremony of monarchy to the drama of experience. He undertakes to change his sister's name and comes to doubt his own. Unable to dominate his feelings or to transform their object, he sinks beneath a contradiction he can articulate but not resolve: 'I shall but languish for the want of that, / The having which would kill me' (III, i, 202–3). Shattered when experience throws off the heroic shapes he would impose upon it, he finds his kingliness, indeed his humanity, threatened.

> Such an ungodly sickness I have got,
> That he that undertakes my cure must first
> O'er throw divinity, all moral laws
> And leave mankind as unconfined as beasts.
>
> (III, i, 195–8)

Arbaces has attempted to remake the world; not only is he powerless to do so, he is made ridiculous by having tried. His efforts lead those around him to mock him as a madman and the scene becomes a burlesque of majesty. Arbaces has driven nails with a sponge, fabricated a divinity and is shamed by its collapse. He had earlier boasted that he would 'teach the neighbor world humility' (I, i, 133); in act III, the world teaches hm. For all his arrogance and pride, he is more foolish than wicked. Still the dilemma he confronts is a false one. He remains a comic figure who struggles with the world and gets no closer to its truth. He peels away one layer of deception only to lose himself at another. He has found that words do not confer existence on the things they name; he continues to be hobbled and humiliated by the names he gives himself and others.

What is involved here, I suggest, goes beyond character and plot. In a necessarily cautious but insistent probing of notional or ideational terms, the play illuminates with startling precision the ambiguities and uncertainties that remain embedded in the language and fictions of kingship. It does this in various ways beginning with the paradoxical title by which it names itself. It does so again by locating Arbaces' dilemma in the abstracting or notional property of language and in the peculiar distortions that find a foothold there. Arbaces' reluctance to venture beyond *a priori* assumptions, beyond the whole established order of things, to hold himself, as it were, hostage to what are essentially verbal constructions, a network of named relationships, is a distinctive feature of his character and the source of much trouble in the play. Language imposes an impossible burden on his ability to maneuver in or adjust to the situations in which he finds himself. Arbaces struggles with relational terms, with common names, throughout much of the play; those sanctioned by tradition and a social group clash with those answering to experience and the unexpectedness of things. *Arbaces* and *Panthea* are proper names – their referents unique and unrelated.[14] *King, subject, brother, sister* are abstracting terms that assert relationships between bearers of proper names. Abstract terms organize experience, impose an order on events and things, and, in their application, are susceptible to error. The term *brother* names, but mistakes Arbaces' relationship to Panthea; it fails to meet the requirements of normal usage. Thus it introduces a relatively simple kind of semantic confusion. Terms of mixed or contested meanings involve matters more elusive to analysis or control. *King* is such a term and its capacity to sort and organize social and psychological phenomena is very much in question. *King* like *brother* classifies; it implies relationships between what is named and other terms or set of terms. But it asserts relationships of a much higher order of abstraction. The referents or terms which figure in those relationships extend from earth to heaven and claim to touch a secret scheme of things. The failure of ceremony in act III diminishes or redefines the name of *king*, radically changing the relationships it customarily implies. So do the actualities of passion as they assault the image of authority. Together they cast a shadow that involves the awesome power and special status claimed for kingship, unsettling in the process some of the more extravagant meanings encompassed by the word.

If the audience responds to this demonstration of the distorting influence of language, Arbaces does not. Enlightenment comes to him much later in the play, provoked by the dismantling of his 'fictional' identity and the collapse of the deceptions, linguistic and otherwise, with which it is entangled. Until that happens, Arbaces remains bound by his unques-tioned acceptance of named relationships. The strain thus imposed is painfully felt in act IV when he laments his powerlessness to change the language and the categories by which he knows the world and his position in it. He finds himself entrapped by words and by the relational concepts to which those words refer: 'The very reverence of the word comes cross me / And ties mine arm down' (v, iv, 121–2). It is perfectly in line with his attention to abstractions and the conceptual mode that he should falter before the rigidities of named relationsips. Because they are named, they exist. But when he cries out that these words are more elusive than the things they classify, he almost stumbles upon the source of his distress, the kind of error he has not yet learned to reckon with. When Panthea demands to know the reason of her imprisonment, Arbaces confesses his love and learns that she returns it.

Arbaces.   Is there no stop
  To our full happiness but these mere sounds,
  'Brother' and 'sister'?
Panthea.   There is nothing else,
  But these, alas, will separate us more
  Than twenty worlds betwixt us.
Arbaces.   I have liv'd
  To conquer men, and now am overthrown
  Only by words – 'brother' and 'sister'. Where
  Have those words dwelling? I will find 'em out
  And utterly destroy them, but they are
  Not to be grasp'd.

                                         (IV, iv, 112–21)

Earlier Arbaces had dressed out his pride with words he claimed were
transcendentally effective. Now his defiant rhetoric burns itself out on
words he cannot seem to change. His formal lament makes effective use of a
number of rhetorical devices. The figure of repetition or *anaphora* links three
clauses and serves to underscore a perfect parallelism shaping the whole
speech. The figure of vehement supplication or *optatio* marks the expression
of an ardent wish or desire. Arbaces cries out against the abstract and
elusive enemy he wants to fight, but cannot. Each complaint except the last
one follows the general pattern: Would that things were otherwise and, if
they were, then victory would be easy.

       Let 'em be men or beasts
  And I will cut 'em from the earth, or towns
  And I will raze 'em and then blow 'em up.
  Let 'em be seas, and I will drink them off
  And yet have unquench'd fire left in my breast.
  Let 'em be anything but merely voice.

                                         (IV, iv, 121–6)

Hyperboles project a perfect victory over men, beasts, towns, seas, not
over words. Arbaces would act against a world of things. The tone grows
more plaintive than defiant. His final exhortation arises from despair and
sounds its own defeat: 'Let 'em be anything but merely voice.' The
arrangement of parallel members throws full weight and emphasis on an
authority which Arbaces is not prepared to question or dispute. This final
term of the series somewhat modified and set off by quotation marks
appears as the first line of Yeats's poem 'King and No King'. The poem
fastens upon one aspect of Arbaces' dilemma, his reluctance to challenge
the ideal of a fixed and abiding order reflected in language.

'Would it were anything but merely voice!'
The No King cried who after that was King,
Because he had not heard of anything
That balanced with a word is more than noise;
Yet Old Romance being kind, let him prevail
Somewhere or somehow that I have forgot. . .[15]

Of concern here is the aspect of character Yeats chooses to recall: Arbaces' near-fatal determination to uphold the order of words against all the clamour of experience. Arbaces is reluctant to engage whatever capacity for accommodation or adjustment he might otherwise muster precisely 'because he had not heard of anything that balanced with a word is more than noise'. He is persuaded that words derive their 'legitimacy' from a transcendental, unalterable order, that they assert absolute social and political relationships, 'not in the power of any force / Or policy to conquer...' (IV, iv, 127–8). The play argues against that belief by exposing the inevitable distortions and betrayals to which it leads. There develops an acute sense of the opposition between the rigidities of language and the whirling, streaming eventuality of things against which they struggle. One further effect is a renewed appreciation of just how those rigidities thwart the play of human experience itself, encouraging, in Richard Hooker's splendid phrase, 'every mans fashioning of his owne life contrary unto the customs and orders of this present world'.[16] Arbaces has greater cause than he knows to ask: 'Where have those words dwelling?' Jonson remarks that 'there is much more holds us, than presseth us. An ill fact is one thing, an ill fortune is another: Yet both often-times sway us alike, by the error of our thinking'.[17] It is an ill fact masquerading as an ill fortune that becomes the chief determiner of action in *A King and No King*. Conflict arises more from what Arbaces and Panthea think they know than from what they feel. They lose their way not in the wilderness of passion but in the concealments of language. Release from artfulness and error, not from passion, brings recovery and a comic resolution.

That release is won when Arbaces turns upon Gobrius, the chief minister and Lord-Protector of the kingdom, accuses him of treason and demands to know why he had so praised Panthea 'that I doted / Something before I saw her' (v, iv, 91–1). Gobrius' aside 'Now it is ripe' (v, iv, 64) has prepared us for the *dénouement*. He defends himself against the charge of treason by proving Arbaces no brother and no king. Panthea is discovered the only child of the late king and, thus, the lawful heir to the throne. Hard truths reveal themselves as verbal fictions. But before the play is done, Arbaces returns once more to the rhetoric of royal authority. This time he does so as the agent of satire, not its target. This later recapitulation leaves little doubt about the attitude the play intends us to take toward the ceremonial role Arbaces has so long struggled to sustain. Arbaces has by now been told he is no king, but when he meets Ligones, the Armenian ambassador, who seeks to negotiate the release of Tigranes, he assumes the role in order to parody it, dwelling on the mysteries and miracles a king is empowered to perform. It is a striking conclusion to the satire of kingly ritual and ceremony. Arbaces promises the ambassador that he shall be sent home 'on a horse cut out of diamond / That shall be made to go with golden wheels, I know not

how yet' (v, iv, 318–20). The figure may have for its example the hyperboles
which carried Marlowe's hero in triumph through Persepolis. Ligones,
taken in by the fiction, delights in the thought that with such a gift he 'shall
be made forever'. Thus encouraged, Arbaces promises to bestow an even
greater gift upon Ligones' daughter: 'She shall have some strange thing;
we'll have the kingdom / Sold utterly and put into a toy / Which she shall
wear about her carelessly / Somewhere or other' (v, iv, 323–6). In this
marvelous bit of mock-work, the debts of courtesy are paid with counterfeit
coin. The risk falls to those credulous enough to count on such a reckoning.
The action of the play has brought home to Arbaces the absurdity of his
earlier belief in the vaunted powers of monarchy. Here his performance
recalls that belief and exposes it to ridicule. It seems unlikely that the wider
implications of that performance would be lost to a contemporary audience
or fail to signify a sharply declining reverence for royal authority.
Throughout the play, the role of Arbaces seems too closely matched to a
model of monarchical authority not much different from that to which
James had repeatedly and insistently appealed for the audience to have
mistaken its drift.

MONARCH AND THE LAW

There is, however, another impulse beyond this satiric one that tries to
decipher some cherished notions about linguistic privilege and the unalterable order of words. That second, related impulse conveys an ideological
point. Behind the glossy cover of overdressed emotions, *A King and No King*
stages a conflict between two sharply drawn, opposing views of kingship.
The conflict enforces an investigation of themes touching not only a mode of
discourse but also the position of the monarch in relation to the law of the
land. It builds toward an eventual release from the tyranny of linguistic and
political absolutism by invoking a familiar, if controversial, ideological
construct that places the royal prerogative under the rule of law. Thus the
play rehearses and attempts to resolve what was, perhaps, the most
unsettling political and legal issue of the period, that of the position and
power of the king.

James brought the issue into prominence by declaring his contempt for a
limited monarchy. He maintained that the royal will was absolute, that he
was gifted with absolute sovereignty, that his word was the law, above
contest or review by Parliament or the courts. To combat that view, the
opposition appealed to legal tradition and parliamentary sovereignty,
holding that no law was to be promulgated except in full Parliament of king,
Lords, and Commons. Political theorists of the period, Hooker and
Buchanan among them, were prepared to defend the traditionally legal
aspects of kingship, not its sacred or priestly ones. They resolutely argued

against the king's right to make law by proclamation or to exercise his authority over the determinations of the Common Law courts. They contended that the king's sovereignty is limited by law, that the law stands superior to the monarch by reason of an authority derived ultimately from the collective efforts of a society to establish rules necessary for the attainment of the common good.[18] They sought to limit prerogative power and to escape the rigidity of laws made by proclamation by vesting authority in such extra-textual sources as judicial precedent and the customs and ideals of the community, in the silent testimony of experience, in 'what usage had approved'.[19] Rules so derived had proven their utility and adaptability by surviving over time. That they had survived implied sufficient popular consent to confer legitimacy. This appeal to 'worldly experience and practise', 'to the customes and the orders of this present world', is most eloquently and comprehensively set forth by Richard Hooker in *Of the Laws of Ecclesiastical Polity*, the foundation of which, we are told by one contemporary, 'was laid in the Temple' and in the Common Law tradition.[20] James's own teacher had similarly argued that the law is grounded in something beyond the royal will and justly acts to constrain that will.

> The most loathsome monsters, anger and lust, are clearly apparent in mankind. And what else do laws strive for or accomplish than that these monsters be made obedient to reason. And where they do not conform to reason, may not the laws most justly impose limits upon them? He, therefore, who releases a king, or anyone else, from these bonds does not merely release a man, but sets up two exceedingly cruel monsters in opposition to reason and arms them that they may break down the barriers of the law.[21]

Against the background of contemporary controversy and debate, the close attention *A King and No King* focuses on the rule of law and on the consequences of its abuse by those in power must have stirred the audience to reflection. Calculated to enforce such reflection and especially to create concern over what follows when prerogative power overreaches the law is the sudden disclosure (in III, iii) of what Arbaces is prepared to do in the grip of passion. When his absolutist rhetoric is emptied of meaning, when, in effect, words fail him, he seeks to fulfill his dark intent by intrigue and deception. He turns first to Mardonius: 'I would desire her love / Lasciviously, lewdly, incestuously, / To do a sin that needs must damn us both / And thee too' (III, iii, 77–80). Mardonius refuses to take part, protesting that private crimes are public ones as well, that they strike at the heart of judicial authority: '... if you do this crime, you ought to have no laws, for after this it will be great injustice in you to punish any offender for any crime' (III, iii, 98–100). Undaunted by the rebuke, powerless to resist his 'loathed fate', Arbaces enlists the aid of the sycophantic Bessus, willing to 'do anything without exception, be it a good, bad, or indifferent thing' (III, iii, 140–1). But Bessus' bland indifference in the face of what Arbaces proposes so horrifies him that he drives Bessus from the stage, resolving to stand against his own intended lawlessness. He falters before the moral wilderness he is about to enter, the image of his corruption reflected in another person. The result is decisive and he abandons the whole sordid business, humiliated by the discovery of what he has become.

> Know I will die
> Languishing mad, as I resolve I shall,
> Ere I will deal by such an instrument.
> Thou art too sinful to employ in this.
> . . . .
> If there were no such instruments as thou,
> We kings could never act such wicked deeds.
> Seek out a man that mocks divinity,
> That breaks each precept both of God's and man's
> And nature's too and does it without lust
> Merely because it is a law and good,
> And live with him, for him thou canst not spoil.
>
> (III, iii, 176–9, 185–91)

Arbaces' new-found respect for the law, his reluctance to violate bonds and obligations which even he is disposed to acknowledge in relations between individuals, sexes, and social groups or classes, springs from his encounter with one indifferent to both law and custom. The derision he heaps upon Bessus recoils upon himself.[22]

From this point forward, Arbaces presents himself as first among the targets of his rage, an outcast, banished from the coasts of light and the company of men. He responds with increasing horror and disgust to what he supposes to be a sickness within, helpless in the throws of a mad agony 'thou wound'st me in / To such a strange and unbeliev'd affection / As good men cannot think on' (v, iv, 94–6). Finally in despair of his capacity to endure further shame, he resolves to end his life in a crescendo of violence against those who woke him from the dream of majesty.

> It is resolv'd. I bore it whilst I could;
> I can no more. Hell, open all thy gates,
> And I will through them; if they be shut,
> I'll batter 'em, but I will find the place
> Where the most damn'd have dwelling.
>
> (v, iv, 1–5)

The self-condemned, bewildered monarch staggers to his doom:

> Why should the hasty errors of my youth
> Be so unpardonable, to draw a sin
> Helpless upon me?
>
> (v, iv, 62–4)

Mardonius' not quite plausible 'What tragedy is near?' (v, iv, 11) merely enforces the self-conscious and ironic quality of this final scene, bringing to

mind the kind of play we are watching, the sudden shifts and turns that are
the stock and trade of tragicomedy. Mardonius' question and the flowing
cadences of Arbaces' near perfect iambic verse help to drain off whatever
emotional intensity the scene generates. The stricken Arbaces continues to
rail against the slings and arrows of outrageous fortune, but his speech lacks
conviction and we have reason to believe that all may be well in the end.
When, for example, he declares: 'There is a method in man's wickedness; /
It grows up by degrees ...' (v, iv, 36–7), what strikes us is the highly
generalized, impersonal diction, the flat, unequivocal tone, further indication, I think, of the distance between what is said and what the context
would seem to require. The resulting irony warns us that Arbaces' situation
is more ambiguous and uncertain than he is able to report, that the full story
is yet to be told. Disclosure comes when he turns upon his benefactor
demanding to know why

> thou didst save me
> Only till thou hadst studied out a way
> How to destroy me cunningly thyself.
> This was a curious way of torturing.

(v, iv, 79–82)

Gobrius has stage-managed the events of the play to produce this seeming
impasse, a state of affairs to which Arbaces now grudgingly capitulates:
'Get out I cannot where thou hurl'st me in' (v, iv, 106).[23] Gobrius brings
Arbaces to his senses by exposing him to what bears some resemblance to
the stormy climate of an uncertain world. His medium is obviously a
theatrical one, the message less exclusively so. In this respect, if not so
precisely in others, the play approaches what Sidney terms 'the right use' of
tragedy

> that openeth the greatest wounds, and sheweth forth the Vlcers that are
> couered with Tissue; that maketh Kinges feare to be Tyrants, and Tyrants
> manifest their tirannicall humors; that, with sturring the affects of admiration
> and commiseration, teacheth the vncertainety of this world, and vpon how
> weake foundations guilden roofes are builded.[24]

The play, of course, draws back from the irrecoverableness of tragedy; it
does, after all, find a way out of the dilemma it poses. It is significant, I
think, that the escape route leads from identifiable absolutes – political,
moral, and linguistic – through a succession of provisional adjustments,
corrections, and acceptances. In the nick of time and to the immense relief
of all concerned, Gobrius intervenes with the truth of Arbaces' birth,
dispelling in an instant the conditions and confusions against which
Arbaces has so painfully contended. A festive, egalitarian mood suddenly
engulfs the play's conclusion: 'Mardonius, the best news... I am found no
king!' (v, iv, 263–4); 'I am Arbaces; we all fellow-subjects...' (v, iv, 291).
And Arbaces drops altogether the imperious, commanding tone of his

earlier utterances. The conditional mood replaces the imperative. The crucial instance is, of course, the long delayed proposal to Panthea, the conditional element of which is that it can be shown to accord with custom and the law.

> *Arbaces*. Grant me one request.
> *Panthea*. Alas, what can I grant you? What I can
>   I will.
> *Arbaces*.   That you will please to marry me,
>   If I can prove it lawful.
>
> (v, iv, 329–32)

Arbaces has learned to maneuver in a world of contingent, shifting significations. He turns for guidance to what experience can approve, to what traditionally has seasoned and instructed the exercise of power. Recognition of the value and sanctity of law, neither absolute nor mysterious, but grounded in history and the successiveness of things, is given careful emphasis in the play; it becomes the essential condition the satisfaction of which dispels confusion and makes possible new relationships – Arbaces, 'proved no king', is at long last free to marry Panthea and to reclaim the throne.

The implications are clear. At least within the boundaries of the fictional world, laws based on custom and usage serve to capture, if not altogether to check, an impulse toward self-aggrandizement and overreaching that disables monarchy and puts at risk the goals and interests to which the social world of the play is committed. The values upon which the play settles are much reduced in scale from those absolute ones about which Arbaces has earlier ranted. Hard lessons in humility and dependency reform the monarchy, making it obedient to custom and the Common Law. The play enacts an ideological transformation: king-is-the-law gives way to king-under-the-law. Monarchy is redefined and then approved. That the law itself is sovereign is a proposition to which both Arbaces and his audience are urged to give assent.

NOTES

1 Una Ellis-Fermor, *The Jacobean Drama*, 3rd edn. (London: Methuen, 1963), p. 4.
2 Robert K. Turner, Jr, Introduction, *A King and No King*, by Beaumont and Fletcher (Lincoln: University of Nebraska Press, 1963), p. xvii.
3 Margot Heinemann, *Puritanism and Theatre* (Cambridge University Press, 1980), p. 37.
4 Turner, Introduction, pp. xxv–xxvi.
5 Heinemann discusses several notable cases of theatrical censorship in the early years of James's reign. She concludes that censorship on behalf of the Crown in Jacobean times was much tighter than it had been under Elizabeth (*Puritanism and Theatre*, pp. 36–47).

6 Heinemann makes the point that, despite a censorship which severely limited expression of political dissent, 'there is a clearly discernible line of dramatic production (albeit a minority one) which appeals to and encourages anti-establishment, generally Parliamentary Puritan sympathies...' (ibid., p. 16). She argues 'that the assumption, in which many later critics have concurred, that all the "better" Jacobean dramatists were naturally aligned with the Crown against Parliament will not really stand examination, and may lead us to misread the plays' (ibid., p. 17).

7 Jonathan Goldberg, *James I and the Politics of Literature* (Baltimore and London: The Johns Hopkins University Press, 1983), pp. 116, 122–4.

8 All quotations from the play are from Robert K. Turner, Jr's edition in Regents Renaissance Drama series (Lincoln: University of Nebraska, 1963).

9 Mardonius considers Arbaces' vainglorious rejection of honest counsel to be a fault of such large proportion that it must necessarily overwhelm whatever claim to victory the king may fashion for himself. His analysis recalls Montaigne's observation that 'a King is not to be credited, when for his glorie, he boasteth of his constancie, in attending his enemies encounter if for his good amendment and profit, hee cannot endure the libertie of his friends words, which have no other working power, than to pinch his learning: the rest of their effect remaining in his owne hands. Now, there is not any condition of men, that hath more need of true, sincerely-free and open-hearted advertisements, than Princes' (*Essayes ... now done into English by John Florio* [1603], pp. 641–2). It is noteworthy perhaps that Florio's printer set this passage and others dealing with kingship in italic type thereby giving to them an emphasis for which there is no precedent in the French editions of 1593 and 1595.

10 *The Political Works of James I*, ed. Charles Howard McIlwain (New York: Russell and Russell, 1965), p. 310. See David Harris Willson's discussion of James's dealings with Parliament in *King James VI and I* (New York: Oxford University Press, 1967), pp. 258–65.

11 *Proceedings in Parliament 1610*, ed. Elizabeth Read Foster (New Haven and London: Yale University Press, 1966), vol. II, p. 101. See also *Parliamentary Debates in 1610*, ed. S. R. Gardiner (London: Camden Society, 1862), vol. LXXXI, pp. 34–5.

12 *The Letters of John Chamberlain*, ed. N. E. McClure (Philadelphia: American Philosophical Society, 1939), vol. I, p. 301.

13 *English Historical Review*, ed. Reginald L. Poole (London: Longmans, Green and Co., 1903), vol. XVIII, p. 673.

14 John Lyons, *Semantics* (Cambridge University Press, 1977), vol. I, p. 216.

15 *The Variorum Edition of the Poems of W. B. Yeats*, ed. Allt and Alspach (New York: Macmillan, 1957), p. 258.

16 Richard Hooker, *Of the Laws of Ecclesiastical Polity*, ed. W. Speed Hill (Cambridge, Mass.: Harvard University Press, 1977), vol. I, p. 43.

17 *Ben Jonson*, ed. Herford and Simpson (Oxford: Clarendon Press, 1947), vol. VIII, p. 564. Bacon regularly attacks a reverence for linguistic forms as an impediment to empirical inquiry: 'Here, therefore, is the first distemper of learning, when men study words and not matter: . . . for words are but the images of matter: and except they have life of reason and invention, to fall in love with them is all

one as to fall in love with a picture' (*The Advancement of Learning: Book I*, ed. William Armstrong (London: Athlone Press, 1975), p. 71).

18 Lawrence Manley, *Conventions 1500–1750* (Cambridge, Mass.: Harvard University Press, 1980), pp. 96–104.

19 Henry de Bracton, *On the Laws and Customs of England*, trans. Samuel E. Thorne (Cambridge: Belknap, 1968–79), vol. II, p. 2.

20 Izaak Walton, *The Lives of John Donne, Sir Henry Wolton, Richard Hooker, George Herbert, and Robert Sanderson* (London: Oxford World Classics, 1927), p. 208.

21 George Buchanan, *The Powers of the Crown in Scotland*, trans. Charles F. Arrowood (Austin: University of Texas, 1949), p. 128.

22 In addition to the sinister face shown in the scene just described, Bessus wears a comic one in a series of elaborate ceremonies he performs in his own behalf. The sub-plot exhibits his attempts to maintain a reputation won by accident. Running from battle, he stumbles upon the enemy and claims a victory for which he had not fought. The field bears his name, Bessus' Desperate Redemption. Old enemies, once able to ignore his insults because all knew him to be a great coward, now must press their cause for honor's sake. Bessus becomes the victim of his reputation; to put off his challengers, he resorts to court etiquette and the rules of courtesy. He stands to gain from challenges by selling the paper on which they are written to the grocers. He will catch as catch can and hopes for more paper. He regrets that he can learn 'but a little skill in the comparing of styles' (III, ii, 95) since all the challenges are written by the same scrivener. His buffoonery continually mocks the solemnities more earnestly performed by others. His cynical exploitation of ritual forms anticipates the decline of Arbaces' own reverence for ceremony and ritual. Plot and sub-plot move in one direction, if not to one end. When Bessus is finally stripped of his disguise, we are not much disturbed because, even for him, it held so little meaning to begin with.

23 When Gobrius projects the end to which he directs the course of events, his immediate rhetorical motive is to persuade Panthea that she must 'labour out this tempest' until Arbaces 'shall once collect himself and see / How far he has been asunder from himself, / What a mere stranger to his golden temper' (IV, i, 15, 19–21). The promise of Arbaces' eventual self-recovery is embodied in the figure of a tree whose roots 'though somewhat stopt with humor' will renew themselves and shoot again the branches of their government 'high as our hopes can look at, straight as justice, / Loaden with ripe contents' (IV, i, 22–6). The figure seems to have its origin in Nebuchadnezzar's vision of his empire and in the interpretation of that vision by the prophet Daniel. By far the fullest elaboration of the figure is found in Edmund Dudley's anti-monarchical *The Tree of the Commonwealth*. Shakespeare uses the figure in *Cymbeline* to express the theme of restoration. In *Henry VIII*, the figure is the vehicle for an elaborate compliment to James I. A seventeenth-century Nebuchadnezzar is called upon to remind himself that 'we in our worke resemble should a tree / In branches that beare most fruitfullie' (*Nebuchadnezzars Fierie Furnace*, ed. Margarete Rösler, *Materials for the Study of Old English Drama*, Louvain, 1936, vol. XII, p. 2).

24 Sir Philip Sidney, *An Apology for Poetry* in *Elizabethan Critical Essays*, ed. G. Gregory Smith (Oxford: Clarendon Press, 1904), vol. I, p. 177.

Dialogue into drama: Socrates in eighteenth-century verse dramas*

K. J. H. BERLAND

I

According to the first-hand witnesses Plato and Xenophon, Socrates loved to talk, and he apparently had a dry sense of humour. He was condemned to death unjustly, resisted dishonourable alternatives to his sentencing, and died nobly. All this ought to provide ideal subject material for theatre, but there have not been many outstanding plays written about Socrates since Aristophanes wrote *The Clouds* in the philosopher's own lifetime. However, a number of eighteenth-century authors did attempt to dramatize the story. Their versions of the story are based partly on the earliest versions, and partly on popular tradition.

The plays all seem to have been intended for private readers instead of public audiences, allowing a different kind of effect than theatrical presentation affords. There is little or no stage history, but the plays employ a powerful vocabulary of historical image and allusion, and they merit some attention.

II

The difficulties inherent in translating the dialogue form into drama can be seen in Samuel Catherall's Εικων Σωκρατική; or, a Portraiture of Socrates, Extracted out of Plato (1717). Catherall draws primarily on the *Apology*, *Crito*, and *Phaedo*; however, the author has largely abandoned the dialogical form, and in its place appear several varied approaches. The work is divided into four parts, like acts (though they are not so designated), complete with directions specifying location. The first section is a monologue by 'Socrates at the Bar';[1] though loosely based on Plato's *Apology*, the speech follows neither the order of the argument nor the question-and-answer method of the original. Catherall himself explains that he wrote for a lay audience, 'to let the Illiterate Part of Mankind know, what elevated Thoughts a *Heathen* entertain'd concerning the Nature of Vertue, and Vice, and the Certainty of

* A draft of this paper was read at the *Themes in Drama* International Conference held at the University of California, Riverside, in February 1988.

future Rewards and Punishments in another Life' (sig. [A3]ʳ). Like many other writers, Catherall intends that his readers should be impressed by the great goodness of this man, achieved without the benefit of revelation – the example of the heathen wise man serves as a reproach to inconstant Christians.

Dialogue, especially as practised by Plato, requires of its readers a fairly complex process of inferential activity. We can only come to understand Plato's Socrates with study and careful speculation. The dialogues are oblique: Plato never tells us directly what we are to make of Socrates, as novelists employing the privileges of commentary and access to the minds of their characters might do. Rather, he shows us Socrates at work, and we arrive at our understanding inductively.

Catherall expects something less complex from his readers. This expectation is reflected both in the image of Socrates he presents and in the form of the poem itself. His Socrates is a moral hero whose significance is to be found in the example he offers. Much of what we have come to think characteristic of Socrates – his questioning method, his assumed ignorance, his irony, his dry wit – simply have no part to play. Instead, we are shown an already completed portrait, a character already fully judged and explained. Sometimes this explanation comes from the mouth of the principal character himself. Catherall's Socrates simply tells us what he's up to. Consider the opening lines:

> Simplicity of Speech, and naked Truth,
> Not varnish'd with the Charms of Eloquence
> Or cover'd with the Gloss of Rhetorick,
> Belong to Me: *Athenians*, think no more
> That Pride, and Self-Conceit, that dire Disease!
> Sophistick Wrangling, intricate Dispute,
> Peculiar Notions, groundless Mysteries,
> Fetch'd from among the Clouds, or else the Product
> Of a wild Fancy, and distemper'd Brain
> Make up the Character of *Socrates* 1

(p. 1)

He goes on to insist he has never taught 'Erroneous Tenets', has never denied the existence of the gods or pursued forbidden knowledge. Nor has he 'instill'd bad Notions into Youth', or 'confounded the Ideas / Of Justice, and of Truth, with artful Shuffle, / So as to make a Cause, that's stamp'd with Vice, / Shine under the Disguise of Lovely Vertue' (p. 2). This speech clearly addresses the trumped-up charges levelled by Anytus and Melitus, even though the specific terms are never provided. But it is Catherall's reader, not the ostensible audience of Athenians, who is to benefit from the speech.

Thus, Catherall's portraiture involves a process of transformation that extends beyond casting Socrates' defence into blank verse. One of the great attractions of Plato's *Apology* is the way it shows Socrates in action; even when his life is in danger, he cannot resist the challenge of applying his method to his accusers and even to the jury. Plato's early dialogues are dramatic; the action (the interplay of ideas) is presented directly before the readers, whose participation is necessary to complete the picture. Xenophon's presentation, on the other hand, is usually much closer to narrative form, so that in his Socratic writings we are usually aware of Xenophon's presence as an intermediary, a voice telling us (rather than showing us) what Socrates did and meant. Catherall, too, is involved in a kind of summing up. Socrates tells the Athenians straight out what they are to think of him. The end result is hardly a portrait extracted from Plato. Instead, it is a synopsis of *current* notions of the significance of Socrates.

Catherall does take certain arguments unchanged from Plato, especially the conversation with Crito (about escape and the law) in the second section, and the conversation with Crito and Simmias (about the after-life) in the third section. Here the portrait is relatively faithful to its sources in Plato's *Crito* and *Phaedo*. However, there are a number of significant changes. First, Catherall's historical perspective allows him the benefit of hindsight. He transforms Socrates' brief suggestion in the *Apology*, that the Athenian people will regret their part in his destruction, into a full-fledged tirade of the 'Prophetick Spirit'. Socrates foresees terrible consequences:

>   ... if Poison be my Doom,
> And instant Death must snatch me from the World;
> Then dire Calamities will fall on *Athens*.
> How will it mourn too late the loss of Me,
> And curse the Day, the Hour, the fatal Moment,
> When it condemn'd me to Eternal Silence!

The Athenians' regret goes beyond the sorrow and shame attendant upon the loss of a valued teacher or exemplary moral figure. The action develops along conventionally tragic lines; injustice in the tribunal produces civil unrest:

> What Fears will shock each guilty Breast! I see,
> Methinks, vast Crowds of unexpected Friends
> Combine together to support my Cause,
> (The Cause of Truth!) and breathe out dire Revenge!
> I feel the City shaken with Alarms,
> And all my Adversaries stand a ghast ...
> I see Death rage, and the destructive Sword
> Deep glut it-self with Blood, to expiate *Mine*!
> I see those gen'rous Youths with Fury burn
> Who once *Socratick* Doctrines did imbibe,
> And thence corrupt become (so Fame reports,
> That Publisher of Lies!) I see them rave!
> Cursing my dastard Foes they scour along,
> And strive with Blood to appease my angry Ghost.

(p. 5)

This is only a small sampling of the fare. The revenge speech occupies upwards of 100 lines – and Socrates keeps returning to the subject all through the play. This aspect of the work clearly owes more to the revenge play tradition – and to a sense of what is appropriate to the prophetic tone – than to any historical account of the death of Socrates.

It is the author's sense of appropriateness that brings about the most striking alterations of the historical material. By the early eighteenth century, the view of Socrates as a proto-Christian 'martyr for the unity of the godhead' was widely accepted. Just such a notion informs Catherall's entire work: Socrates, the wisest of the heathen wise men and exemplar of natural religion, must be assigned the appropriate beliefs. Thus, Socrates' tentative exploration of the possibility of life after death in the *Apology*, and his discussion of the Elysian Fields and Tartarus in the *Phaedo*, here appear to fit the Christian eschatology exactly; inevitably, the metaphysics is also adjusted. Catherall follows Plato in drawing a strong distinction between the corruptible body and the incorruptible soul, but he superimposes a redemptive pattern. Since the immortal part is untouched, Socrates explains, we should labour to make the soul happy 'Not for a Moment, but Eternity' (p. 34). The account of the afterlife that follows resembles Dante and Milton more than Plato.

Very loosely grounded on the *Phaedo* (110d–114c), the *Portraiture* is fully Christianized. According to Plato, the guilty dead suffer in Tartarus until their victims forgive them; according to Catherall's Socrates, they are punished by the active agency of 'Wrath Divine', and they are punished eternally. The good move upward, skipping Plato's intermediate stage on the earth's surface, going directly to a bodiless state in 'more beautiful Habitations' (pp. 37–9).

While his disciples praise him for the sublimity of his notions, which must surely spring from divine Inspiration (p. 36), Socrates insists that the existence of a state 'of future Bliss and future Woe' should convince men to pursue only that wisdom 'that will purchase Heav'n!' (p. 40).

In the last section, Catherall modifies his 'dramatic' technique, introducing speeches including narrative passages, and appending the conventional epic tag, 'he spoke', at the end of the speeches of Socrates and the jailer. The point of view becomes external, and the play closes with an instructive apostrophe:

> O *Socrates*! Thy Thoughts were so refin'd,
> Such Shining Vertues did adorn thy Mind,
> As all th'admiring World might blush to see,
> And ev'n the *Christian Hero* learn of *Thee*!

(p. 53)

Catherall's verse-play is not precisely hagiography. It is, rather, polemical biography, dedicated to the educative function proclaimed in the preface. There the author declares that the force of Socrates' example should be sufficient to 'awaken the stupid *Atheist*, convince the obstinate *Free-Thinker*, and shame the ungodly *Christian!*' (sig. [A3]ʳ). By casting Socrates as a proto-Christian martyr, Catherall allies himself with a long humanist tradition proclaiming the value of reason in approaching and assenting to the truths of religious teaching. Naturally, it is necessary to 'stretch' the historical evidence to make it fit, but Catherall has no difficulty in accounting for this. 'Wheresoever it appears, that I have enlarged too freely upon *Plato*'s Sentiments, give me Leave to say, it was owing only to the ungovernable Efforts of a transported Genius. For who can read that glorious Author with any manner of Taste, and not be ravish'd, and carry'd away onto boundless Thought, and Speculation?' (sig. [A3]ᵛ).

This is not simply a tribute to Plato's writing – it is a critical declaration of interpretive poetics. Catherall attributes to Plato's words a potent force, which in turn gives him licence to share his enthusiasm. In the poem, Crito tells Socrates that his every word is 'An Oracle, and stirs up Rapture in us' (p. 37). Perhaps Catherall is alluding to the rapture or frenzy of inspiration that Ficino and the Cambridge Platonists found in the influence of Socrates. In any case, it is a forthright declaration that the author's view of the significance of Socrates allows him considerable freedom to adjust his sources to fit the requirements of his polemic. The result is a Socrates who talks in blank verse with the voice of a liberal Anglican divine of the early eighteenth century.

III

A similar approach to source material appears in Amyas Bushe's *Socrates, A Dramatic Poem* (1758).[2] Bushe prefaces his poem with this caveat:

> The system and sentiments employed in the following poem ... are no farther embraced by the author, nor recommended to the reader, than as they agree with sound morality and Christian principles: they are considered as the nearest approaches made by uninspired reason, to that perfect dispensation, which the gospel affords to mankind. The name of Socrates will in some measure sanctify the doctrine he delivers...   (sig. [A3]ʳ)

The author's principle of selection – that which governs the choice of material from historical and traditional sources – is immediately apparent. Like Catherall, Bushe includes any material he can mine from the earliest sources that fits his conception of Socrates. Likewise, he draws on a long-standing (and somewhat procrustean) tradition that turns Plato's suggestions and ambiguous statements into Christian certainties. Bushe's poem is set in standard dramatic form, complete with acts, scenes, and dialogue assigned to speakers. Most of the lines, of course, feature Socrates holding forth on such proto-Christian (or anachronistically Christian) teachings as the argument from design: 'The works of God / Indeed are great, and shew a wond'rous hand' (p. 4); the notion that reason is God's image in man (p. 5); divine providence (pp. 7–10 *et passim*); the presence in the human mind of innate notions of God's existence and of the nature of virtue (p. 22); death as 'entry through heaven's blest gate' (pp. 33, 70); the daemonic voice as heavenly inspiration (p. 39).

Socrates was the first to bring Philosophy down from the heavens, providing instead 'moral lectures' (p. 42); nonetheless, here he encourages natural philosophy, arguing (like the most devout New Scientist) that studying and admiring God's handiwork is a form of praise.[3]

Preparing for death, Bushe's Socrates avails himself of consolations obviously based on the Christian tradition (pp. 57–60), focusing on the manifest presence of God in the physical world and the need for submission to his providence. He tells Crito he cannot break the law of Athens by fleeing punishment – an argument familiar from Plato's account – but here Socrates insists that law must be respected because of its divine source. It stems from God, 'Who gave it Being' (p. 76). He chastens his disciple Crito in Christian terms for wanting to revenge himself on Athens: 'Crito, too much zeal / In friendship's cause, has made you pass the bounds / Of virtue's law, which bids you not return / Evil for evil; nor requite offence / By the like usage; nor repair a wrong / By foul misdeeds' (p. 84). Bushe has transformed the Socratic paradox (that the perpetrator of wrong-doing is more unfortunate than the victim) into something very close to Christianity's Golden Rule.

Finally, his death is not only noble, but markedly pious, in terms appropriate to the proto-Christian martyr:

> Hold, hold me up – ye winged ministers –
> To Thee, thou God supreme – to Thee I give –
> Thou source of life – but O my soul is thine –
> Take back this portion of thyself – take back –
> Let Socrates be thine – for ever –

(p. 96)

The poem's last words are given to an angelic 'Chorus of etherial Spirits', who praise Socrates rhapsodically and report that they have seen his soul, 'the living part ascend / Bright as the pure etherial ray, / And tow'rd the court of heav'n, with soaring effort tend' (p. 97).

The effect of placing Christian teachings in Socrates' mouth, and of surrounding him with Christian epic machinery, is to establish a potent myth of his significance. Thus, Bushe effectively *reverses* the critical stance he asserts in the 'Advertisement'. In practice, the doctrine Bushe's Socrates here delivers sanctifies his name.

IV

In 1759, only one year after the publication of Bushe's play, Voltaire published his own *Socrate*. The preface asserted that it was an English play written by 'the late J. Thomson' and translated into French by 'the late M. Fatema'. When the play was published in an English translation in the following year, the attribution was denied.[4] Nevertheless, it was a prudent tactic, Raymond Trousson has noted, since the work was (in the spirit of Voltaire) truly 'une machine de guerre'.[5]

The central figure is a new Socrates, noteworthy not for the substantive content or the method of his teaching, but for his principled resistance to the machinations of the powerful, hypocritical priests of the city. At the heart of the play is a sentimental plot: Socrates has two wards, Aglae and Sophronime, who are in love with each other. Anitus, the high priest of Ceres and a swaggering, domineering bully, also courts Aglae. His suit is assisted by the socially ambitious Xantippe, who is very impressed by the priest's 'great interest among the grand folks' (p. 49). Anitus tells his mistress, Drixa, why he is courting Aglae: '*Agaton* her father, they say, left her a large fortune. *Aglae* is adorable, and I idolize her; I must marry her...' (p. 7). It is obviously her fortune that makes her adorable, and is the true object of Anitus' idolatry. But Agaton, unfortunately, was (like his friend Socrates) a 'sober, serious fool' who was 'tainted with ... principles', and was therefore one of the priests' 'sworn enemies; who imagine they have fulfilled all their duties, when they have worshipp'd the divinity, assisted humanity, cultivated friendship, and studied philosophy' (p. 6). Worse, he even dared to ridicule the mysteries of Ceres. In Anitus' account of Agaton's unacceptable beliefs (which match those of Socrates), Voltaire sets up a satiric opposition between priestcraft and right thinking.

Anitus courts Aglae with pomp and bluster. The courtship begins, significantly, with the guardian, not the young woman herself. Anitus demands that Socrates give his consent, but he in turn insists Aglae 'has a right to dispose of her own heart. I look upon constraint as an outrage' (p. 13). When she independently refuses to marry the priest, he threatens her with the displeasure of the gods. She answers calmly, 'I am persuaded the Supreme Being concerns itself very little, whether I marry you or no' (p. 21). Anitus is outraged, and cries out:

> The Supreme Being! 'tis not thus, my dear girl, you ought to talk; you should say the gods and goddesses; be cautious, I find you have some dangerous opinions, and I perceive very well who hath inspired them. Know, that *Ceres*, whose high priest I am, can punish you for the contempt offered to her worship, and her servant. (p. 22)

Aglae is polite but unimpressed, coolly stating again that she cannot believe Ceres would 'concern herself about my marriage' (p. 22). Anitus cajolingly offers her what he considers happiness: 'Youth decays but fortune remains, and ... riches and honours ought to be your only consideration' (pp. 23–4). This formulation turns upside-down the ethical tradition associated with Socrates, who told his accusers, 'I tried to persuade each one of you not to think more of practical advantages than of his mental or moral well-being' (*Apology*, 36c).[6] Anitus holds the wrong things to be truly valuable; in the place of moral well-being, he seeks only material advantages, becoming a scathing caricature of Voltaire's principal enemy, self-interested priest-craft. His attitude is a compound of greed, hypocrisy, ambition, and abuse of power.

Throughout the play, Anitus identifies his own interests with the will of the gods. Urged to revenge himself on Socrates, he answers, 'That's my intention; 'tis the cause of Heaven: This man undoubtedly despises the gods, since he contemns me' (p. 56). The hireling accusers level grave charges: 'He is an infidel. He hath offered no cakes to *Ceres*. He says, that there is too much silver and gold lying useless in the Temple. He believes only in one God; he is an atheist' (pp. 63–4), and he has been heard to 'cut jokes upon the owl of *Minerva*' (p. 65).

Voltaire's version of the *Apology* encapsulates his own beliefs at the time of writing. His Socrates adjures the people of Athens 'to love true virtue, and to shun the miserable philosophy of the schools' (p. 785). Voltaire's ancient philosophe, naturally enough, is an outspoken theist:

> Judges of *Athens*, there is but one God... 'Tis his property to be infinite; no being can share his infinitude with him. Lift up your eyes to the celestial bodies, and turn them toward the earth and the seas; every thing corresponds, one part is made for another, and every being is intimately connected with other beings: All is but one same design, and there is therefore but one only Architect, one only Preserver.   (pp. 75–6)

He reads the stories of gods and goddesses emblematically: Minerva is the wisdom of God, Neptune 'only his unchangeable laws that give the seas to ebb and flow' (pp. 786–7).

Most importantly, Socrates is an advocate of simple ethics and an enemy of superstition. He insists, 'The only way of being the children of God, is by endeavouring to be just and to please him. Obtain this title by never giving unjust judgments' (p. 78). His judges angrily call his words insolent, blasphemous, and absurd, and, as if his ethics were beside the point, they pursue the question of his disrespect for Minerva's owl. To this line of questioning, Socrates replies,

> Judges of *Athens*, look well to your owls. When you propose for our faith things that are ridiculous, it determines too many people to believe nothing at all. They have sense enough to see that your doctrine is absurd, tho' not enough to look up to the true Law. They know how to laugh at your little divinities, tho' not to adore the God of all, who is sole, incomprehensible, eternal, all just, as well as all powerful.   (p. 79)

The priests label this as subversive blasphemy, and pressure the judges (including several who were initially sympathetic to the defendant) to condemn Socrates to death. One judge, in his enthusiasm to rid Athens of troublemakers, actually proposes 'while our hands are in, to put to death all the geometricians, who pretend that the three angles of a triangle are equal to two right angles, and offend much the populace who read their books' (pp. 83–4). Voltaire thus uses the trial of Socrates as a fable of the perils of superstition and the absurd intolerance of the priestly caste.

At the end, Socrates stoutly refuses Anitus' offer to trade a pardon in return for Aglae's hand. Preparing to die, he discourses upon immortality and tells Crito that poison will always be turned against 'the worshippers of God, and enemies of superstition' (p. 91). Xantippe has a change of heart, crying out against the 'grand' folks of the tribunal: 'These are the polite sort of people who poison you. – O my dear husband!' (p. 90). Aglae and Sophronime struggle successfully through a series of rather conventional obstacles, and are united at last. Socrates addresses them with his last words:

> Amiable *Aglae*, kind *Sophronime*, the law ordered me to drink the poison. I have obeyed the law. I die, but the example of friendship, and greatness of soul, which you give to the world, shall never perish. Your virtue rises superior to the iniquity of those who accused me. I bless what is called my misfortune, since it hath displayed the force of your noble sentiments. (pp. 94–5)

Voltaire's Socrates is a sentimental *philosophe*; his 'tragedy' is the fate of the speaker of truth surrounded by hacks and narrow wielders of power. The play really concerns Voltaire's own interests; it is not about Socrates at all, except insofar as Socrates and Voltaire share circumstances.[7] When the circumstances differ, Voltaire simply alters them to suit his polemic. In mounting a play loosely based on the death of the father of philosophy, Voltaire very nearly casts himself in the title part.[8]

The play is thus much more than a translation of the past into a new context – it is no longer interpretation, but reinvention.

v

There is even less of the historical Socrates in the anonymous *Socrates Triumphant; or, the Danger of being Wise in a Commonwealth of Fools* (1716).[9] A very uneven work, this play is a pastiche of styles and forms ranging from an attempted Shakespearian set-piece – the play's opening scene, in which two priests exchange accounts of prodigies of nature (the Great Chain of being upset) – to choral songs to Cupid, to burlesque in the brawlings of Xanthippe, to a satirical gallery of meretricious types dressed down by the Pythian Sibyll in a brusque, Juvenalian manner. She delivers her home-truths in a humorous tone, deflating in turn a Tyrant, an Apostate, a High

Priest, a Prime Minister, a Principal Secretary, a Scribler, a Fop, a young
Woman who has allowed herself to be seduced and has since been
abandoned, a greedy Youth waiting for his inheritance, and a Mechanick
cursed with a scolding Wife. And it is this very oracle who proclaims that
there is 'none more free, / More wise, more just, or innocent' than Socrates
(p. 217).

The *saeve indignatio* informing the Sibyll's wisdom extends to the Socrates
she sponsors. When he speaks to his disciples, it is with the voice of the
satirist, verbally lashing the abuses of pride in society. He chides Plato (not
Crito) for recommending that Socrates either leave Athens or keep silent for
a while:

> And would you have me silent? Does not the General
> Who never yet saw Battle rang'd, nor heard
> The Trumpet sound, unless in Merriment,
> Look on his Fellow-Creatures, as he walks,
> As if they were not worthy the beholding,
> And he the only Gem of the Creation;
> When she indeed can hardly shew a viler.
> And would you have me silent? Nay, has not he,
> Who in his Prosperity foreswore the Gold,
> His Master lent him in Adversity,
> Run through a Catalogue of Crimes since that,
> Enough to damn the Nation that forgave him,
> And call Almighty Justice into Question.
> And would you have me silent? No, my Friends;
> As long as Merit at the Foredore waits,
> And Interest's slily at the Back slip'd in;
> Or formal Fools for wise Men pass, and Knaves
> Would palm themselves for Patriots on their Country,
> Accepting that which they condemn'd in others.
> So long shall *Socrates* his Course pursue,
> And maugre Hell and Malice, question all
> He meets, and thinks has need of his Advice.
>
> (p. 225)

In this speech, and others very like it, Socrates rails against the manifold
corruptions of Athenian society. There is very little about this version of
Socrates to distinguish him from any other historical figure whose
principles come into conflict with the practice of the dominant culture. He
is a generic satirist-philosopher, much closer to the traditional reputation of
Diogenes the Cynic, with his penetrating and mocking answers, than to
Socrates, with his professed ignorance and constant questioning.

But the author of the poem claims that Socrates continues to insist on
asking questions. Does this mean that the author has built the Socratic
method into his poem? Not at all. It is a satiric technique whose model
seems more likely to have been Lucian's *Dialogues of the Dead* than any

philosophical dialogues, as a typical example will demonstrate. Socrates asks Meletus what he believes, and he answers:

> I hold,
> That the Hat nicely press'd beneath the Arm
> The Sword directly with the Elbow's Point,
> The Hands thus in the Wasteband of the Breeches;
> A single Roll, a red Top, and a high Heel,
> Are all essentially necessary
> To form a compleat Gentleman.

(p. 226)

Socrates angrily calls him a Fop, and insists that he speak about his beliefs concerning the soul,

> That noble Part,
> Which of coelestial Origin, and Frame,
> Must unto all Eternity remain
> A blessed Angel, or a cursed Fiend,
> According to its Behaviour here.

(p. 226)

Melitus obtusely insists on interpreting Socrates' inquiries superficially, and continues to talk about fashion and other worldly things. When finally it comes home to him that Socrates is asking him about the state of his soul, he exclaims in surprise that it is 'the last Thing upon Earth I should have thought on' (p. 227). Socrates, out of patience, calls him 'stupider than old *Deucalion*'s Brood' (p. 227), and 'vile Trash' (p. 229).

Like his patroness the Sibyll, this author's Socrates is more interested in chiding errant Athenians than in seeking or teaching truth in the manner set forth by Plato. To a certain extent, this version is based on the tradition of the Christianized Socrates in the dogma preached and implicit in his many harangues. The focus of the play, however, is quite different from that of the others we have been examining. For Catherall and Bushe, the tradition serves as a vehicle for moral teaching; for Voltaire, it serves as a starting point for improvising a new battle strategy. Here it simply serves as a normative point of reference against which the satire's negative characters are measured and found wanting.

The author's handling of Socrates' defence bears out this analysis. The largest part of the scene is devoted to the farcical intervention of Xanthippe. Socrates' own 'Apology' is less than a quarter of the length of her furious diatribe, and even here the few points drawn from the originals are nearly supplanted by still more satirical thrusts:

> Death (were there no Hopes of a future State,
> And much more such a glorious one, as we have)
> Were to be wish'd for, rather than Eternity,
> On such base Terms as these. No *Athens*, no

Squeeze-Agents, Treasurers, and Paymasters,
Rogues, that like Mushrooms spring up in a Night,
And like them too, ought to be cropt next Morning,
And not the Man, who looks upon this World,
But as a Stage that leads him to a better...

(p. 254)

The author, as might be deemed appropriate for a military man, gives a prominent place in his gallery of rascals to those who have power over the military, rogues such as senior politicians, 'Paymasters', and the inexperienced but arrogant general of the earlier speech.

The play ends with a fifth act crammed with farce, pathos, and oratory. As Socrates dies, the Athenians revolt, take his accusers prisoner, and the play closes with a eulogy delivered by some Ambassadors who have appeared on the scene like Fortinbras at the end of *Hamlet*.

VI

It would be easy enough to dismiss the last play out of hand. To begin with, the 'Socrates' it represents distorts the image left by history. Perhaps because Socrates is such a compelling figure, he has continued to appear in the works of a wide variety of writers, his appearance often altered by the limitations of the author's historical sense or adjusted to fit certain historically determined polemical ends. These alterations, considered together, occupy a marginal zone in the historiography of philosophy, the zone of creative anachronism. Here we find a vast profusion of narratives left us by authors who have succumbed to the powerful temptation to translate the historically unfamiliar into familiar terms.

Of course, the situation was complicated from the first, since the contemporary accounts of Socrates in the writings of Plato, Xenophon, and Aristophanes differ widely. Then, over the centuries, there grew up around the image of Socrates what sometimes seems to be an impenetrable forest of conflicting stories. For many writers after the Renaissance, the figures of the past, and especially the heathen wise men, were significant only so far as they could be made to appear relevant to current issues. Since the instructive function of such interpretations is paramount, what we have since learned to call 'historical accuracy' and 'objectivity' falls by the wayside. The past seems to exist in order to provide *topoi* to support a worthwhile argument. Thus Socrates becomes a vehicle for instruction, rather than a source.

Generic vehicles of instruction tend to be neutral in themselves; as rhetorical instruments they can be turned to nearly any sort of task. Under these conditions the image of Socrates multiplies into protean variety. Very few of these versions can offer much to the student of the historical Socrates, but I am convinced that they are worth studying as reflexive tools of historical enquiry. After all, the history of philosophy is not simply a record of what the great philosophers have said or written. There is much to learn from what their successors *thought* they meant. P. O. Kristeller has commented on the presence, among the main streams of the historiography of philosophy, of a distinct history of misrepresentation:

> Before setting forth his own treatment of a given subject, Aristotle often summarizes and criticizes the views of his predecessors, and he sometimes distorts their doctrines to justify his own position. We cannot and should not curtail the right of a philosopher to criticize and also to misrepresent the views of his predecessors. Such misinterpretations are often interesting, and they help us to understand the thought of the later critic.[10]

While he acknowledges that we can learn from misinterpretation, Kristeller rightly insists that ultimately we must see past (or through) them when studying the initial subject. 'They must be disregarded for a historical interpretation of the earlier thinker' (p. 161).

We must study Plato and Xenophon to learn about Socrates; what Aristotle says about him is more useful in coming to understand Aristotle. However, Kristeller has obliquely suggested a new area of study in literature and the historiography of philosophy: understanding later critics through their polemical misrepresentations of their predecessors.

The plays I have surveyed here all misrepresent Socrates, but their very misrepresentations offer the careful reader a striking view of the authors' values. Samuel Catherall (who also published a similar poem about Cato based on Cicero's *De Senectute*[11]), is primarily concerned with presenting a morally exemplary hero. His polemic requires that the words of Socrates approximate Christian doctrine; in this manipulation of the historical evidence and tradition we can see the great synthetic power of liberal Anglicanism. Amyas Bushe labours in the same vineyard, but he adds to the declamatory mode a few new touches, including a few more speaking parts and an extended apology for research into natural phenomena. The only biographical information about Bushe I have been able to track down is that he was a Fellow of the Royal Society, which accounts for the apology. Voltaire's play is perhaps the most transparent, since it makes the least pretence of representing the Socrates of Plato (or of any other tradition). And the 'officer'-author of the last piece simply seems to have seized upon Socrates as a kind of archetype of the good man under attack by a corrupt society. In the shadow of this archetype, he can satirize both conventional and personal targets.

Earlier in this paper, I suggested that it is difficult to translate the dialogue form into drama. The action of the philosophical dialogue is the interplay of ideas, which is difficult to portray in dramatic form. Even if the ideas are put into the mouths of characters – a device common to dialogue and dramatic form – there are severe limitations. Generally, such works are limited to two equally unsatisfying options: the use of an exemplary character whose life somehow embodies or symbolizes a philosophy, or the use of set speeches proclaiming or summarizing a philosophy. As we have seen, these approaches are singularly ineffective in portraying the *development* of ideas. Perhaps the least appealing aspect of the plays discussed here is the way in each case Socrates is forced to stand up and tell us exactly what we are to think about him. What is missing is the delight of inference, the excitement of following an argument toward discovery. It seems likely that the experience of dialogue cannot be translated across genres into drama.

However, the works I have discussed are neither producible on stage, nor intended for a play-going audience. Rather, they are directed to the private reader, as 'closet drama'. The interplay of ideas is not weighed down by the mediation of a full dramatic production. The plays, like dialogues, are loaded, in that they carry the potential for communicating the author's notions. But to a certain extent the approach is heuristic: they all seek to elicit a personal response of concentration, recognition, and assent. In this sense, though they are cast in a form that approximates the dramatic, the plays retain something of the interaction of the dialogue.

Apparently Socrates does not offer ideal material for the theatre; at least we have yet to see a reliable or convincing representation. In its place, though, we have a number of instructive misrepresentations. This brief account, an exercise in the historiography of misunderstanding, should help to shed some light on the tradition of re-inventing Socrates in our own image, a tradition still very much with us.

NOTES

1 Samuel Catherall, *Εἰϰὼν Σωϰρατιϰή, or, a Portraiture of Socrates, Extracted out of Plato* (Oxford: by L. Lichfield, for A. Peisley, and are to be sold by J. Knapton, *et al.*, 1717), p. 1. Subsequent references will appear in the text.

2 Amyas Bushe, *Socrates, a Dramatic Poem* (London: for the Author, and sold by R. and J. Dodsley, 1758), sig. [A3]ʳ. Subsequent references will appear in the text.

3 For a discussion of Bushe's version of Socrates as a devout natural philosopher (in the later seventeenth-century mould), see my essay, 'Bringing Philosophy Down From the Heavens: Socrates and the New Science', *Journal of the History of Ideas*, 47:2 (1986), 299–308.

4 I have referred to the first English edition of the next year, which includes a translator's 'Advertisement' denying the attribution to 'Thomson' and assigning authorship to Voltaire. *Socrates, A Tragedy of Three Acts* (London: for R. and J. Dodsley, 1760), sig. A2ʳ. Subsequent references will appear in the text.

5 Raymond Trousson, *Socrate devant Voltaire, Diderot, et Rousseau: la conscience en face du mythe* (Paris: Lettres Modernes Minard, 1967), p. 34.

6 *Socrates' Defense (Apology)*, tr. Hugh Tredennick, in *The Collected Dialogues of Plato*, ed. Edith Hamilton and Huntington Cairns (Princeton University Press, Bollingen Series LXXI, 1961), p. 21.

7 Concerning Voltaire's opinion of Socrates, see Raymond Trousson's chapter, 'Voltaire et le "sage au nez epate"', *Socrate*, pp. 31–44; and Oscar Haac, 'A "Philosophe" and Antiquity: Voltaire's Changing Views of Plato' in *The Persistent Voice: Essays on Hellenism in French Literature Since the 18th Century in Honor of Professor Henri M. Peyre*, ed. Walter G. Langlois (New York University Press, 1971), pp. 15–26. For an account of the controversy which pitted Voltaire (as Socrates) against Palissot (as Aristophanes) and the 'persecutions' of critics, see Mario Montuori, *Socrates: The Physiology of a Myth*, tr. J. M. P. and M. Langdale (Amsterdam: J. Gieben, 1981). There were several other French plays written to address polemical issues, including Billardon de Sauvigny's *La Morte de Socrate, Tragedie* (Paris: Duchesne, 17863), and J. M. Collot d'Herbois, *Le Proces de Socrate, ou Le Regime des Anciens Temps. Comedie* (Paris: Chez la Veuve Duchesne et Fils, 1791). This last piece, a revolutionary revision of the trial of Socrates, features a last-minute rescue of the philosopher by the freedom-loving people.

8 Haac discerns in Voltaire a 'pragmatic' devotion to the classics, in that he 'tends to seek out in the past those authors whom he can cite in support for the cause he is advancing at a given moment' (p. 23). Although he shared the tradition in which 'Socrates' martyrdom had become a rationalist's equivalent to the passion of Christ' (p. 15), Voltaire was displeased with Dacier's Christianized version of Plato (p. 15). Although Voltaire criticized Dacier as a translator (p. 18), his objections were hardly based on historical or linguistic accuracy. Rather, as Haac's study tends to suggest, Voltaire respects Socrates as a prototype of the iconoclastic, persecuted theist. In Voltaire's play, Socrates is transformed or transvaluated into 'a philosophe, a spokesman of enlightenment' (p. 22), a shift actually just as radical as Dacier's.

9 *Socrates Triumphant; or, the Danger of Being Wise in a Commonwealth of Fools* (1716). The Huntington Library copy, which I have worked with, is disbound from the first edition (1716) of the collected works of the author, identified only as 'An Officer of the Army'. The pagination runs from pp. [201]–271. Subsequent references will appear in the text.

10 Paul Oskar Kristeller, 'Philosophy and its Historiography', *Journal of Philosophy*, 82 (1985), 161. Subsequent references will appear in the text.

11 Samuel Catherall, *Cato Major. A Poem, Upon the Model of Tully's Essay of Old Age* (London: for J. Roberts, 1725).

Theatre as temple in the 'New Movement' in American Theatre*

WILLIAM F. CONDEE

Many people dedicated to the reform of the American theatre in the early decades of this century believed that the theatre would eventually take the place of the temple in society. The theatrical experience would provide a mystical communion among the spectators and would attain the level of religious experience. While the material goals of the reform movement are more well-known, the subject here is their spiritual goals. Though perhaps less noted, these spiritual goals provide the philosophical underpinnings to their material objectives. What makes this spiritual aspect especially interesting today is the reformers' great – even grandiose – expectation for the theatre. Critics today mourn the state of the contemporary theatre as much as the reformers did then, but few today prophesy the phoenix of theatre will rise, let alone lift society and religion with it. The cynicism of today, right or wrong, must be contrasted with the unflagging optimism then. We may look back at these reformers as naive, but I think we must respect the audacity of their goals for the American theatre.

The 'New Movement', as the reform effort was then known, was an attempt during the first three decades of this century to move the theatre away from its realistic, naturalistic, illusionistic (all three terms were used and denounced) and commercial course. These self-styled reformers wanted an invigorated, non-commercial art theatre, intimate or mass, dedicated to symbolism, suggestion, simplicity and synthesis. They saw the nineteenth-century theatre as having no greater role in society than that of commercial entertainment and diversion; they wanted their theatre to be central to society and culture and to address major issues facing human-kind. The new playhouse was to provide an environment conducive to a feeling of unity among the spectators and with the performers.

The reformers marked the inception of the New Movement with the works of Adolphe Appia and Edward Gordon Craig, just before and after the turn of the century. While each had unique ideas about theatrical production, certain common elements in Appia and Craig's designs had

* A draft of this paper was read at the *Themes in Drama* International Conference held at the University of California, Riverside, in February 1988.

great effects upon the American reformers. Foremost was the idea that all elements of the production should be unified: scenery, lighting, costumes and acting should all be developed with a single, clear artistic goal in order to create a unified effect on the audience. Appia and Craig's scenery was simplified and pared-down, using simple architectural forms that evoked, rather than realistically depicting, the setting for the play. Renderings by both designers show unadorned vertical and horizontal planes of three-dimensional masses, sculpted by light and shadow. Appia emphasized the use of light, modulation of the floor into levels, ramps and steps, and concentration on the actor as the 'measure of all things', while Craig's scenery tended toward looming towers.

The American reform movement was most vigorous in the 1910s and 1920s, following tours by European theatre groups and pilgrimages by critics and designers to the European sources. Critics such as Sheldon Cheney and Kenneth Macgowan perceived a lack of experimentation in the American theatre. After excursions across the European theatrical land-scape, they wrote hortatory works to inspire their countrymen to work in comparable theatrical veins. Several English writers were so widely published and quoted in America that they must be considered among the reformers of the American theatre; most influential were Craig and the critics Huntly Carter and Alexander Bakshy. The resulting American reform movement was more homogeneous than in Europe. There was no formal reform 'organization', but neither was there a plethora of schools and manifestos. America had a self-styled reform movement with ident-ifiable spokesmen, practitioners, theatres and tenets.

The New Movement was in part a reaction to the theatre of the late nineteenth century; the reformers objected both to the mode of performance and to the theatres in which plays were presented. They saw nineteenth-century realism and naturalism as a 'cramp upon art',[1] and called for the theatre to rid itself of the 'chains in the illusionism of naturalistic settings'[2] and the 'evils of representation'.[3] Eugene O'Neill wrote that the 'old "naturalism"' represented

> our Fathers' daring aspirations toward self-recognition by holding up the family kodak to ill-nature... We have taken too many snap-shots of each other in every graceless position; we have endured too much from the banality of surfaces. We are ashamed of having peeked through so many keyholes, squinting always at heavy, uninspired bodies – the fat facts – with not a nude spirit among them.[4]

In practice, these American reformers had their greatest success in the area of scene design. Foremost among the designers of the 'New Stagecraft', as it was known, were Robert Edmond Jones, Norman Bel Geddes, Joseph Urban and Lee Simonson. Like Appia and Craig, their scenery was simplified, suggestive and evocative, eschewing an illusionistic depiction of reality. Hiram Moderwell, a chronicler of the New Movement, described the elements of this approach to design as 'lines and masses – nothing more'.[5] Influenced by Appia, they wished to place the emphasis in theatrical production on the actor; according to Cheney, their purpose was to highlight 'the actor and action above all else'.[6] The design might consist of the 'space stage', a relative void backed by a curving cyclorama, in which the actor could be emphasized by the use of light. Cheney described the space stage,

> not as an area surrounded with decorations but as a shaped volume of space, with surroundings suppressed as far as possible to afford the impression of a void, into which the action is placed and picked out with light... Living light and movement are the basic elements of decoration.[7]

The three watchwords were simplicity, suggestion and synthesis. While simplicity was a goal in itself, it was also an effort to purge the clutter and ornamentation of the nineteenth-century stage. Just as in architecture, where the modernist urge was to strip buildings of ornamentation that did not express structure and function, the reformers called for a stripped-down, architectural style in scenery. In calling for simplicity, Jones quoted Michelangelo: 'Beauty is the purgation of superfluities.'[8]

Suggestion was important because, as Macgowan explained, one object could 'suggest a wealth of spiritual and aesthetic qualities.'[9] Instead of realistically depicting the play's locale, the designer could use minimal scenery to symbolize a place, with a single evocative arch, for instance, representing an entire cathedral. The designer could also use suggestive scenery to symbolize the intended meaning of the production, as Jones did with his three witches' masks looming over the action of *Macbeth*.

The final tenet was synthesis, to give unity to the 'complex and rhythmic fusion of setting, lights, actors and play', Macgowan explained. Again, this was in opposition to the nineteenth-century theatre that often used stock scenery without any overall 'concept' for the production. For Macgowan, synthesis was the goal of theatre itself: 'The creation of a mood expressive of the play is, after all, the final purpose in production.'[10]

The ultimate purpose of the New Stagecraft was to create the proper mood for the new drama the reformers wished to produce. Theatrical production was to convey a unified mood that would sweep the spectators into a world of emotion and spirit. Cheney wrote that the New Stagecraft was

> designed to foster one single sustained mood. The artist of the theatre is eliminating from the setting everything that ... might call the attention away from the spiritual essence of the production ... so that unconsciously the spectator is put into a state of receptivity.[11]

Macgowan made explicit the spiritual aim of the New Stagecraft: 'The line, mass, and color of Robert Edmond Jones ... liberates the soul.'[12]

The drama these reformers wished to produce would emphasize rhythm, movement, action and music. Instead of literary drama, this new thatre was to appeal to the senses. Cheney wrote: 'This new form makes its sensuous appeal to eye and ear – mainly through pure beauty of sight and sound. Its essence is action in the visual sense: physical movement rather than story-development.'[13] This drama would carry the spectator 'into an ecstasy of the senses'.[14]

Macgowan summed up these new approaches by turning to the circus, a form that includes the audience in a frankly 'theatricalist' performance, acknowledging the audience and the theatrical nature of the experience:

> The theatre of the circus opens up possibilities for the playwright that seem singularly broad and singularly pregnant with the spirit of the age. Such a theatre enables him to write in terms of movement as well as of words, to dramatize life upon varying levels of consciousness and of actuality, to reach ever closer to the life-giving vigor of vast audiences, to arouse in such mighty gatherings emotions which sweep in one gigantic swell to the players and are thrown back in still more majestic power to the audience again. In such a playhouse is born a sense of drama which transcends individual action.[15]

These goals could not be achieved, however, in the nineteenth-century 'peephole' theatre, as the reformers loved to call it. The picture-frame proscenium arch enforced a rigid line of separation between the audience and the performance, with each occupying its own, discrete space. To these reformers, such a theatre was emblematic of an art not in touch with the lives of the spectators, and the unity they desired could therefore not be achieved. Appia noted that, in contrast to the open stages he promoted, 'we have placed the production beyond the boundary because, not being artists, we deliberately separate ourselves from the work of art.'[16] According-ing to Cheney, society gets the kind of theatre it deserves: the ancient Greek theatre was characterized by 'openness and nobility', while the theatre of his time was 'cramped and trivially fussed up'. He saw the contemporary theatre as a reflection of his materialistic age: 'Perhaps never, we think, has the stage been farther from the divinity with which it was marked in other eras.'[17] This theatre was not only bad for the drama they wanted produced, it was in fact unholy.

One common solution to this modern 'house of bondage',[18] as one critic called it, was to fish through history for theatres that offered a more congenial audience–performance relationship. One reformer wrote, 'We are now beginning to suspect that our people of the theatre missed the turn three centuries ago and that in order to go forward we may have to go back. We may have to retrace our steps to the place where the mistake was made ... and go on from there.'[19]

The historical precedent chosen most often was the theatre of ancient

Greece. It was a period of universally acknowledged great drama; it was not based in realism as it was known in the nineteenth century, and it was central to the society and religion of its time. That it was not 'religious drama' in the medieval sense made it all the more appealing; instead of teaching church dogma, Greek drama addressed major philosophical issues.

The ancient Greek theatre also answered the calls of these reformers because they saw in it the spiritual and physical unity they sought. They saw a spiritual aspect to the drama insofar as Greek theatre had emerged from religion and had maintained that religious element (though some now might question the validity of this theory of theatre's origin). The spiritual communion the reformers perceived in the ancient Greek performance had its counterpart in the theatre form in which the drama was presented. The performance occured on a stage thrust out into the midst of the spectators; it was not separated from the audience by a proscenium arch.

This religious aspect lies at the heart of the reformers' concerns: they wanted new theatre forms not only in order to reinvigorate the drama, but also to address what they perceived as modern religious needs. These reformers were addressing the perceived spiritual crisis of the time – secularization and the often stated view then that modern man had lost the religious dimension; that 'God is dead.' O'Neill wrote about 'the sickness of today ... the death of the Old God and the failure of science and materialism to give any satisfying new One'.[20]

Because of this spiritual dilapidation, these reformers believed the Western world was yearning for the lost Dionysian unity of the Greek theatre. They saw the New Movement not merely as a group of theatre reformers, but as part of an emerging 'New Spirit' in society as a whole. From the abyss of secularization, these reformers saw a spiritual reawakening. Humankind was seeking a new spiritual relationship with the supernatural, apart from the orthodox religions. Their goal was not, though, to reinvigorate Christianity; they saw a new spirituality, linked to theatre, emerging. Macgowan observed a 'ferment' of activity in the contemporary theatre, and believed that

> the new forces in the theatre have been working towards a spiritual change ... I cannot escape the conviction that there is something inherently and humanly mystical in the coming of a new movement in art.[21]

The mystical nature of this New Spirit is apparent in the writings of these reformers. Mysticism remains elusive to attempts at definition. Cheney noted that no definition of the 'rapturous reality that is the mystic experience' was possible, but he described it as ' "union with God," "intuition of the Divine," "realization of the Eternal," and "mergence of the soul in the Absolute." ... It is the pure spiritual experience.'[22]

This mystical bent can be seen in the writings of Appia and Craig, and then traced through the English and American reformers who followed them. Art, according to Appia, could 'unite our souls by uniting ... *our common body*'.[23] O'Neill referred to himself as 'a most confirmed mystic', and wrote: 'I'm always acutely conscious of the Force behind – Fate, God ... Mystery certainly ... And my profound conviction is that this is the only subject worth writing about.'[24]

These reformers believed that the art most capable of expressing this emerging mystical awareness was theatre. It is perhaps paradoxical that the very real and actual human body should be used to depict virtual states of the 'spirit world'. While other art forms can blur and distort the human image in order to throw the emphasis onto 'inner states' or 'expression', theatre runs up against the necessity of the human body, which forces its actuality onto the attempt to depict states of mind, not body. To these reformers, however, that human presence was instead theatre's strong point in conveying mysticism. Their view was that ineffable issues of the spirit could best be communicated via an actor-centered, non-illusionistic theatre. According to Cheney, the theatre was the 'most human of the arts and nearest to the soul' and best able to convey 'the human-divine intimacy'.[25]

With this mystical dimension, theatrical performance was therefore to be a religious activity in itself. Theatre was not simply to contain a religious point of view; theatre was to be, in a new way, religious. Macgowan summed up these views in his call for that spiritual, mystical essence of all religions to become the dominant force in theatre:

> It is the conviction of some of us that there has resided in the theatre – and our hope that there may reside once more – something akin to the religious spirit. A definition of this spirit is difficult. It is certainly not religion. It goes behind religion... To-day we might call it the spirit of life... It is not: Can religion make itself theatrical? But: Can the theatre make itself – in a new sense – religious?[26]

Because this new theatre was to be a form of religious activity, its job was not simply to stage a new kind of drama, but in fact to bring about a change in the spectator – a new mystical awareness and a communion with others. Theatre, as a mass grouping of people together to undergo a common experience, was seen by these reformers as well suited to bringing about this mystic communion. It was not enough that the creators of the theatrical performance have some mystical awareness; they were to bring the audience into that very experience. The members of the audience should no longer be spectators, detached and passive, but participants taking part in the communion. Cheney described this ability of theatre to draw the spectator to

1 Wyndham's Theatre, London (1899)

the realm of beauty, wisdom, and perfect understanding... For a few moments we have known a cessation of the outward life of the world. We have known an intensification of the life of the spirit... This is the moment toward which all drama tends... This is as near as we are likely to come to the divine and the spiritual. It is the Dionysian experience, our ecstatic participation in the divine life... For we are humans, and during some moments the actors have made us gods.[27]

2 Edward Gordon Craig: *Macbeth* (1906)

This theatrical–religious concept was what led to the idea that the new theatre would be the temple of the future – the locus of humankind's spiritual aspirations. The church, with its rituals, had been the focus for conventional religions, but churches were not appropriate focal points for the kind of mystical communion sought by these reformers. Now the new theatre, with its new rituals, would take the church's place. Appia called for theatre to be a 'cathedral of the future'.[28] Craig believed that this new theatre would 'be the first and final belief of the world',[29] and he called the theatre a 'famous temple'.[30]

3 Robert Edmond Jones: Arnold Schönberg's *Die glückliche Hand* (1930)

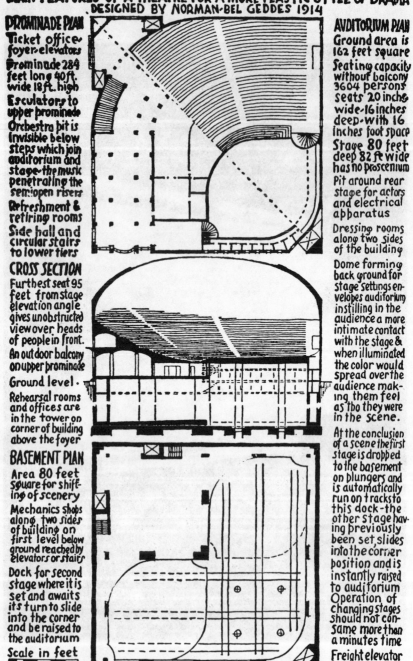

4 Norman Bel Geddes's plans for a theatre fit for the new spirit in drama

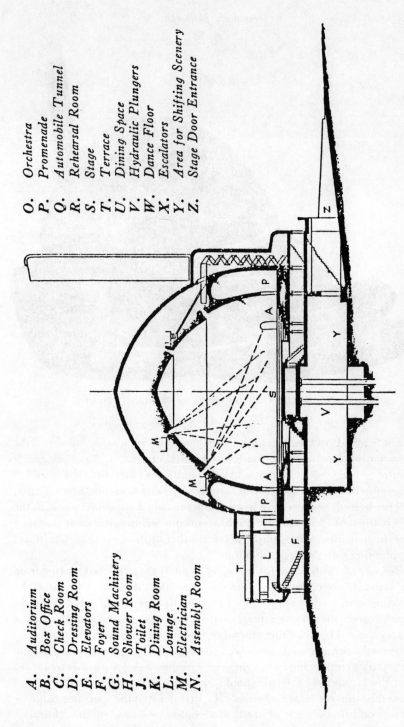

A. Auditorium
B. Box Office
C. Check Room
D. Dressing Room
E. Elevators
F. Foyer
G. Sound Machinery
H. Shower Room
J. Toilet
K. Dining Room
L. Lounge
M. Electrician
N. Assembly Room

O. Orchestra
P. Promenade
Q. Automobile Tunnel
R. Rehearsal Room
S. Stage
T. Terrace
U. Dining Space
V. Hydraulic Plungers
W. Dance Floor
X. Escalators
Y. Area for Shifting Scenery
Z. Stage Door Entrance

5 Norman Bel Geddes's plan for an intimate theatre

6 Norman Bel Geddes's sketch for an intimate theatre

English and American reformers took up this cry. Carter called for 'the elevation of the theatre to the level of the Church'.[31] O'Neill wanted 'a theatre returned to its highest and sole significant function as a Temple'.[32] Cheney believed that the reformers were beginning to create 'a theatre that will be, indeed, not less than a new cathedral in its appropriateness to the uses of the soul'.[33] In Cheney and Macgowan's writings it is clear that they saw the new theatre not simply being another form of worship, but in fact supplanting conventional religion.

Reformers insisted that the design of this new theatre should spring from the standards of ecclesiastical architecture. Most important was that the building convey the mood of a church, with repose and serenity as the watchwords. Cheney denounced existing theatres as failing to provide the proper mood. He called these theatres 'ornate, overdecorated, and vulgarly gorgeous',[34] 'opulent, fat, shallow',[35] 'fleshy, superficial and gaudy' having the 'fat obscenity of the Paris Opera'.[36] This new role for the theatre meant that the façade and interior should be composed with a combination of modernist and ecclesiastical simplicity, in order that the spectator could be carried off into the state of mystical abandon treasured by the reformers.

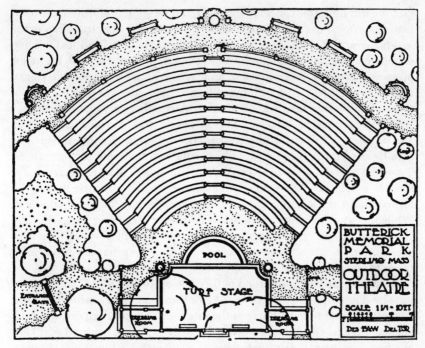

7 Frank A. Waugh's plan for the Butterick Memorial Theatre

Carter said that the theatre should have the 'consecration and dignity' of the church, the 'essential mood of religious ecstasy', and an 'air of mysticism'.[37]

The audience–performance configuration should also enhance this mystical communion. The proscenium theatre, with the spectators all facing roughly in one direction and separated architecturally from the performance by an arch, had to go. Instead they advocated various forms of 'open stages', with the audience 'gathering around' the performance rather than 'looking on', and with the spectators and performers sharing the same architectural volume. Such theatres, known then as 'Shakespeare' and 'circus' stages, have come to be known as thrust stages and theatres-in-the-round.

The creation of these new theatre forms was essential to the fulfillment of the reformers' goals; new dramatic forms – the stuff of new ritual and religion – would wither and die behind proscenia. Thus while their goals were decidedly spiritual and metaphysical, the means were – literally – concrete.

Few theatres that matched the reformers' goals were actually built in America before World War II, but the unrealized projects of Norman Bel

Geddes are important in that they were among the first fully developed plans to incorporate these ideals. These projects lacked the trappings of the 'old-fashioned' theatre – proscenium arch, footlights and facilities for flying scenery – and also aimed to unite audience and performance. All his major projects contained the auditorium and stage within an unadorned, single, unified space. In a Geddes-designed theatre, according to the architect, 'a sense of unity, intimacy and audience-participation pervades the theatre, arising in part from the fact that the same great domed ceiling spans actors and audience'.[38] This Geddes trademark, the single domed ceiling, was seen by the reformers as serving to unite the spectator and performer.

Geddes also designed the New York production of Max Reinhardt's *The Miracle*, in what could be called an example of environmental theatre: he turned the entire Century Theatre into a cathedral for the production. While this was in a sense a mingling of religion and theatre, the specifically Christian nature of this spectacle and that fact that it was set in a proscenium theatre, even if the use was novel, meant that it was not what the reformers envisioned.

The other specific implication of the New Spirit for theatre architecture was the new emphasis placed on outdoor theatre. Cheney called this form 'communal' and noted, 'There is the intangible spiritual aspect, a subtle, almost religious effect on each individual... For man is never so near God as when certain sorts of dramatic beauty are revealed to him under the open sky.' These theatres would 'remind men that once the church and the theatre united to give dramatic expression to man's innate spirit of worship'.[39]

Not only were there few 'reformist' theatres actually built, there was little of the ritual-drama that the reformers had hoped would emerge from these new theatre forms. Maurice Maeterlinck and other Symbolists attempted to depict mystical states dramatically, but few carried on with their approach. Reinhardt experimented with his mass 'Theatre of Five Thousand', but the effect was more spectacular than communal and ritualistic.

There was resistance, and finally a reaction, to this New Movement. Alexander Bakshy, writing contemporaneously with the reformers, denounced the 'fallacy of this identification of art with religion'. Bakshy, a 'pure' theatricalist reformer, wanted 'not a temple or a conjuring shop, but just a theatre'. According to Bakshy, theatre should strive to attain theatricality, not religion or anything else. He pointed out an important distinction between theatre and religion: while theatre has separate performers and audience, in a religious service all are participants; the intrusion of religion into theatre, therefore, 'destroys the fundamental division between the actors and the audience; it destroys the theatre itself'.[40]

By the early 1930s, a strong reaction had set in. A book on scene design, published in 1930, stated: 'It seems today that in the domain of art every manifestation born swiftly, full of hope, and with pretensions to a durability reaching to eternity, dies in equal swiftness.' So soon, the authors dismissed Craig and others as belonging 'to the long past'.[41]

The primary leader of this counter-revolution, though, was Lee Simonson – ironic insofar as he was one of the New Stagecraft designers and was associated with one of the reformist theatres, the Washington Square Players/Theatre Guild. In a book published in 1932 he wrote: 'I cannot foresee the features of this new divinity with whom we are to be so humanly intimate. Nor can I anticipate the ritual with which a new godhead will be worshipped in a theatre-temple.'[42]

Simonson's essential argument with the reformers was that a new religion either would or would not emerge, but in either case, theatre was irrelevant to that process. Instead the theatre would play its historic role of representing the nature and symbols of religion:

> The theatre, even in epochs when religious faith flourished, did not create a picture of a universe. It reflected a picture already created. Modern designers must abandon their ridiculous pretence that by manipulating coloured lights and blank screens they can evolve a new religion or a substitute for one. They may succeed in illustrating whatever picture of the universe a modern religion evokes, if such a religion is ever evolved.[43]

It is self-evident that the prophecies of the reformers did not come to pass: theatre is not the new religion; the theatre is not the new temple. It could not be more easy to mock these failed objectives.

More interesting, however, are the ways in which their prophecies have taken root. One of the major developments in twentieth-century theatre is the growing emphasis among theorists and directors on theatre's relationship to ritual. Directors such as Tyrone Guthrie, Peter Brook, Jerzy Grotowski and Richard Schechner emphasize the ritualistic aspect of theatre. Countless open stages have been built in America and Europe since World War II. Directors, designers and architects strive to have the audience play a role greater than that of passive spectators peering through a peep-hole. Theatre productions and structures are often designed with the aim of involving the audience, on some level, in a ritual-based performance.

There is a crucial difference, however. These theatre artists are, in effect, 'quoting' ritual: incorporating ritual into or emphasizing the ritualistic aspect of theatre, not attempting to create wholly new rituals. Brook's *The Cherry Orchard* or *Carmen* is not attempting to make a modern ritual out of Chekhov or Bizet. Instead, he and other directors are trying to show Western audiences the ritualistic aspects of even the most realistic or refined drama.

Thus, while the reformers in the New Movement did not achieve their spiritual objectives, they did provide a theoretical adumbration of the work of many later directors, designers, critics and architects. As many continue to consider our theatre to be essentially tangential to society, these reformers are to be admired for envisioning a theatre of great expectations. Their effort was to create a new theatre that would address the cultural and even spiritual needs of modern society.

NOTES

1 Kenneth Macgowan and Robert Edmond Jones, *Continental Stagecraft* (New York: Harcourt, Brace, 1922), p. 7.

2 Alexander Bakshy, *The Theatre Unbound* (London: C. Palmer, 1923), p. 15.

3 Huntly Carter, *The New Spirit in Drama and Art* (New York: Mitchell Kennerley, 1913), p. 8.

4 Eugene O'Neill, 'Strindberg and Our Theatre' in Oscar Cargill, N. Bryllion Fagin, and William J. Fisher, *O'Neill and His Plays* (New York: New York University Press, 1961), pp. 108–9.

5 Hiram Moderwell, *The Theatre of Today* (New York: John Lane, 1914), p. 85.

6 Sheldon Cheney, *Stage Decoration* (New York: John Day, 1928), p. 110.

7 Ibid., p. 111.

8 As quoted in Robert Edmond Jones, *The Dramatic Imagination* (New York: Theatre Arts Books, 1941), p. 69.

9 Kenneth Macgowan, *The Theatre of Tomorrow* (New York: Boni and Liveright, 1921), pp. 22–3.

10 Ibid., p. 23.

11 Sheldon Cheney, *The New Movement in the Theatre* (New York: M. Kennerley, 1914), p. 212.

12 Macgowan, *Tomorrow*, p. 217.

13 Cheney, *New Movement*, p. 18.

14 Sheldon Cheney, *Modern Arts and the Theatre* (Scarborough-on-Hudson, NY: Sleepy Hollow Press, 1921), p. 11.

15 Macgowan, *Tomorrow*, p. 273.

16 Adolphe Appia, *Music and the Art of the Theatre*, trans. Robert W. Corrigan and Mary Douglas Dirks, foreword by Lee Simonson, ed. Barnard Hewitt (Coral Gables, Fla.: University of Miami Press, 1962), p. 52.

17 Sheldon Cheney, *The Theatre, Three Thousand Years of Drama, Acting and Stagecraft* (New York: Tudor, 1935), pp. 5–7.

18 Edith Isaacs, ed., *Architecture for the New Theatre* (New York: Theatre Arts, 1935), p. 10.

19 Roy Mitchell, 'The House of the Presence', *Theatre Arts*, 14 (1930), 575.

20 Eugene O'Neill, 'On Man and God' in Cargill, et al., *O'Neill*, p. 115.

21 Macgowan and Jones, *Continental*, pp. 213, 220.

22 Sheldon Cheney, *Men Who Have Walked with God: Being the Story of Mysticism through the Ages* (New York: A. A. Knopf, 1945), pp. x, xiii.

23 Adolphe Appia, *Work of Living Art*, trans. H. D. Albright, ed. Barnard Hewitt (Coral Gables, Fla.: University of Miami Press, 1960), pp. 71–2.

24 Eugene O'Neill, 'Neglected Poet' in Cargill, et al., *O'Neill*, pp. 125–6.

25 Cheney, *The Theatre*, pp. 540–1.

26 Macgowan and Jones, *Continental*, pp. 215, 218.

27 Cheney, *The Theatre*, pp. 7–8, 10.

28 Appia, *Music*, p. 5.

29 Edward Gordon Craig, *On the Art of the Theatre* (Chicago: Brownes Bookstore, 1911), p. 52.

30 Edward Gordon Craig, *The Theatre Advancing* (London: Constable, 1921), p. 66.

31 Carter, *New Spirit*, pp. 229, 44.

32 Eugene O'Neill, 'Memoranda on Masks' in Cargill, et al., *O'Neill*, p. 121.

33 Sheldon Cheney, *The New World Architecture* (New York: Longmans, Green, 1930), p. 351.

34 Sheldon Cheney, *New Movement*, p. 208.

35 Cheney, *The Theatre*, p. 491.

36 Cheney, *World*, pp. 348–9.

37 Carter, *New Spirit*, pp. 105, 133.

38 Norman Bel Geddes, *Horizons* (Boston: Little, Brown, 1932), p. 150.

39 Sheldon Cheney, *The Open-Air Theatre* (New York, M. Kennerley, 1918), pp. 10, 63, 130.

40 Bakshy, *Theatre Unbound*, pp. 20, 21, 31, 32.

41 Walter Rene Fuerst and Samuel J. Hume, *Twentieth Century Stage Decoration* (Philadelphia: Lippincott, 1930), p. 4.

42 Lee Simonson, *The Stage Is Set* (New York: Harcourt, Brace, 1932), pp. 5, 20, 22.

43 Ibid., p. 47.

Images of women and the burden of myth: plagues on the houses of Gorky and O'Neill*

PATRICIA FLANAGAN BEHRENDT

Generic drama criticism typically justifies a comparative study of Maxim Gorky's *The Lower Depths* (1904) and Eugene O'Neill's *The Iceman Cometh* (1940) by citing the structural and thematic similarities: the naturalistic portrayal of the bottom rung of the social scale; the emphasis upon dialogue rather than action; the introduction of a truth-bearer who brings frustration and anguish to others by heightening an awareness of the terrible disparity between pipe-dreams and reality. However, in the popular study, 'Circe's Swine: Plays by Gorky and O'Neill', Helen Muchnic concludes that in spite of the similarities, philosophically, the two works differ substantially:

> One of them (*The Lower Depths*) has as its aim to state a temporary ethical problem affecting men in an unsatisfactory society which might be changed; the other (*The Iceman Cometh*) to scrutinize the eternal dilemma of how conscious man is related to unconscious nature – aims so divergent as to make these two samples of Western art in the twentieth century almost as dissimilar as those produced by the cultures of Byzantium and of ancient Greece.[1]

Muchnic's argument is one of form and content in which she suggests that the superficial, formal similarities imply similarities in content which do not, in fact, exist. Regardless of the methods employed in analysis, scholars, perhaps following Muchnic's lead, often returned to similar versions of the same conclusions: Gorky – a religious agnostic praised as a social realist by the communist regime during the demise of imperial Russia – is, essentially, a social propagandist while O'Neill – a spiritually troubled former Roman Catholic in a capitalistic society – is a seeker of psychological insight, a propagandist for spiritual understanding.

In fact, a fundamental relationship exists between the two plays that has been overlooked. It is a commonplace of criticism, for instance, to compare the primary male characters that function similarly in both plays. Luka and Hickman, for example, are the truth-bearers who seem to have discovered some fundamental truths about life which make them apparently

---

* A draft of this paper was read at the *Themes in Drama* International Conference held at the University of California, Riverside, in February 1988.

reconciled in their relationships to the world. The remarks of Satin and Slade, on the other hand, provide a cynical counterpoint which fore-shadows the unhappiness which the truth-bearers precipitate in their respective communities. Basically, the major theme of both plays – the necessity of the pipe-dream as a life-force antidote to harsh reality – seems to be conveyed primarily through the characterizations and the dialogues of the men who represent a wide variety of social types.[2] The fact that the women in *The Iceman Cometh* either occupy minor roles or exist in the memories of the men has diverted critical interest from a comparison of the views and functions of women in the two plays. However, O'Neill believed that he and Gorky shared a specific philosophical perspective on one segment of humanity which by definition includes both sexes. After reading *The Lower Depths*, O'Neill wrote:

> Many of the characters in my plays were suggested to me by people in real life... Gorky's 'A Night's Lodging' [*The Lower Depths*], the great proletarian revolutionary play, is really more wonderful propaganda for the submerged than any other play ever written, simply because it contains no propaganda, but rather shows humanity as it is – truth in terms of human life.[3]

O'Neill suggests that he shared Gorky's view of the 'submerged' as an embodiment of a particular 'truth' in terms of human life. The nature of this truth for both authors is related specifically to the phenomenon of the pipe-dream; since the submerged, reduced to their desperate circumstances through personal or societal dissolution, still cling to their pipe-dreams, they demonstrate the necessity of the pipe-dream as a human truth, a transcendent human need no matter how illusory. Then what of the relationship of women to this need? What are the actual images of women in the two plays? And most important, what is the relationship of the images of women to the enigmatic concept of truth?

Although the male roles outnumber the female roles in each of the plays, the portrayal of gender relationships, especially gender conflict, is fundamental to both plays. Of the twelve male roles in *The Lower Depths*,[4] ten are described in terms of their minor professional roles or functions within the community. Kostylev, Medvedev, Kletch, Bubnov, Luka, Aleksa, Screwy, and the Tartar are a lodge owner, a policeman, a locksmith, a cap maker, a tramp, a cobbler, and a longshoreman respectively. The Baron and the Actor carry references to their relationships to the world in their 'names'. The two male characters whose social roles are unspecified in the cast list are the central figures of Peppel and Satin, a petty thief and a self-appointed social commentator respectively.

Of the five women in the play, four are described in terms of their familial roles or their relationships to male members of the community. Anna and Vasillisa are wives, Natasha is a sister, and Nastya a prostitute. Although Kvashnya is described in the cast of characters as a street seller, she is described by the men, as the play opens, as a widow between husbands.

While O'Neill describes the men in his cast of characters in terms of their socio-economic relationships to the world he likewise reveals his women according to their relationships to the men of the community. The three women who appear on stage (Cora, Margie, and Pearl) are prostitutes. However, much of the male conversation concerns reminiscences about specific women whose lives fundamentally influenced their own. Jimmy Tomorrow and Hickman remember their wives; Harry Hope sentimentalizes about his sister; Parritt recalls his relationship with his mother.

Superficially, the central aspect of each female character's image, in both plays, seems to be her relationship with a specific man or with men in general. This formula is obviously the creative prerogative of two male authors concerned primarily with the male voice. However, critics have overlooked the fact that the exploration of the nature of women is a major theme which motivates a great deal of the action and much of the dialogue in both plays. Both authors are significantly concerned with images of women filtered specifically through the sensibilities of the male characters.

Each of Gorky's female characters embodies a specific quality associated with traditional views of women in Russian mythic and religious thought. Structurally, the play opens and closes with the presence of two women, Kvashnya and Nastya, who formally represent opposite values and world views. Kvashnya is a large, outspoken widow capable of both earthy vulgarity and spiritual compassion. The Baron and Kletch ridicule her insistence that she will never remarry. Eventually, she succumbs and marries Medvedev, demonstrating that the two men know her better than she knows herself. In marrying Medvedev, she becomes the traditional image of nurturing protectiveness, even though Medvedev proves to be a drunk and a profligate. Although she marries Medvedev because she thinks that as a policeman he will protect her, she in fact becomes both his slave and his guardian. Speaking to her, Medvedev summarizes the attitudes of the Baron and Kletch as well: 'you're a wonderful woman, all flesh, fat and bones – weigh four hundred pounds – and have no brains at all' (p. 551). Kvashnya reflects the traditional Russian association of woman with the mindless, dark, fertile, nurturing and protective processes of the earth.[5] In some translations Kvashnya is simply called 'Dough Pan'. In marrying Medvedev in violation of her own vow never to become a man's slave, she suggests that her will is not her own but is subject to the ebb and flow of nature's endless cycle.

Nastya's thin and pale image, like the images of female saints in Russian religious icons, is the opposite of Kvashnya's corpulent earthiness. Like Kvashnya, Nastya is ridiculed by the men. Regarded as a 'good girl', she is nevertheless considered a fool for her absorption in a fanciful, romantic novel called 'Fatal Love'. Although Nastya is described in the cast of characters as a prostitute, suggesting a very material relationship to the world, the play focuses upon her preoccupation with love as a purely romantic, spiritual ideal. She cherishes memories of love in which events in the material world symbolize extraordinary spiritual commitment. She relates the tale of Raoul, for example, who threatened to kill himself for her love. Unlike Kvashnya, Nastya engages in a spiritual idealization of the nature of love relationships. Though far less complex, Nastya is reminiscent of Flaubert's Emma Bovary, who developed her preoccupation with ideal love while reading romantic novels in the convent school. Dostoevsky's Lisa, in *Notes from Underground*, is more paradigmatic, for she too retains a spiritual belief in ideal love despite having been reduced to prostitution as a means of survival.

The label of prostitution itself does not link Nastya with Cora, Margie, and Pearl, the prostitutes in *The Iceman Cometh*.[6] Nastya belongs to the tradition in Russian literature of women who, although reduced to prostitution out of economic necessity, retain a pure or chaste spirituality. Sonia Marmeladov, in *Crime and Punishment*, epitomizes the tradition. Although her father, a drunkard, coerces her into prostitution to help support the family, Sonia has a spiritual dimension to her character which proves to be the source of religous redemption for other characters in the novel. Nastya belongs to this tradition in which the pejorative connotations associated with prostitution are rendered irrelevant in the face of her overwhelming spiritual idealism. The fact that Nastya's spiritual idealism is ridiculed by the men of the community reflects another late nineteenth-century philosophical theme. Having become disillusioned with the economic hardships of a still near-feudal nation, many Russian thinkers including Gorky began to believe that people could improve their lot by channeling the energy reserved for spiritual and religious pursuits into the belief in the natural right to a better life on earth. Rather than focus on the vague rewards promised by an afterlife which religion promoted, Gorky believed in the people's right to invest themselves with the respect and affection usually reserved for divinities. As a result, Gorky belonged to a movement which deified humanity.[7] Nastya's idealism and Kvashnya's earthy simplicity were ridiculed by the men of the community because they represented forms of mental impotence and the mindless acceptance of reality in Gorky's thought.

O'Neill's prostitutes, on the other hand, are a flashy, gum-snapping, wise-cracking trio – promiscuous but likeable. If they share anything with Nastya, they share the stereotypic image of the 'good prostitute'. As characters grounded in the material world, they lack Nastya's spiritual dimension. Their objectification by the men around them is characterized by Larry, who calls them his 'big, beautiful dolls' (p. 106). The image of the good prostitute merely combines the notion of prostitution (implying the inherent evil idea of woman as temptress) with otherwise good human qualities. The prototype for this image can be traced back in time through Manon Lescaut and the magdalenes to Eve, to the dualistic image of women as attractive to man and yet repellant, for in the Judeo-Christian myth she is responsible for his fall from paradise.

Other images of women in both plays belong to a symbolic mode of representaion. In *The Lower Depths*, Kvashnya blames Kletch's brutishness for the fact that his wife, Anna, is dying of consumption. But Anna's personality, though only briefly displayed, is quite clear: she is a woman of endless self-sacrifice, the kind of self-sacrifice that ultimately produces ambivalence in those for whom it is exercised. When Kvashnya leaves a few hot dumplings for Anna to eat, Anna – who has been alternately either ignored or ridiculed by Kletch – gives him the food: 'What's the good of me eating? You work – you need to eat' (p. 523). The primary prototype for self-sacrifice as a major theme associated with womanhood is the figure of the Christian Madonna. Since the early Slavic peoples were agrarian worshippers of the earth and matriarchically organized cultures with many female deities, they were predisposed to an affection for the figure of the Christian Madonna whose image entered Russia after the conversion to Christianity in 988. The Madonna is the primary figure in Christian myth who prays and weeps for the sins of the world in a gesture of perpetual self-sacrifice and forgiveness.

Kletch's cruelty toward Anna reveals the ambivalence of his regard for her self-sacrificing nature. He waits for her death to free him to move up in the world. But when she dies, he feels responsible for the disposal of her body. Out of guilt, he sells his tools to pay for her funeral. Without his tools, however, he cannot rise above the lower depths. Therefore, while Anna's guilt-inducing self-sacrifice seems to benefit Kletch in life, in death she becomes his ultimate burden.

Beginning with Kletch and Anna, Gorky illustrates repeatedly that the supposedly benign characteristics associated with the traditional image of woman have a distinctly dark side. When Kvashnya finally marries Medvedev, her care of him is suddenly interpreted by the other men as domination. They enjoy the suspicion that she beats him. The idealism of Nastya's view of love irritates the male community, because it seems unrealistic in their dire circumstances and serves only to heighten their sense of dissolution. In other words, Gorky illustrates a process by which the benign qualities associated with the female image come to be viewed by men as forms of tyranny. This perverted view of nurturance, self-sacrifice, and ideal love will be shown later explicitly to characterize the nature of Hickman's ambivalence toward his wife, an ambivalence which results in contempt leading to murder.

The central female characters in *The Lower Depths*, Vasillisa and Natasha, are sisters. Firmly within Gorky's symbolic mode, they are opposite in nature. Vasillisa is a cruel, manipulative seductress–adulteress. While the other women of the play seem, on the surface, benign, Vasillisa is overtly destructive. She beats Natasha, she seduces Peppel, and out of jealousy over Peppel's love for Natasha, she tricks him into murdering her own husband, Kostelev. Vasillisa suggests a link between animal sexuality and evil, since Peppel becomes disgusted with the manipulative power that her sexuality assumes over him. As the one woman in the play with the power to control worldly events, Vasillisa is the repository of all overt evil.

Natasha, on the other hand, shares Nastya's sentimental idealism, but with destructive results. While Nastya lives in a world of cheap novels, Natasha lives in a world of dreams. She characterizes herself as follows: 'I like imagining things. I dream and dream, and – wait . . . Perhaps someone will come along tomorrow . . . or something's going to happen . . . that never happened before' (p. 539). Her intuition, which characterizes an emotional rather than a rational frame of mind, foreshadows Kostelev's murder, for she remarks, 'I feel strange, uneasy today. Funny aching feeling around my heart . . . as if something is going to happen' (p. 541). Natasha's character contrasts the depth of her dream world with the shallowness of her perceptions about events in the real world. When Kostelev is murdered she impulsively assumes that Peppel and Vasillisa were conspirators even though Peppel had pledged himself to her. She hysterically reveals her suspicion to the police, thereby wrongly and stupidly condemning Peppel, who thought he was acting to save her. She stepped momentarily from her dream world, in other words, in order to commit an act of betrayal in the real world.

Male ambivalence toward the traditional values associated with womanhood is the key to understanding how women function in *The Lower Depths*. The men suffer ultimately at the hands of the women who, superficially, according to the burden of mythical values, represent nurturance, self-sacrifice, the idealization of love, and sexuality. A woman, therefore, is not what she appears to be. But is she consciously duplicitous, according to the play? The answer lies in an exchange btween Natasha and Bubnov. When Nastya and Natasha take pleasure in relating their dreams, Bubnov remarks, 'Why is it people are so fond of lying?' Natasha replies, 'Perhaps it is more fun lying than telling the truth' (p. 539). As a footnote to the exchange, Bubnov turns a woman's use of makeup into a metaphor for the masking of reality or lying: 'people telling lies . . . I can understand it with Nastya. She's used to painting her face; now she wants to paint her soul . . . put rouge on her soul' (p. 539). Behind the male ambivalence toward the traditional values associated with womanhood lies the male suspicion that women delight in duplicity.

Similar concerns about the nature of women permeate *The Iceman Cometh*.

Jimmy Tomorrow's relationship with his wife Marjorie illustrates a cycle of ambivalence. His first reference to her suggests that she represents a female ideal: she 'was beautiful and played the piano beautifully and had a beautiful voice' (p. 141). Initially, he blames his drinking on her duplicity by suggesting that behind the 'beautiful' exterior was an adulteress who drove him to drink. Later he reverses this and says that his drinking drove her to adultery. But he admits that he is glad she left him since this furnished him with 'such a tragic excuse to drink' (p. 230). He was relieved that she shattered the ideal image of himself which he could no longer tolerate because of the guilt that it induced. Marjorie foreshadows the tyranny-of-the ideal represented by Hickman's wife Evelyn.

While Jimmy's Marjorie left him, thereby diffusing his guilty hatred, Evelyn remained to torture Hickman with her presence. According to Hickman, Evelyn embodied all of the benign, traditional values represented by women in *The Lower Depths*. She comforted and nurtured him and forgave all of his transgressions until he began to wish that he would catch her in bed with the 'iceman' as a way of equalizing their relationship. Evelyn's name indicates Hickman's ambivalence toward her presence: 'Eve' invokes the image of the first woman; 'Evelyn' combines Eve and 'evil', thereby stressing the role of Eve as the temptress supposedly responsible for Adam's fall from the grace of God. For Hickman, Evelyn's seeming generosity of spirit becomes a form of oppressive tyranny driving him to further degeneracy. He rationalizes killing her as an act of love intended to put her out of her misery, when, in fact, he seeks to end his own misery by eliminating her as its source. The traditional qualities that attracted Hickman to Evelyn have become the source of his anguish and his humiliation. In his mind, she is not a comforting figure of eternal forgiveness but rather a figure of divine vengeance, echoing the American Puritan view of woman as the guardian of morality. Ultimately, he reveals his hatred of her by admitting that he always wanted to say, 'well, you know what you can do with your old pipe-dream now, you damned bitch!' (p. 241).

Like Jimmy and Hickman, Hope and Parritt reveal ambivalent regard for the women in their lives. Hope relates sentimental memories of his sister Bessy, claiming that he lost his political ambitions when she died. She supported him and guided his decisions. But eventually he reveals that her care of him was oppressive, calling her a 'nagging old hag' (p. 204).

Parrit claims to have loved his mothr, only to admit finally that he informed on her political activities because he hated her. He calls her the 'Mother of the Revolution' that promised freedom for everyone but him. As his mother, she alienated his father and suppressed him: 'You remember what mother's like Larry. She makes all the decisions. She doesn't like anyone to be free but herself. She's always decided what I must do' (p. 247).

Parritt extends his contempt for his mother to include feminists in general. As a justification for his betrayal of his mother, Parritt claims patriotic motives which reveal, instead, a fear of the new roles for women in the political arena. Parritt relates that he informed on his mother because he didn't want 'cranks, bums, and free women' overthrowing the government (p. 128).

Both *The Lower Depths* and *The Iceman Cometh* suggest then, that the benign, traditional values associated with the female image throughout both myth and religious history can be perceived conversely as forces of destruction. The male characters in both plays interact with the female characters *not* as individually drawn personalities but rather as woman collectively, woman as myth. As myth, woman resembles the pipe-dream or the life-lie for she seems to embody ideal values. But unlike the pipe-dream which acts as a life-force which lifts the spirits, woman – through her duality – becomes a life-crushing tyrant.

While other studies have traced the theme of the pipe-dream to Nietzsche, whose works were read by both authors, the theme of the duplicitousness of woman may be traced to him as well. In *Beyond Good and Evil*, Nietzsche wrote that woman 'does not want truth: what is truth to woman? From the beginning nothing has been more alien, repugnant, and hostile to woman than the truth – her great art is the lie, her highest concern is merely appearance and beauty'.[8] Gorky and O'Neill reflect this same distinctly misogynistic train of thought which first insists upon endowing woman with all of the stereotypical qualities long associated with her image and, then, accuses her of not being what she should be when measured against the immense burden of myth associated with her image.

The plays of Maxim Gorky and Eugene O'Neill belong to the traditional canon of literary works of enduring aesthetic importance. In order for us more clearly to understand the history of the gender images, feminist critic Lillian S. Robinson encourages a continual confrontation with the claim that the literary canon embodies truths which subsequent generations should continue to value and approve. Robinson suggests, however, that

> we have to return to confrontation with the canon, examining it as a source of ideas, themes, motifs, and myths about the two sexes. The point in so doing is not to label and hence dismiss even the most sexist literary classics, but to enable all of us to apprehend them, finally, in all their human dimensions.[9]

The consideration of the nature of the images of women in *The Lower Depths* and *The Iceman Cometh* is justified, in part, by Robinson's call for a fuller apprehension of the traditional canon; for the ultimate realization concerning the images of women in the two plays moves beyond recognition of the inherent sexism and the threads of misogyny: more important is the pained and painful ambivalence toward women revealed in the tortured stories presented in both plays. Both works embody formulas which transform the positive qualities associated with womanhood into manipulative, oppressive, and ultimately destructive forces within the community. The plays may be viewed no longer merely as two similar plays which reflect the socio-economic preoccupations of two authors from distinct cultures. In fact, what these two plays share is the portrayal of unresolved gender conflict as the central metaphor for cultural turmoil and cultural angst.

NOTES

1 Helen Muchnic, 'Circe's Swine: Plays by Gorky and O'Neill' in *O'Neill*, ed. John Gassner (Englewood Cliffs, NJ: Prentice-Hall, 1964), p. 109.
2 O'Neill quoted on the necessity of the pipe-dream as a central theme in *The Iceman Cometh* in Croswell Bowen, *The Curse of the Misbegotten: A Tale of the House of O'Neill* (New York: McGraw-Hill, 1959), pp. 310–11.
3 Arthur and Barbara Gelb, *O'Neill* (New York: Harper and Row, 1960), p. 499.
4 Maxim Gorky, *The Lower Depths*, trans. Henry Burke, in *The Modern Theatre*, ed. Robert W. Corrigan (New York: Macmillan, 1964), pp. 522–51. All further references are by page number in parentheses and refer to this text.
5 For full accounts of the traditional views of women in Russian myth see George Fedotov, *The Russian Religious Mind* (Belmont, Mass.: Nordland Publishing Co., 1975) and Sergius Bulgakov, *The Orthodox Church* (Dobbs Ferry, NY: American Review of Eastern Orthodoxy, 1935).
6 All further page references are in parentheses and refer to Eugene O'Neill, *The Iceman Cometh* (New York: Random House/Vintage, 1957).
7 For a complete account see Abbott Gleason, *Young Russia: The Genesis of Russian Radicalism in the 1860s* (New York: Viking, 1980).
8 Friedrich Nietzsche, *Beyond Good and Evil*, trans. Walter Kaufmann (New York: Random House, 1966), pp. 231–2.
9 Lillian S. Robinson, 'Treason Our Text: Feminist Challenges to the Literary Canon' in *The New Feminist Criticism*, ed. Elaine Showalter (New York: Pantheon Books, 1985), p. 119.

Bruno and Beckett: coincidence of contraries*

JAMES E. ROBINSON

In the face of certain remarks by Samuel Beckett, one should approach the application of philosophy to Beckett's work with caution. In headnotes to the text of his film *Film* (published in 1967), Beckett cites Bishop Berkeley's philosophical dictum of being, *Esse est percipi*, and then includes the following commentary which might well serve as a rather thick-tongued statement for the philosophy of *Film*: 'Search of non-being in flight from extraneous perception breaking down in inescapability of self perception.' However, Beckett immediately undercuts such philosophic jargon with this acidic detachment: 'No truth value attaches to above, regarded as of merely structural and dramatic convenience.'[1]

More generally Beckett has expressed his detachment from philosophic 'truth value' in remarks like these: 'I never read philosophers'; 'I never understand anything they write.'[2] There is, however, evidence enough in Beckett's works that he has read a host of philosophers, and scholars of Beckett have been proceeding sporadically but relentlessly to apply philosophies from the pre-Socratics to Sartre in the study of Beckett's art.[3] I select here a now relatively obscure thinker rarely referred to in a Beckett context to formulate a philosophic issue that has interesting applications to Beckett's drama. Beckett read the sixteenth-century Italian philosopher–cosmologist Giordano Bruno evidently at James Joyce's urging as preparation for an essay on Joyce that Beckett contributed to the whimsically entitled anthology of essays celebrating Joyce's 'Work in Progress' (*Finnegan's Wake*): *Our Exagmination Round his Factification for Incamination of Work in Progress* (1929). The youthful Beckett's piece is 'Dante ... Bruno . Vico .. Joyce'. Beckett's essay has much to say about the influence on Joyce of Dante and Giambattista Vico, the eighteenth-century 'scientific historian' as Beckett calls Vico, and in the process of these claims of influence on Joyce, Beckett refers briefly to Bruno's principle of the coincidence of contraries as a basis for Vico's cyclic theory of history.

Before I proceed with some specifics of the parallels between Bruno's

* A draft of this paper was read at the *Themes in Drama* International Conference held at the University of California, Riverside, in February 1988.

philosophy and Beckett's drama relative to the coincidence of contraries, let me remark on certain premises I presume about what it is one is doing when one applies philosophy to theatre, at least when one applies philosophy to Beckett's theatre. Alain Robbe-Grillet furnishes a useful suggestion in his chapter on Beckett's drama and fiction in the study called *For a New Novel* (1965; first published in French as *Pour un nouveau roman*, 1963). Robbe-Grillet sees Beckett's theatre as an especial opportunity to grasp Beckett's 'Man' (*l'Homme*), who in the Beckett novels seems to be disappearing, reduced more and more 'on every page'. I quote Robbe-Grillet:

> The human condition, Heidegger says, is *to be there*. Probably it is the theatre, more than any other mode of representing reality, which reproduces this situation most naturally. The dramatic character *is on stage*, that is his primary quality: he is *there*.[4]

Aside from the claim that theatre is especially conducive to illustrating Heidegger's requirement for being, one draws a more general and simpler point from the above remark by Robbe-Grillet: theatre can give image to what remains in philosophy as idea. In theatre the word becomes image. But there are severe complications involved in this simplification, or oversimplification. Before Robbe-Grillet's chapter on Beckett is finished, he must admit that the stage characters are only seeming presences. As in the fictions, Beckett's stage characters are subject to the 'contagion' of reduction, disappearance, absence.

> The stage, privileged site of *presence*, has not resisted the contagion for long... After having believed for a moment that we had grasped the real man, we are then obliged to confess our mistake. Didi [in *Waiting for Godot*] was only an illusion, that is doubtless what gave him that dancing gait, swaying from one leg to the other, that slightly clownlike costume ... He, too, was only the creature of a dream, temporary in any case, quickly falling back into the realm of dreams and fiction.   (Robbe-Grillet, p. 125)

Robbe-Grillet aptly cites Hamm from *Endgame* saying, 'I was never there. Clov! ... I was never there ... Absent, always. It all happened without me ...'

My first assumption, then, is that theatre can give presence and image to philosophical concepts of being while at the same time it illustrates the ephemeral and illusory quality of that translation of concept into image. One can go further: drama has the erosive (or creative) power to empty concept of meaning. Beckett has said, 'I am interested in the shape of ideas even if I do not believe them.'[5] In theatre, it is the shape that matters. Thus, what I have now to say about Bruno and Beckett and the coincidence of contraries should be understood in the light (or shadow) of these assumptions: when talking about parallels in philosophy and drama, I presume that what is idea or concept in the former is shape or image in the latter and that in the extremities of such a paradigm the ephemeral and illusory presence of theatrical image on the one hand and the theoretic impalpability of philosophic principle on the other are both exposed. However lively, specific, dramatic, or even poetic may be a given process of philosophic thought (and Bruno's thought incidentally was often all of these), a philosophic articulation of a universal perception of being may seem abstractly shapeless in its theoretic structure and conclusion, like an opaque stretch of formless sky. On the other hand, dramatic shapes shadowing forth suggestive senses of being may seem to dissolve even as they form, like shifting clouds in an endless sky. In either case, we appreciate the limitations of the human mind and imagination, even as we admire the adventuresome philosopher or dramatist who seeks to express something that cannot be fully or definitively apprehended.

The best way to summarize Giordano Bruno's concept of the coincidence of contraries is to quote Beckett's explanation of the concept in his essay 'Dante . . . Bruno . Vico . . Joyce'. This passage from the Beckett essay is a concentrated version of a passage in Bruno's dialogue *De la causa, principio e uno* (1584):[6]

> There is no difference, says Bruno, between the smallest possible chord and the smallest possible arc, no difference between the infinite circle and the straight line. The maxima and minima of particular contraries are one and indifferent. Minimal heat equals minimal cold. Consequently transmutations are circular. The principle (minimum) of one contrary takes its movement from the principle (maximum) of another. Therefore not only do the minima coincide with the minima, the maxima with the maxima, but the minima with the maxima in the succession of transmutations. Maximal speed is a state of rest. The maximum of corruption and the minimum of generation are identical; in principle, corruption is generation. And all things are ultimately identified with God, the universal monad, Monad of monads.[7]

In *De la causa* Bruno's coincidence of contraries is part of a discussion of substance as distinct from quantity, measure, number, and other such 'accidents' inherent in multiplicity. Bruno insists that we understand 'substance as essentially without number and measure, and therefore as a unity and undivided in all particular thngs'. On the other hand, says Bruno, 'certain accidents of existence cause multiplication of substance. And similarly certain accidents of being cause multiplication of entity, truth, unity, being, the true, the one' (Lindsay, trans., p. 145). Thus if the mind can perceive those points where multiple contraries touch as one, minimum and maximum, arc and chord, circle and straight line, heat and cold, speed and rest, corruption and generation, one penetrates the mystery of oneness of substance that underlies the multiplicities of accident or appearance. Some of Bruno's coinciding contraries may seem to be merely tricks of geometry, which in his text may be illustrated with diagrams; indeed in one work he shows us how to square the circle.[8] Other of Bruno's contraries are more intensely bearing on human aspects of being, such as the corruption–generation contrary cited in the Beckett passage quoted above. In some contexts Bruno claims life and death among his coincident contraries. In the Fifth Dialogue of *La cena de le ceneris* (1584) [*The Ash Wednesday Supper*], Bruno's philosopher-spokesman Teofila presents an impressive list of social, moral, and existential oppositions that are contained within a unified human reality: 'So, everything within its own kind has every [possible] alternation of dominion and servitude, of happiness ad unhappiness, of that state we call life and that we call death, of light and dark, of good and evil.'[9] In the 'Explanatory Epistle' (dedicated to Sir Philip Sidney) of *Spaccio de la bestia trionfante* (1584) [*The Expulsion of the Triumphant Beast*], Bruno speaks of death as 'nothing but the divorcing of parts joined in a composite'. In a composite of contraries, the accidental features are corruptible, but not the substance: 'necessitated by the principles of dissolution, abandoning its architecture, it [the efficient and formative principle] causes the ruin of the edifice by dissolving contrary elements, breaking the union, removing the hypostatic composition' (Imerti, trans., p. 76). The formative principle of a unit of contraries survives the dissolution (or death) of the unit, and indeed as this passage in *The Expulsion* proceeds in a manner that sounds like a description of a Pythagorean metempsychosis, we understand that further hypostatic unions are continuously reconstituted in such a universe as Bruno postulates. What Bruno postulates over-all is the concept that in this measured, divisible, and corruptible universe there exists an underlying principle of being that is immeasurable, indivisible, and incorruptible. To understand that contraries are the same or touch at a common point is to understand that an underlying monad equates all, a monad beyond the limitations of both division and change, 'Monad of monads'.

Now I examine whether such a concept of philosophy has a coincidence in drama, whether this idea which Beckett found in Bruno and reported dutifully in his essay on Joyce has significant implication when applied to Beckett's theatre. Obviously I make no claims about whether the idea which Beckett conveyed in a 1929 essay stuck in his head as a resource to be specifically and purposefully exploited for plays composed at later dates. Rather the interest here is that Beckett in his own way has been drawn to express images of the tensions between measurability and immeasurability, divisibility and indivisibility, corruptibility and incorruptibility. Unlike Bruno, Beckett does not make a discursive or argumentative case for an ultimate unity of being. Beckett's art is rather to draw lines of measurement, division, and corruption so severely that their opposites might be adumbrated. Bruno's principle of the coincidence of contraries as part of a philosophy of the substantial unity of being is affirmative and reassuring; Beckett's verbal and theatrical images of coinciding contraries are usually unsettling.

Beckett's pairing of characters in his early major drama immediately suggests the coincidence of contraries, for in these pairings Beckett united couples so finely dissimilar and so powerfully linked that they seem to operate together as units, as monads. Thus in *Waiting for Godot* (English version produced 1955; *En attendant Godot*, 1953),[10] we have Vladimir and Estragon (Didi and Gogo) as a duo locked in vaudevillian stichomythia, bound to their single appointment with Godot, fearful of their separation. Then there are Pozzo and Lucky, master and slave, each bound by the rope that defines their being as master and slave. The Pozzo–Lucky pair is particularly corruptible. During the course of the transmutations of the play from act I to act II, Pozzo goes blind and Lucky goes dumb. The Didi–Gogo pair seem to stand in contrast to Pozzo–Lucky as more incorruptible. Didi and Gogo change little through the play, and yet they are subject to corruption: one has 'stinking breath' and the other 'stinking feet' (*Waiting for Godot*, p. 31). A third pair is a more seamless pair than the other two. These are the boys who serve as emissaries from Godot at the end of each act, the one who 'mind[s] the goats', and the other who 'minds the sheep'. These boys are so exactly alike in appearance and speech that we have only the word of the second one that he is not in fact the first one. Here Beckett so diminishes the stage divisibility of the two characters that they represent an image of indivisibility. And further, these boys of Godot as a youthful unit unaffected by the course of the play represent an image of seemingly pure changelessness, incorruptibility. Yet these boys affirm nothing finally about either Godot or the mystery of being. As images of indivisibility and incorruptibility, they only baffle us.

In *Endgame* (1958; *Fin de partie* 1957) Beckett presents again coincident contraries in pairings of characters placed in a context that suggests a diminishing line between the measurable world of the set and the indivisible space beyond. Hamm and Clov are a master–servant unit, the one sitting unable to stand, and the other standing unable to sit (see *Endgame*, p. 10). They play out their game of painful coexistence on a stage of a '*Bare interior*' and '*Grey light*' with '*two small windows*', '*high up*' (stage directions). The windows, we learn in the dialogue, look out to a nearly empty earth on the one side and a desolate sea on the other. Near the beginning of the play, in response to Hamm's question about what time it is, Clov says, 'The same as usual. . . . Zero' (p. 4). Time now and no time coincide. A little later on, when Clov with his telescope looks out the windows to sea and earth, he measures them as 'Zero . . . (*he looks*) . . . zero . . . (*he looks*) . . . and zero' (p. 29). The waves of the sea are 'lead', the sun is 'zero', the day is 'Grey' (p. 31), like the interior of the room. The outside and inside are distinct, yet similar, divisible, yet nearly indivisible. Here and nowhere coincide.

Within the scene of *Endgame* the pairing of Hamm's progenitors, Nagg and Nell, suggests a coincidence of life and death. This pair of lovers exist as stumps of creatures encased in bins on the stage. They still make feeble attempts at kissing and recall old times as young lovers on Lake Como. When looking into the Nagg–Nell baskets near the end of the play, Clov answers to the question of whether the one is dead, 'Looks like it', and to the same question for the other he says, 'Doesn't look like it' (p. 62).

Beckett's imagery of the coincidence of contraries in *Endgame* takes on grim suggestions. If the measurable world borders on the immeasurable, a zero of non-being seems to threaten annihilation of being. If life coincides with death, the latter overwhelms the lingering possibilities of the former. If generation should reconstitute being in the face of corruption, Hamm and Clov would rather have none of it. When Clov announces the discovery of a flea, he quickly goes for the insecticide, because as Hamm says 'humanity might start from there all over again!' (p. 33). When Clov through his telescope sees what might be a small boy outside, he scurries for the gaff and hastens for the door, presumably in an absurd gesture to search out and kill such 'A potential procreator' (p. 78). For Bruno the intersections of contraries, grasped philosophically, affirmed the unity of being. For Beckett in *Endgame*, creating images of the intersections of contraries is a perilous exercise, intensifying the uncertainty of being and evoking the kind of *Angst* that attends the perception of nothing, the vision of zero, the awareness of the possibility of an ultimate fragmentation and disunification of being.

In later plays Beckett's presentation of the coincidence of contraries has evolved into a much more concentrated kind of dramatic technique. *Krapp's Last Tape* (1958) might be considered a turning point, for in this play there is not a pairing of characters, but a single character, Krapp, who is divided into two selves, the younger Krapp age thirty-nine, who is heard on a tape which the older Krapp plays on the occasion of his sixty-ninth birthday as he prepares for his annual recording of the year's memorabilia. The ingenious device of the play imagines a character who so divides and stores his life over the years with the measurements of boxes and spools for the recordings. 'Ah! . . . Box . . . three . . . spool . . . five', begins the play. In the play Beckett presents two aspects of one self not only divided in time but divided in quality. The older Krapp is aging, weary, discombobulated, hard of hearing, cracked of voice, constipated of bowel, corruptible, indeed falling apart before our very eyes. The younger Krapp is pretentious, voluble, vibrant, full of superficial hopes and romantic dreams, recalling among other things a moment with a girl on a punt in a lake when he experienced the feeling of oneness of being, with the girl, with the lake, with himself. 'I lay down across her with my face in her breasts and my hand on her. We lay there without moving. But under us all moved, and moved us, gently, up and down, and from side to side' (*Collected Shorter Plays*, p. 163). In this expression of the intersection of motion and stasis, Beckett offers us a more invigorating image of the coincidence of contraries than he offers in

8 'The coincidence of contraries', Willie and Winnie (Tristan Middleton and Tiffany Murray)

Endgame, as indeed in *Krapp's Last Tape* as a whole the intersections of youth and age and generation and corruption are more deftly maneuvered in delicate balance than are the more threatening maneuvers of perilous balance in *Endgame*.

But, whatever the feeling or texture of the play, the point about *Krapp's Last Tape* that forecasts the technique of much of Beckett's later drama is the

methodology of presenting the contraries of a single character who is
fragmented for exploration of the tensions between duality and oneness
previously embodied in paired characterizations. In several of the later
plays after *Krapp's Last Tape* the contraries, and contraries within contraries, are the contraries of human consciousness, centering in the key
issues of post-Cartesian being, the issues concerning the dualities of body–
mind, subject–object, self–other. In some senses Beckett's theatre images of
the divided consciousness are beyond the philosophy of Bruno, since Bruno
was not of an age where such a theme was a philosophical issue. For Bruno,
the mind was the unifier.[11] In Beckett's later theatre, the mind becomes
both the divider and the thing divided. In Beckett's later theatre, the stage
is the unifier, bringing together in tentative and perilous coincidence at
varying angles various contraries of the divided mind, the divided self. But
still in such division, there is the search for the indivisible, the effort to test
whether something immeasurable, indivisible, and incorruptible can be
revealed or suggested as subsuming the intersections of conscious being.
For illustrations, I refer to two of Beckett's theatre pieces from the 1970s
and one from 1981.

Not I (1973) presents on a dark stage a Mouth, '*faintly lit*', delivering in a
woman's voice a relentless third-person history of her self, 'with veheme-
ment refusal to relinquish third person' (says a note to the text). The
speaking Mouth attempting self-comprehension in language concentrates
attention on a focused point of the tenuous body–mind intersection. The
fact that Mouth speaks in a third-person perspective projected as though
from outside the self enforces the perceiver–perceived division of consciousness. In the monologue of Mouth we get expression of inchoate awareness
in broken language that seems to be trying to articulate a coming into
sentience, but at a late age; Mouth speaks of a person 'practically speechless
... all her days', one who somehow 'lived on and on ... to be sixty ...
something she – ... what? ... seventy? .. Good God!' (*Collected Shorter Plays*,
p. 221). Thus the play suggests a compression of being from sentient birth
into dissolution, as though such divisible progression were one indivisible
experience. The angles of the play's presentation of being are complicated
by the presence of an Auditor in '*loose black djellaba with hood, fully faintly lit. . .
diagonally across stage*' from Mouth. On four of the occasions that Mouth
pauses at the pronoun 'she' (refusing 'to relinquish third person'), the
opaque Auditor makes a coincident 'gesture of helpless compassion' (see
note to text and stage directions – mysteriously on the fifth and last occasion
that Mouth pauses at the pronoun 'she' in resistance of the pronoun 'I',
Auditor does not respond). Presumably Mouth and Auditor represent the
division of perceiver–perceived or subject–object in the figuration of the
spoken and the heard. However divided, Mouth and Auditor meet at
certain theatrically gestured points of oneness, expressing a shared

sympathy, suggesting a hypostatic union in combat against that very unity, trying to refuse the isolated cohesion of the conscious self into the monad of the pronoun 'I', fearful of losing the angles of perception that locate the self in being. *Not I* is a disturbing play about the intersections of being and non-being within a divided consciousness. In *Not I* the resistance of the character to be 'I' suggests that to be indivisible, to be one 'I', to be only 'I', is to relinquish being, to relinquish the consciousness of being. The painful paradox in Beckett's later plays is that the stage figures seem to fear loss of consciousness even as they desire flight from consciousness.

In *A Piece of Monologue* (1979), the Speaker, '*White hair, white nightgown, white socks*', situated near a '*skull-sized white globe*' and a '*white foot of a pallet bed*', soliloquizes on the theme 'Birth was the death of him', again refusing the first person,[12] compressing in relentless monologue as he describes his movements on stage the coincidence of contrary images of generation and corruption, birth and death, the bed perhaps suggesting the scene of both, birth and death.

During the course of *A Piece of Monologue*, the Speaker describes his efforts to keep lit the '*skull-sized white globe*', evidently a kerosene lamp which keeps going out. The lamp, then, becomes an arena for an alternating coincidence of light and dark. As a '*skull-sized . . . globe*', the lamp suggests further a space wherein mind and matter, head and universe, congeal, where skull is globe and globe is skull.

The Speaker's last few lines in *A Piece of Monologue* form a stunning exercise in the compression of opposites into as singular a coincidence as language allows:

> Never were other matters. Never two matters. Never but the one matter. The dead and gone. The dying and the going. From the word go. The word begone. Such as the light going now. Beginning to go. In the room. Where else? Unnoticed by him staring beyond. The globe alone. Not the other. The unaccountable. From nowhere. On all sides nowhere. Unutterably faint. The globe alone. Alone gone.

Here as the 'word go' becomes the 'word begone', all matters become one matter, 'Never but the one matter': the divisibility of multiplicity and the measure of time nearly disappear. And nowhere borders the here, 'On all sides nowhere': the absence in nowhere borders the presence of the 'globe alone', and the divisions of place nearly disappear. The light of the globe becomes 'Unutterably faint', and light and dark, life and death nearly merge. And then the incredible articulation that compresses oneness (aloneness) and absence (goneness) into that powerfully suggestive but inconclusive two-word 'sentence': 'Alone gone.'

In *Ohio Impromptu* (1981), a Listener and a Reader appear on stage, '*As alike in appearance as possible*' (say the stage directions), the Reader as subject reading a story of another to himself as Listener and Object. The story told includes a sequence of visitations to the 'he' of the story by still another who came on several occasions to give comfort to the 'he' of the story by reading him a 'sad tale' from a volume whereafter each reading the visitor 'disappeared without a word'. Eventually the visitor–reader and the listener of the inner text ebb to a silence, 'So the sad tale a last time told they sat on as though turned to stone.' At the end of the play the Reader and Listener of the outer text, the figures on stage, imitate or repeat the ebbing into stony silence of the inner text: the play ends with this stage direction for Reader and Listener: '*Simultaneously they lower their right hands to table, raise their heads and look at each other. Unblinking. Expressionless. Ten seconds. Fade out.*' Between its opening words 'Little is left to tell' and its closing words 'Nothing is left to tell', the play gives figuration of the intersection not only of saying and hearing, but also of words and wordlessness, sound and silence. Consciousness depicted in a double layer of subject–object is held in tension between such oppositions, the wordlessness and silence that surround the inner and outer texts of the play being as much a part of the play as the figures and words of the play. The divided stage figures of Listener and Reader and the measurable words of the Text stand in coincident opposition to the immeasurable and indivisible silence, 'Nothing is left to tell.'

In all of these plays, and others, the Beckett stage of the later part of his career becomes typically more and more a concentration of narrow light in the limited part of the stage where aging figures play against a background of enveloping darkness. Beckett's later theatre thus presents an image of confining light suggesting diminishing consciousness surrounded by the uncertain and extending darkness, the shapeless zone of non-being. If the Beckett stage is a place of unification of contraries, or more precisely a space where the intersections of oppositions within human consciousness meet, the tonal suggestions of diminishing figures ebbing toward assimilation into the darkness of non-being would seem to present an erosive if not grimly disturbing sense of unification. Moreover, the ebbing toward the darkness seems to be an infinite process without hope of either consummation or release.[13] Give me Bruno's more reassuring concept of contraries, one might say at this point, wherein the mind releases the tension of contraries with the saving grace of philosophic declarations that make oppositions to be of an accidental order of reality and true substance to be a deducible, inherent indivisibility that underlies all being.

But the Beckett theatre, however inconclusive it is, need not be all that disturbing or depressing. Beckett's quest for some kind of apprehension of the puzzlements and suffering of being is of itself an intriguing if not exhilarating adventure in theatre, just as Bruno's sometimes wildly conjectural postulation of an infinite, animate universe unified with a world soul was an adventure in philosophy. However contrary Bruno and Beckett are in century and circumstance, training and instinct, tone and approach, I claim as tenuous coda for this essay their coincidence as adventurers, both responding to the human urge to find a way to express or configure something perceived as the immeasurable, the indivisible, the incorruptible.

NOTES

1 *The Collected Shorter Plays of Samuel Beckett* (New York: Grove Press, 1984), p. 163.

2 From a 1961 interview with Gabriel D'Aubarède in *Nouvelles litteraires*, trans. Christopher Waters in Lawrence Graver and Raymond Federman, eds., *Samuel Beckett: the Critical Heritage* (London, Henley, and Boston: Routledge and Kegan Paul, 1979), p. 217.

3 Without attempting to distinguish studies of Beckett's fiction and drama, I offer in this note a few examples of scholarship relating philosophy to Beckett's art. In a section on 'Beckett and the Philosophers' in his book *Samuel Beckett's Art* (London: Chatto and Windus, 1967), John Fletcher reviews Beckett's borrowings from the pre-Socratics to philosophers of the eighteenth century: e.g. Heraclitus, Democritus, St Augustine, Campanella, Descartes, Geulincx, Malebranche, Leibniz, Berkeley, and Hume. Hugh Kenner in *Samuel Beckett: a Critical Study* (New York: Grove Press, 1961) made famous 'The Cartesian Centaur' (man on bicycle = mind and body) as a touchstone for the importance of Descartes in understanding Beckett; numerous other critics have developed the Descartes–Beckett connection. Richard N. Coe in *Beckett* (Edinburgh and London: Oliver and Boyd, 1964) applied in different sections of his book Descartes, Wittgenstein, and Sartre to Beckett. A recent study totally devoted to Beckett and the philosophies of Hegel, Heidegger, and Sartre is Lance St John Butler's *Samuel Beckett and the Meaning of Being: a Study in Ontological Parable* (New York: St Martin's Press, 1984). And to suggest the marvelous variety of philosophers who can be invoked in a study of Beckett, I quote from David H. Hesla's Preface to his book *The Shape of Chaos: an Interpretation of the Art of Samuel Beckett* (Minneapolis: University of Minnesota Press, 1971): 'In my view, Beckett's art is finally ontological: it asks the question, What is the being of that entity we call man? In asking it, he has drawn on the ideas of the pre-Socratics, the rationalists of the seventeenth and eighteenth centuries, on Schopenhauer and Bergson, and the group of thinkers collected under the heading "Existentialists". In order to talk about his work I have thought it necessary to draw on these thinkers, as well as on Hegel, Kierkegaard, Heidegger, Sartre, and Edmund Husserl, among others.'

4 Alain Robbe-Grillet, *For a New Novel: Essays on Fiction*, trans. Richard Howard (New York: Grove Press, 1965), p. 111.

5 As reported by Harold Hobson, 'Samuel Beckett: Dramatist of the Year', *International Theatre Annual*, 1 (1956), 153. Beckett is commenting on the two thieves crucified aside Christ, a situation turned into comic dialogue in the opening phases of *Waiting for Godot*. The fuller context of Beckett's remark is this:

'I am interested in the shape of ideas even if I do not believe them. There is a wonderful sentence in Augustine: I wish I could remember the Latin. It is even finer in Latin than in English. "Do not despair; one of the thieves was saved. Do not presume; one of the thieves was damned." That sentence has a wonderful shape. It is the shape that matters.'

6 See Jack Lindsay, trans., *Five Dialogues by Giordano Bruno: Cause, Principle and Unity* (New York: International Publishers, 1964), pp. 145–9.

7 From 'Dante ... Bruno . Vico .. Joyce' in *Our Exagmination Round his Factification for Incamination of Work in Progress*, second edn (New York: a New Directions Book, 1962), p. 6.

8 Giordano Bruno, *The Expulsion of the Triumphant Beast*, trans. Arthur D. Imerti (New Brunswick, NJ: Rutgers University Press, 1964), p. 221.

9 Giordano Bruno, *The Ash Wednesday Supper*, trans. Edward A. Gosselin and Lawrence S. Lerner (Hamden, CT: Archon Books, 1977), p. 214.

10 These are the texts used for my citations from Beckett plays in the rest of this essay: *Waiting for Godot* (New York: Grove Press, 1954); *Endgame* (New York: Grove Press, 1958); *Krapp's Last Tape, Not I, A Piece of Monologue*, and *Ohio Impromptu*, in *Collected Shorter Plays of Samuel Beckett* (New York: Grove Press, 1984). My indications of the dates of the plays are dates of first production.

11 Note this comparison by Bruno of the human intellect to the unifying cosmic intellect in *De la causa, principio e uno*: 'The universal intellect is the innermost, most real and essential faculty and the most efficacious part of the world soul. It is the one and the same thing, which fills the whole, illumines the universe, and directs nature in producing her species in the right way. It plays the same role in the production of natural things as our intellect does in the parallel production of rational systems' (Lindsay, trans., p. 81). For an understanding of how the mystical or magical learning associated with 'Hermes Trismegistus' influenced Bruno's conception of the universe reflected in the human mind, see Frances A. Yates, *Giordano Bruno and the Hermetic Tradition* (London: Routledge and Kegan Paul, 1964), pp. 31–2, 191–9.

12 At one point toward the end of the play, Speaker draws a questioning emphasis of concern or puzzlement upon his use of the pronoun 'he'. Jane Alison Hale makes this remark about the complications of consciousness involved in that moment: 'The Speaker of *A Piece of Monologue* has used the pronoun "he" on numerous occasions up till this point. The third-person form has thus far presented no problems to him, since he perceives and expresses the self he is pursuing as an object separate in both time and space from the pursuing subject, whose name would be the absent "I". The grammatical difficulty arises here because the perceiver/perceived dichotomy has been transferred to another level: the subject, Speaker, is perceiving the object, "he", who is in turn engaged in the process of perceiving himself, through "the words falling from his mouth."' *The Broken Window: Beckett's Dramatic Perspective* (Lafayette, IN: Purdue University Press, 1987), p. 122.

13 See my essay 'Samuel Beckett's Doomsday Play: the Space of Infinity', in *The Theatrical Space*, ed. James Redmond, *Themes in Drama 9* (Cambridge: Cambridge University Press, 1987), pp. 215–27. In a recent essay, Martin Esslin explains Beckett's themes of permutative and entropic infinity, and then counterpoints

these themes with an assertion of Beckett's pursuit, 'however impossible, however hopeless', of the kind of salvific eternity of mystical release expressed by Dante at the end of *Paradiso*. As example of an exhilarating (and astonishing) rendition of Beckett's philosophic yearning, I would certainly recommend Esslin's exuberant last paragraph of this essay: 'Samuel Beckett – Infinity, Eternity' in *Beckett at 80 / Beckett in Context*, ed. Enoch Brater (New York and Oxford: Oxford University Press, 1986), pp. 110–23.

The Devils and its sources: modern perspectives on the Loudun possession

JANE GOODALL

For contemporary as well as for more recent commentators, the principal fascination of the Loudun possession has been its interpretative challenge rather than its sensational events, and they have been as much concerned to take issue with each other's hermeneutic biases as to study the facts of the case. Cardinal Richelieu's vested interest in the conviction of Grandier, the priest accused of diabolism, made it politic for chroniclers of the time to employ their ingenuity in finding evidence of the genuineness of the nuns' possession. Sister Jeanne, Grandier's principal 'victim', and her exorcist Father Surin both left autobiographies which were earnest retrospective attempts to understand the significance of what they had experienced. These and other contemporary accounts became the subject of renewed interest in the late nineteenth century, when developing research into non-rational areas of the mind began to offer new forms of insight into the condition of both the possessed and their extravagantly credulous observers. An account by De Nion first published in 1634 was translated in 1887 by Edmund Goldsmid, a Scot working on a history of magic and superstition who presented it as an illustration of the kind of specious argument that undermined rational judgement.[1] In the 1870s, Gabriel Legué and Gilles de la Tourette, two students of the Parisian psychologist Charcot, began to study documents relating to the case in quest of material to contribute to his research on hysteria. Grandier was a character whose disparate motivating forces presented an intriguing challenge for them but more intriguing still was Sister Jeanne, in whom they found a textbook case of hysterical psychosis. In 1886, they published an annotated edition of her autobiography with an introduction giving a detailed psychoanalytic explication.

Aldous Huxley's account, *The Devils of Loudun* (1952), drew heavily on the work of Legué and Tourette, but his wide-angle lens ranges over philosophical, moral, political and theological as well as psychological issues. His interpretation of these issues is dualistic and a comparative treatment of Grandier and Surin is essential to his perspective. Surin is introduced in chapter 3 as Grandier's alter-ego:

> Grandier and Surin – two men nearly of an age, brought up in the same school, by the same masters, in the same humanistic and religious discipline, both priests, one secular, the other a Jesuit, and yet predestined to be the inhabitants of incommensurable universes.[2]

Grandier set out in the egocentric pursuit of worldly advancement and sensual gratification, whilst Surin 'with heroic perseverence... addressed himself to the task of Christian perfection'.

The chain of events with which these two life courses are bound up demonstrates for Huxley a whole range of archetypal polarities. Physical and spiritual awareness, contradistinguished in the figures of Grandier and Surin, are confused in the experience of the possessed nuns and their exorcists whose exploits prove that 'sex mingles easily with religion'. The possession itself highlights the antitheses of diabolism and divinity, revelation and delusion, tragedy and comedy. Surin's behaviour exhibits a blend of ascetic self-denial and pathological solipsism and Huxley sees such paradoxes as central to human motivation:

> On all levels of our being, from the muscular and sensational to the moral and intellectual, every tendency generates its own opposite. (p. 33)

This can create a profound division in the psyche:

> Even among those whom nature and fortune have most richly endowed we find, and find not infrequently, deep-seated horror of their own selfhood.
> (p. 78)

Thus, although *The Devils of Loudun* is a well-researched documentary, Huxley's primary interest in the story is not historical. He finds it an ideal vehicle for the exposition of a thesis based on this dualistic interpretation of the human condition, a thesis which has theological implications and strong polemical overtones:

> Without an understanding of man's deep-seated urge to self-transcendence, of his very natural reluctance to take the hard, ascending way, and his search for some bogus liberation either below or to one side of his personality, we cannot hope to make sense of our own particular period of history or indeed, of history in general. (p. 361)

Grandier achieves self-transcendence through suffering inflicted upon him, Surin through suffering which is self-inflicted, and elsewhere in the narrative instances of 'bogus liberation' abound. Most striking of these is the possession itself, the interpretation of which is central to Huxley's thesis. He argues that the metamorphosis of a community of nuns into a troupe of savage, blaspheming exhibitionists is a classic instance of 'downward transcendence' fuelled by herd intoxication and liberating all the basest instincts from the responsible control of the ego. To their contemporary audience, the nuns were victims of a diabolic tormentor; Legué and

Tourette still saw them as victims, but victims whose torment was autogenous; Huxley goes one stage further and, inverting the ethical perspectives of the seventeenth century, unequivocally blames the nuns for the persecution of their 'tormentor', contending that the truly diabolical phenomenon is the abdication of the ego in favour of a chaotic melange of bestial impulses. Huxley is no fatalist. The impetus of his narrative derives from his didactic insistence on the moral responsibility of the individual and his enduring fascination with the exercise of deducing where the blame should be laid for each link in the grim train of events which took place at Loudun. With the satirical acuity of an experienced novelist, he reconstructs and dissects a whole range of characters who play nefarious supporting roles in the drama.

It would be reasonable to assume that the appeal of Huxley's book to a dramatist under contract to write 'a full-scale costume drama'[3] was largely in these vivid character sketches, but John Whiting never chose his sources for conventional reasons or used them in predictable ways. Only two of Huxley's caricatures survive in recognizable form in Whiting's dramatis personae. It is the long passages of thematic extrapolation which really caught his imagination, for they offered an analysis of the problems he himself had been concerned with since the writing of *Saint's Day*, fifteen years earlier: the discordance of physical experience and spiritual apprehension, the perversion of Christian ideals, and the desolate condition of man attempting to live in a world poisoned by a myth gone bad.

Physical and spiritual considerations are in dynamic conflict from the opening scene of *The Devils* and this is established visually by the symbolic juxtaposition of church and sewer, the two institutions which, in diametric opposition, govern the lives of the characters. Grandier emerges from the church, having just preached a sermon 'very rousing to the spirit', to be given the benefit of a sermon of another kind.

> *Sewerman.* Well, every man is his own drain. He carries his main sewer with him. Gutters about him carry off the dirt –
> *Grandier.* They also carry the blood of life.
> *Sewerman.* Mere plumbing. Elementary sanitation. Don't interrupt.[4]

It is in more senses than one that this encounter leaves 'shit on the holy purple'.

The third important symbol incorporated into the set of the opening scene is that of the hanging corpse. The young man on the gallows, cut down in his glorious physical prime, is transformed into a dehumanized obscenity. His remains provoke contrasting speculations. Adam and Mannoury wonder 'what resides', what vestiges of humanity may be discovered in this physiological specimen and, having obtained the severed head for a small price, probe for the answer with their scalpels:

> *Mannoury.* I might stumble upon the very meaning of reason. Isn't it possible
> that the divinity of man, enclosed in an infinitesimal bag, might rest upon the
> point of my knife?   (p. 147)

Philippe's question, 'does death unmask the face in heaven?', represents an
antithetical perspective: the physiological specimen belies the true nature
of man which may be revealed only when the body is discarded. Grandier
has known the man as a living, acutely sentient being capable of fusing
physical and spiritual responses in a profoundly individual way. From the
beginning of the play, when he is assailed by the sewerman, Grandier is the
figure on whom these contradictory ideas of human existence are focused.
Where Huxley explores such contradictions by setting Grandier and Surin
against each other as alter-egos, Whiting makes an idiosyncratic decision to
fuse them and their antithetical patterns of motivation, so creating one
highly complex, ambiguous personality, a man torn between two worlds.

   Huxley's rationalization of the stages in Grandier's downfall is based on
a carefully researched analysis of their political background. Richelieu's
plan to destroy all the provincial fortresses in the realm was to be put into
effect at Loudun, and Grandier boldly supported D'Armagnac, the town
governor, in his resistance to it. As represented in Huxley, his motives for
doing this were straightforwardly self-interested. Being a close friend of
D'Armagnac, he had gained considerable influence in the administrative
affairs of Loudun and had, on occasion, been unofficially deputed to act for
the governor in his absence. This, combined with the fact that most of his
private enemies were Cardinalists, accounted naturally enough for his
involvement in the defence of the Loudun fortifications. Whiting's
Grandier acts upon a much more unorthodox logic. He recognizes from
D'Armagnac's initial explanation of the affair that it offers him a means of
externalizing the discord within himself:

> Conflict attracts me, sir. Resistance compels me.   (p. 157)

His inversion of normal reasoning is at this stage beyond D'Armagnac's
comprehension. 'Don't smile', he warns, 'they can also destroy you.' But it
is this very possibility that makes Grandier smile. His only hope of salvation
is through the destruction of his worldly self, and this idea is deftly
suggested in metaphorical terms in the preceding discussion:

> *D'Armagnac.* Ignorant and crafty provincials like us cannot see beyond the city
> walls. So we have this order from the Cardinal to tear them down. Will it
> broaden our view?   (p. 156)

Grandier's first soliloquy shows that his attempts to discern 'the way' are
thwarted by more immediate awareness of his physical impulses. Perhaps
he will only gain spiritual awareness by demolishing the prison of the body.
That he should seek the means of his own physical destruction by

campaigning for the preservation of the walls and castle keep at Loudun is one of the symbolic ironies Whiting builds into the story.

This reconception of the primary underlying motive in Grandier's behaviour entailed a range of important adjustments in the representation of those who were instrumental in his downfall. The roles of his more sigificant enemies are transformed as the accent is shifted away from personal malice and animosity. Richelieu's agent, De Laubardemont, appears in Huxley's narrative as a lurid villain, a Uriah Heep:

> The long squirming body, the damp hands incessantly rubbed, the constant protestations of humility and goodwill – all were there. And so was the underlying malignity, the ruthless eye to the main chance.   (Huxley, p. 66)

The 'underlying malignity' emerges in his sadistic interest in the treatment of Grandier after his arrest: to make the place of imprisonment 'devil proof' he has the windows bricked up; he personally supervises a search for witch marks in which Grandier is 'systematically pricked to the bone with a long sharp probe'; he tries to persuade the barber who comes to shave the prisoner in preparation for his trial that the procedure should include removal of the fingernails. His behaviour during the actual torture is fanatical, culminating in hysterical demands for 'cruelty beyond the merely extraordinary' (Huxley, p. 247). Whiting's Laubardemont is the classic civil servant: shrewd, efficient and genuinely diplomatic. There is no mention in the play of the bricking up of the prison cell, the search for witch marks or the orders for Grandier's premature subjection to torture. Laubardemont's only comment during the scene in which Grandier is shaved is 'order of the court' and during the torture itself he remains in the background until deciding peremptorily to call a halt. It seems beneath him to involve himself in such methods of persuasion, when he is so skilled at working on the mental weaknesses of the victim:

> let me tell you what you will think. First: how can man do this to man? Then: how can God allow it? Then: there can be no God. Then: there is no God. The voice of pain will grow stronger and your resolution weaker. Despair, Grandier. You used the word yourself. You called it the gravest sin.   (p. 211)

Laubardemont is of central importance in that he manages the actual process of Grandier's destruction and his mode of operation reflects the larger political machinery which he represents. By characterizing him as a cool-headed professional rather than as a malignant sycophant, Whiting is therefore implying that Grandier's political enemies are far more pragmatic than vindictive in their motivation. More stress is also laid on the extraordinary nature of Grandier's intention by pitting him against a man of reason in the final stages of his strange pilgrimage.

The corruptness of the political system which pushed the Loudun affair to its appalling conclusion is not an issue in the play. Nor is the way in

which this system perverts individuals by fostering cunning and ruthlessness, a prime example of which is the behaviour of the jailer, Bontemps.
According to Huxley Bontemps treated Grandier with 'unwavering
malignity' (Huxley, p. 152). Whiting sees him as efficient and
dispassionate:

> Look, this is your system. Just be thankful that you can get men to do the job.
> Don't ask that they should be humane as well. (p. 201)

For Whiting to have characterized the villains of the piece in the way that
Huxley does would have meant deflecting concentration from Grandier's
inner struggle. He must be seen as his own most determined adversary.

> All worldly things have a single purpose for a man of my kind. Politics, power,
> the senses, riches, pride and authority. I choose them with the same care that
> you, sir, select a weapon. But my intention is different. I need to turn them
> against myself. (p. 184)

Here, the full significance of Whiting's decision to fuse the figures of
Grandier and Surin becomes apparent. It enables him to explore the
bizarre paradox of a man who applies to his quest for salvation the tactical
ingenuity of a politician, the ruthlessness of a profound egotist and the
deviousness of an experienced seducer. The internal struggles of an ascetic
are not easy to dramatize, whereas Whiting's idea of representing a quest
for salvation which is bound up with dangerous politics and intense
personal relationships is inherently dramatic, if theologically bizarre.
Before Grandier discovers 'the way', he takes one major wrong turning.
This leads him to the realization that the worldly things which are his
suicide weapon must never be mistaken for a means of transcendence in
themselves, and that if there is a way of salvation through another human
being, it is to be in the form of mutual destruction, not mutual affirmation.
Huxley's narrative dwells at some length on the subject of Grandier's illicit
love affairs, showing how the jealousy, bitterness and moral outrage they
aroused served to expand the circle of his personal enemies. Whiting's
portrayal of the affair with Philippe Trincant as a false start in Grandier's
quest for salvation integrates it in a more sophisticated way with the central
line of the drama: it serves as an ironic parallel to Sister Jeanne's sexual
fantasies and a counterpoint to the violence which proves to be the real
means of Grandier's deliverance from his baser self.

Whiting's Philippe, like his Grandier, is a composite of two antithetical
figures from Huxley's account. Huxley characterizes her as coquettish,
spoilt and light-minded, in contrast to Madeleine De Brou, Grandier's next
mistress, who was 'quiet and enigmatic', 'religious almost to scrupulosity'
and 'virtuous not only in principle, but by habit and temperament'
(Huxley, p. 51). Whiting creates a character in whom Madeleine De Brou's
spirituality is fused with Philippe's ingenuous sensuality and who is thus

ideally qualified to inspire Grandier's first and most serious illusion. Placing his faith in her, he temporarily succeeds in achieving a unified vision of his own course, believing that there is a 'way of salvation' through human love. This optimism has its logical culmination in the marriage ceremony which is their collaborative act of faith, but the true significance of the ritual is revealed by the sewerman's appearance with his caged bird:

> He's my saviour. Who's yours? (p. 172)

It seems that there are more ways of salvation through another than thus far have been dreamed of in Grandier's philosophy:

> You know the pits at the edge of the town? Where even your beloved here sends in my buckets. Well, there are days when the place gives off poison. So I always approach it with this creature on a pole before me. His many predecessors have died in the miasma. When this happens I know it's no place for me. So I let the drains run foul for a day or two, and I spend my time catching another victim to shut up here. You'll understand what I mean. (p. 172)

And it is true that Grandier does not need the parable spelled out any more explicitly:

> I have put my trust in this child. She is not a victim. (p. 172)

In Whiting's first draft for this scene, the reference to a 'saviour' is construed in doctrinal terms:

> *Grandier.* Your intended analogy appals me. Do you mean that because of the death of God this[5] is no place for me?
> *Sewerman.* Is it? From what I know of the scriptures, and from what I see of the images you put up in your churches, he died in despair.
> *Grandier.* But later, my son. What happened later?
> *Sewerman.* That happened in the minds of men. Men who were not brave enough to despair.[6]

Grandier is being warned against the church on the grounds that the experience of its founder, the original 'saviour', has proved its influence to be poisonous to life and hope. As in the final version of the play the Sewerman is presented here as the enemy of delusion, but in the revision his overt dialectical challenge is cut and his role takes on a subtler, more ironic cast. To make him an active myth-breaker and an enemy of faith per se was to externalize the struggle Grandier has with himself in some of the most intense phases of the drama, and to pre-empt issues which could be raised more naturally in relation to the development of the action. Grandier's rude awakening occurs in the most predictable form: the announcement of Philippe's pregnancy proves that, after all, the relationship is essentially physiological and therefore essentially sordid. She, like the Sewerman's bird, must be relinquished to the miasma of physical corruption.

After he has effectively been shown the dangers of attempting to achieve self-transcendence through human love, Grandier embarks upon the search for someone who can release him from rather than entrench him in the material plane of existence he is so desperate to escape. Richelieu, 'excellent enemy' though he may be, will not, however, resolve the ethical dilemma associated with Grandier's objective. D'Armagnac is percipient enough to define the predicament:

> D'Armagnac. I can see that the obvious short cut, self-destruction, is not possible. But isn't creating the circumstances for your own death, which is what you seem to be doing, equally sinful?
> Grandier. Leave me some hope.
> D'Armagnac. The hope that God will smile upon your efforts to create an enemy so malignant as to bring you down, and so send you – up?
> Grandier. Yes. (p. 184)

This latter suggestion is crucial to the thematic logic of the play. In order to find the means to his own destruction and salvation, Grandier must make an enemy whose malignancy will draw off all the guilt which necessarily attaches to the killing of a man.

The first to recognize the true identity of this figure is the Sewerman, who achieves a kind of clairvoyance through cynicism. During the scene in which he warns Grandier that Philippe will be a passive sacrifice, he also, by a cryptic association of ideas, warns him that 'some very odd things are going on up at the convent' (p. 173). These 'odd things' are the first signs of the vigorous involvement of another participant in Grandier's destiny, Sister Jeanne. Philippe's kind of love cannot save him, as it merely entrenches him further in the material plane of existence he is so desperate to escape, but in Jeanne love has united with hatred so that it has the potential to destroy and thereby release its object. Her role is thoroughly paradoxical: she is Grandier's destroyer and his saviour; the question of which is the quarry and which the prey is at the outset a confused issue.

Whiting is as fascinated as Huxley is by dualism and paradox, but his conceptual models are far more idiosyncratic. He seems to have had little affinity with Huxley's way of thinking, and rather to have been stimulated by a kind of dialectical response to the thematic perspectives in *The Devils of Loudun*. A much stronger influence on his own thinking was his reading of De Montherlant, whose exploration of Jansenian ideas about salvation, especially in *Port-Royal*, bears a close affinity with the central thematic concern of *The Devils*. *Port-Royal* is also a convent drama set in seventeenth-century France (the events Montherlant dramatizes took place in 1664, thirty years after the death of Urbain Grandier) and concerns a community at the centre of an affair which has important political and metaphysical implications. Like Grandier and Sister Jeanne, the nuns at Port-Royal are engaged in an uncompromising quest for salvation and the crisis they face makes it imperative for them to define their faith in a way which will enable them to resist extreme trials. In attempting to do so, they have to engage with anomalies of moral logic which make their own position wretchedly confusing. In an interview about *The Devils* in 1961, Whiting said 'We talk about good and evil as if they are poles apart, but in fact they're virtually the same thing.'[7] At the conclusion of an essay on Saint-Simon, Montherlant, too, observes that 'good and evil are mixed indistinguishably together', and he links this with a Jansenian point about salvation:

> How true are the words of the Scriptures, which can be understood to apply to virtue no less than to wisdom, 'As it happeneth to the fool, so it happeneth to me: and why was I then more wise'?[8]

The idea that God's grace is meted out in an arbitrary process which defies human understanding and which no human endeavour can hope to influence has obvious dramatic implications. It invites realization in terms of the lives of two individuals set in opposite courses, and this is precisely how Montherlant has conceived the underlying structure of his drama:

> Le sujet de cette pièce est le parcourse que fait une âme conventuelle vers un certain événement dont elle prevoit qu'il créera en elle une crise de doute religieux, et par ailleurs le renversement d'une autre âme conventuelle qui, sous l'effet du même événement, passe d'un état à l'état opposé. Le Soeur Françoise est mise, à l'improviste, devant 'la lumière'. La Soeur Angelique s'achemine, d'un cours logique et prevu, vers 'les Portes des Ténèbres'.[9]

The Devils has the same underlying conceptual structure, but Whiting reinforces its ironic implications much more harshly than Montherlant, by exploiting the ironies inherent in the Calvinist/Jansenist assertion that good works are of no avail in the quest for salvation. Jeanne is destined for 'an infinite desert of eternal bestiality' in spite of her aspirations to purity and her instinct for self-sacrifice, whilst Grandier attains grace in spite of his egocentric and licentious mode of living. Grandier dismisses the thought that his fate is to be bound up with 'a farce such as the convent's putting on' (p. 176) but Jeanne's first soliloquy, like his own, expresses a determination to find 'the way' to salvation and invites the inference that there is to be a profound association between her quest and his. At this point she seems calmer, more hopeful than he.

> By your grace I have come young to this office. Have mercy on your child. Let her aspire.   (p. 154)

Grandier, speaking 'in the weariness of thirty-five years... years scandalously marred by adornment and luxury' has no such source of reassurance. Both are distracted from their meditations by an awareness of immediate physical problems: the 'usual ... manifestations' which Grandier experiences at four o'clock on a Tuesday afternoon occur regardless of his more abstract preoccupations and Jeanne's plea for grace cuts off in favour of a prosaically abrupt request:

> Please God, take away my hump so that I can lie on my back without lolling my head.   (p. 155)

But Jeanne's physical problem is not, like Grandier's, irreconcilable with spiritual aspiration:

> O my dear Lord, I find it difficult to turn in my bed, and so in the small and desperate hours I am reminded of your burden, the Cross, on the long road.
>   (p. 154)

She ends on a note which in comparison with Grandier's anguished cry, 'salva me, salva me', is almost complacent:

> There is a way to be found. May the light of Your eternal love ... (*whispers*).
>   (p. 155)

But no evidence of God's grace is manifested in the subsequent stages of Jeanne's quest. In her search for love, she discovers only obscenity and exploitation and in her search for the way to enlightenment she wanders further and further into the darkness. It is not Jeanne but Grandier who will become identified with Christ through redemptive suffering. Jeanne's 'burden' is a symbol only of the guilt whish she is to take upon herself in becoming the instrument of Grandier's salvation. Like Philippe, she is Grandier's 'victim' whose innocence must be sacrificed in order to free him of the sinful elements in himself.

The first half of the play is structured so that the stages in her downfall are depicted alternately with the stages in Philippe's and her first soliloquy indicates that she is the apex of a triangle, reflecting Philippe's predicament as a woman in quest of love as well as Grandier's predicament as a soul in quest of grace. It is juxtaposed with the scene in which Philippe, under Grandier's tutelage, also begins to manifest yearnings which are to disrupt the ordered surface of her life. Philippe is moved to a profane image of 'everlasting' love which travesties the forms of expression normally reserved for spiritual devotion. Jeanne seeks 'eternal love' as a sublimated form of sexual desire:

> You will enfold me in Your sacred arms. The blood will flow between us uniting us.   (p. 155)

The true onset of Jeanne's possession, coincides with her vision of the scene in which Philippe surrenders her virginity. It is she, not Philippe, who understands the real nature of this encounter and experiences the spiritual violation which it symbolizes. Her subsequent mental images of Grandier cannot be confused with the image of an all-embracing divinity, for they speak 'jeering, contemptuous, hurtful obscenity'. Similarly, Philippe's failure to register the sacrilegious implications of her marriage is offset by Jeanne's vision of a ceremonial union which is luridly sacrilegious:

Jeanne. Oh, my dear Father, think of our little chapel, so simple, so unadorned,
That night it was a place of luxury and scented heat. Let me tell you... We
were beautifully dressed. I wore my clothes as if they were part of my body.
Later, when I was naked, I fell among thorns. Yes, there were thorns strewn
on the floor. I fell among them. Come here. (*She beckons to Barré, who leans
towards her. She whispers and then laughs.*)
Barré. She says that she and her sisters were compelled to form themselves into
an obscene altar, and were worshipped. (p. 179)

Tests are then made to determine the form of this 'worship' and Barré's
declaration, 'There's been fornication!... Lust! She's been had!',
grotesquely foreshadows the announcement of Philippe's pregnancy. The
clash between Barré's cry of triumph and Philippe's subdued resignation
serves to give the audience a more acute sense of the humiliation to which
she and Jeanne are being subjected. Both have fallen among thorns, as
wasted seed of the omnipotent distributor. Philippe presages her confession
with a sudden diabolic laugh, an unmistakable echo of Jeanne's and a
further hint of the strong parallel between their respective crises.

In creating a profound empathy between Grandier's 'enemy' and his
mistress, Whiting deviates boldly from Huxley's account, which records
that Jeanne was furiously jealous of both Philippe and Madeleine de Brou.
Whiting's Jeanne is the virtual antithesis of Huxley's: her transformation is
a key element in Whiting's thematic design, which requires not only that
her progress towards her destiny should finely counterpoint Grandier's
progress towards his, but also that it should be a matter of equally intense
concern. Huxley unequivocally discounts such a possibility. He represents
her as shallow, unscrupulous, vulgar minded and motivated by a 'craving
for superiority' (Huxley, p. 101). The predominant traits in her behaviour
are hypocrisy and exhibitionism, which find their perfect medium in the
masquerade of the possession.

There is no indication that Whiting's Jeanne finds the experience of
being possessed anything other than the most degrading torment. The
impression of purity violated and innocence perverted is essential to the
conception of Jeanne as a sacrifice, and actually more consistent with a
psychoanalytical interpretation of the possession than Huxley's conclusion
that 'as well as naturaliter Christiana, the feminine soul is naturaliter
Drum-Majoretta'. Whiting has her explain herself as one of the 'children of
misfortune', destined to show by her own example 'the glory of mortality,
the purpose of man: loneliness and death' (p. 286). But this is not to be the
limit of her suffering. With naive tenderness, she allows Grandier to become
a parasite on her body and her soul – and realizes too late that she has been
duped:

Did Satan take on the person of my love, my darling, so as to delude me? ... I
have such a little body. It is a small battleground in which to decide this terrible

struggle between good and evil, between love and hate. Was I wrong to allow
it?   (p. 292)

She has submitted herself to a Providence which metes out destiny with the
cavalier indifference of the Judge in Genet's *Le Balcon*:

> Je vais être juge de tes actes! C'est de moi que dependent la pensée, l'équilibre.
> Le monde est une pomme, je la coupe en deux! Les bons, les mauvais. Et tu
> acceptes, merci, tu acceptes, d'être la mauvaise!... sous vos yeux: rien dans les
> mains, rien dans les poches, enlever le pourri, et le jeter.[10]

For her, though, there is none of the extasy which 'Saint Genet' finds in such
strange martyrdom. The notion that Grandier receives the gift of divine
grace at Jeanne's expense casts a sinister shadow over his progress towards
redemption, so that the moral vision of the play remains deeply ambiguous
and its climax arouses disturbingly contradictory emotions in the spectator.

Jeanne is to be cheated of her aspirations to purity and destroyed by a
process far more insidious and degrading than any Richelieu and his agents
might devise, yet each time Grandier is at risk of being diverted from 'the
way', he is brought back to it by the intervention of others, as though his
progress were decreed by divine providence. The Sewerman arrives to
disabuse him of his folly when he tries to place his faith in marriage, and
provides a sceptical audience for his second grave delusion, which threatens
to reassert the validity of every element in his being which he has set out to
eradicate in the cause of his spiritual advancement.

> I created God!
> (Silence)
> I created him from the light and the air, from the dust of the road, from the
> sweat of my hands, from gold, from filth, from the memory of women's faces,
> from great rivers, from children, from the works of man, from the past, the
> present, the future and the unknown. I caused him to be from fear and despair.
> I gathered in everything from this mighty act, all I have known, seen and
> experienced. My sin, my presumption, my vanity, my love, my late, my lust.
>   (p. 199)

Transported with his own eloquence, he advances to adore this God 'in his
shrine' but meets instead Laubardemont and his forces, lounging against
the altar like emissaries of Providence, waiting to enforce his diversion back
to harsh reality.

In the last stages of this progress Grandier receives vital assistance from
an aged confessor, Father Ambrose, who induces in him at last the
consciousness that:

> There is meaning after all ... It is not nothing going to nothing. It is sin going to
> forgiveness. It is a human creature going to love.   (p. 205)

By having Father Ambrose assist in the epiphany, Whiting reinforces the
suggestion that Grandier's insight and determination, whilst enabling him

to exploit every opportunity which is offered him, would not of themselves have led him to salvation. It is convincing, too, that Grandier should need the help of a simple and steady thinker to steer his own vacillating perception between the extremes of vainglorious delusion and abject despair.

In the preceding scene, another old man is Jeanne's last resort in her search for comfort, but he succeeds only in reinforcing her fear and confusion:

> These very thoughts are put in your mind by the forces of dread. It's wrong to believe that Hell always fights with the clamour of arms. It is now, in the small hours, that Satan sends his secret agents, whispering, with their messages of doubt. (p. 202)

As they are shown simultaneously in the throes of their darkest hour, Grandier is able to cling to Ambrose's guarantee, 'Christ is now. You suffer with him', but in doing so he begs a strange question:

> Attendite et videte si est dolor sicut dolor meus. (p. 214)

The audience are being made acutely aware of sorrow like unto his sorrow, but an identification with Christ is not Sister Jeanne's prerogative.

She appears at the end of the play's final apocalyptic movement, to confront the Sewerman. With her question 'Do you know who I am?', she parodies the risen Christ, but she is Whiting's last and most tragic nomad. Even the mortal remains of her 'enemy' can offer her no symbol of hope. As the Sewerman assures her, they are not relics with power for spiritual healing, but totems for those who 'want to cure their constipation or their headache'.

In comparison with previous interpretations of the Loudun case, the Jansenian perspective offered in *The Devils* constitutes a bold thematic interpolation. Whiting is certainly taking greater imaginative liberties than Montherlant does in his dramatization of the story of Port-Royal, where similar themes are explicitly related to the historical situation. From a historical or psychoanalytical point of view, Whiting's interpretative twist may seem over-ingenious, but in artistic terms it is inspired, for it enables him to impose rigorous dramatic and intellectual unity on a diffuse historical narrative with diverse conceptual implications.

NOTES

1 De Nion, *The History of the Devils of Loudun*, ed. Edmund Goldsmid (Edinburgh: 1887).
2 Aldous Huxley, *The Devils of Loudun* (London: Chatto and Windus, 1952), p. 74. All subsequent page references are to this edition.

3 Peter Hall commissioned Whiting to write *The Devils* for the Royal Shakespeare Company's first London season at the Aldwych.
4 John Whiting, *The Devils* in *The Collected Plays*, vol. 2, p. 143. All subsequent page references are to this edition.
5 Grandier is standing in front of his church as he speaks.
6 First draft for act II dated 18 July 1960, in Box 29, File 2 of the John Whiting papers held by the Theatre Museum, London.
7 'The Devils', an interview with Richard Findlater in *The Art of the Dramatist* (London: London Magazine Editions, 1970), p. 171.
8 Henry de Montherlant, 'Saint Simon' in *Selected Essays* (London, Weidenfeld and Nicolson, 1967), p. 241.
9 Henry de Montherlant, '*Port-Royal*' in *Théâtre* (Paris: Gallimard, 1972), p. 843.
10 Jean Genet, *Le Balcon* (Saint-Amand: Folio, 1979), p. 35.

Drama as philosophy: *Professional Foul* breaks the rules*

MICHAEL ELDRIDGE

Tom Stoppard's *Professional Foul* is a play about rule-breaking. In three professions – sports, politics and philosophy – we see, within the span of a few days, instances of various rules being violated. The sports foul provides the metaphor – and name – for the play; some of the violations in the other two areas help make the case for the primacy of individual rights over societal rules. In advancing his case through character and plot, Stoppard challenges the conventions that would rule out philosophizing and moral advocacy in an entertaining play. Moreover, he does so in a most unlikely form for a drama of ideas. *Professional Foul* is a mystery! That a dramatist could write a *suspenseful* play of ideas, and have it work as a thriller, is a surprise indeed. Yet Stoppard devises a mystery that is both philosophically interesting and dramatically effective.

I will analyse the play dramatically, as many have already done.[1] I must take the plot, action and characters seriously for two reasons: One, unless the play is taken seriously as play, my contention that this *drama* is to be regarded as philosophy cannot even get underway. Two, if, as I shall argue, the philosophy is integral to the play, then I cannot give a nod to the drama and move quickly to the 'serious business' of philosophy. To do so, would be to regard the philosophy as detachable and the play itself as ultimately irrelevant. While I may think that one could philosophize in a more discursive manner, I think that the philosophical points that Stoppard has to make gain force, if not cogency, from the form he has employed. But I must do more than dramatic analysis. I must extend the work of the dramatic analysts, identifying with some precision the philosophical moves that Stoppard makes dramatically. In arguing that *Professional Foul* is a philosophical enterprise, I will not rely on some vague notion of 'philosophy' as 'having to do with ideas' or 'using philosophical materials' or even a Wittgensteinian understanding of 'philosophy' as showing what cannot be said. Rather I will argue that Stoppard, albeit in an unconven-

* A draft of this paper was read at the *Themes in Drama* International Conference held at the University of California, Riverside, in February 1988.

tional manner, philosophizes in a way that is consonant with the understanding of 'philosophy' in contemporary academic philosophy.[2]
Professional Foul is not academic philosophy. But, and this may be considered faint praise indeed, it is philosophizing that is worthy of my
discipline.

FROM CIVIL DETACHMENT AND MORAL INEFFECTIVENESS . . .

Professional Foul was originally shown on British television, winning the
British Television Critics' Award for the Best Play of 1977. The play opens
with a scene on an airplane, in which we are introduced to three British
philosophers on their way to a philosophical conference in Prague. Only
two, however, Anderson and McKendrick, have any dialogue; the third,
Chetwyn, is asleep in the back of the plane. McKendrick is a with-it sort of
academic who writes on jazz and sex for popular magazines. In the paper he
will read at the colloquium, 'Philosophy and the Catastrophe Theory',
McKendrick argues that a rational person will abandon a moral principle
when it is inadequate to a situation. This sort of catastrophe point is indeed
reached by McKendrick's seatmate, Anderson, during the course of the
play. An Oxbridge professor of moral philosophy, Anderson is a polite,
detached sort. When asked by McKendrick, 'Do you know Prague?',
Anderson replies, 'Not personally. I know the name.' He then wakes up to
what is going on and corrects himself, 'Oh, *Prague*. Sorry. No, I've never
been there.' But then he is not sure, recalling that he may have changed
planes there once on his way to Bratislava (p. 47).[3] A few moments later,
Anderson fails to notice that the paper which McKendrick is attempting to
discuss with him is in fact the paper that Anderson is to give at the
conference, 'Ethical Fictions as Ethical Foundations' (p. 48).

But Anderson, unlike the moral philosopher George Moore of Stoppard's
earlier play, *Jumpers*, is not a complete bumbler, for, we later learn,
Anderson has planned to combine his participation in the Prague
philosophical meeting with an important soccer match between England
and Czechoslovakia. The moral philosopher, contrary to his own professed
ethics of 'correct behavior', is shrewdly taking advantage of the Czech
government's hospitality to indulge his favorite pastime – soccer.

Anderson, however, does not hesitate to invoke his 'good manners' ethics
when he is confronted (in scene 3) by Pavel Hollar, a former student.
Hollar, in spite of – or perhaps because of – his training as a philosopher in
England, is now reduced to cleaning lavatories in his native
Czechoslovakia. Hollar finds Anderson in the latter's hotel room in Prague
and asks him to smuggle a manuscript out of othe country. Anderson
declines:

Anderson. ... I'm sorry ... I mean it would be bad manners, wouldn't it.
Hollar. Bad manners?
Anderson. I know it sounds rather lame but ethics and manners are interestingly related. The history of human calumny is largely a series of breaches of
   good manners.   (p. 60)

Anderson then tries to excuse hmself, but Hollar, not surprisingly, insists. His manuscript defends the thesis that individual rights are prior to the collective ethic. It is wrong, he thinks, for the state to suppress his thought, and it is wrong for Anderson to invoke rules of civility that aid civil oppression. Although Anderson will not consent to smuggling the manu-script out of the country, he does consent, reluctantly, to taking the manuscript to Hollar's apartment the next day. Otherwise, Hollar may be stopped on the way from Anderson's hotel room and the manuscript, of which there is no copy, would be irretrievable. Far from being an act of courage or defiance on Anderson's part, his possession of the manuscript is just more evidence of his own passivity.

Once again, we must notice that Stoppard does not portray Anderson as being totally ineffective. In scene 5, at the philosophical conference, which is the official reason for his presence in Prague, Anderson is apparently paying little attention to a paper being read by a Professor Stone on the adequacy of a logical language. Needing to make a phone call, Anderson stands up at the end of presentation, attempting to leave. Instead, the chairman, assuming he wants to ask a question, recognizes him. Although, as Stoppard notes, Anderson is 'caught like a rabbit in the headlights', he ingeniously twists Ludwig Wittgenstein's dictum, 'Whereof we cannot speak, thereof we must remain silent', to make a Wittgensteinian point: language can obscure reality, particularly ethical reality. Anderson's 'impromptu' response is worth quoting in full, not only for what it reveals of Anderson's character, but also because it shows Stoppard's adept use of philosophical language:

> Ah ... I would only like to offer Professor Stone the observation that language is not the only level of human communication, and perhaps not the most important level. Whereof we cannot speak, thereof we are by no means silent.
>   Verbal language is a technical refinement of our capacity for communica-tion, rather than the *fons et origo* of that capacity. The likelihood is that language develops in an ad hoc way, so there is no reason to expect its development to be logical. (*A thought strikes him.*) The importance of language is overrated. It allows me and Professor Stone to show off a bit, and it is very useful for communicating detail – but the important truths are simple and monolithic. The essentials of a given situation speak for themselves, and language is as capable of obscuring the truth as of revealing it. Thank you.   (pp. 74f.)

One could regard this and other obviously philosophical remarks as sufficient evidence that Stoppard is engaged in philosophy in *Professional Foul*. But I think the philosophical dimension of the play is more structural than this. For, as it will turn out, Anderson's eventual resolution of his own inconsistent thinking about the import of simple but difficult-to-express moral truths – are they fictions or facts? – will lead to decisive moral action.

. . . TO SKILLFUL ADVOCACY

Anderson's decision to become morally engaged does not come all at once. It begins in scene 6 in the Hollar apartment. Anderson, attempting to return the manuscript on his way to the soccer match, discovers Czech plainsclothes police searching the apartment. Now he becomes an object of questioning himself and is reduced to hearing the match broadcast on the radio in Czech. Important developments are summarized for him by one of the policemen while they are interrogating him and searching the apartment for evidence that Hollar has engaged in illegal currency transactions. It is at this point that the event occurs which gives the play its name.

The Czech team is winning because of an inadequate English defense. Finally, in frustration, one of the English defenders tackles a Czech player on his way to a sure goal. One of the policemen, relaying what he is hearing on the radio, says,

> *Policeman.* Penalty . . . for us, I'm afraid . . . Broadbent – a bad tackle when
>   Deml had a certain goal . . . a what you call it? A necessary foul.
> *Anderson.* A professional foul.   (p. 85)

Nothing is made of this at the moment. Rather, Stoppard shows us Anderson outwitting the police. They want to know what Anderson was bringing to the apartment. With his wits about him, Anderson opens his briefcase and gives them two papers from the conference. But moments later, as Anderson is being permitted to leave, a policeman 'discovers' a bundle of American dollars that had allegedly been hidden under the floorboards. Anderson is outraged at this second 'professional foul' and leaves with Pavel's manuscript still in his possession.

The next day, in scene 9, we see Anderson meeting with Mrs Hollar and her son, Sacha, in a park. At first Anderson appears to be committed to taking Hollar's manuscript back to England, but Hollar's wife and son are afraid that Anderson is now under suspicion and will be caught. They ask him to give the manuscript to a friend who will be at the philosophy meeting on the next day. Anderson agrees, but then he is taken aback by the boy's behavior. Anderson had been speaking to Mrs Hollar with her son translating. Although the boy was but a medium for the adults' conversation, Anderson had been treating him as if he were an adult. But then the boy begins to cry. Just why is not clear. Perhaps, it is at the mention of the likelihood that his father will go to jail. Or, perhaps, in this stressful situation he can sustain adult, restrained behavior for only so long.

We, however, are to recall an earlier, unfinished comment by the boy's father. In scene 3 Anderson had asked Hollar to justify his assertion that individual rights are primary. Hollar replied, 'I observe. I observe my son for example' (p. 62). But Anderson's unwillingness to get involved at that point was not conducive to an exploration of Hollar's point, and so the discussion ended. Now, in scene 9, with the boy's inarticulate, yet expressive crying, we almost see an example of the sense of a natural right that the father had in mind. It is not until the next day (in scene 14) that we see the example clearly.

In scene 9 Anderson had been sufficiently struck by this difficult, painful interchange with Hollar's family to respond to Mrs Hollar's urgent request, 'Please help Pavel –', by declaring: 'Mrs Hollar – I will do everything I can for him' (p. 103). This Anderson contrives to do. First, he skillfully manages to find a typewriter and secretly re-write his presentation to the philosophical conference. Then, in a third 'professional foul' (in scenes 11 and 14), he reads the new paper, one that argues Hollar's thesis!, in place of the submitted paper, causing much consternation among the Czech officials. No longer the distracted professor, Anderson forthrightly reads his new paper, fending off the chairman's protestations long enough for us to get a glimpse of his argument. Individual rights are neither derived from the state, given by God nor the product of our language. They are pre-linguistic:

> A small child who cries 'that's not fair' when punished for something done by his brother or sister is apparently appealing to an idea of justice which is, for want of a better word, natural. And we must see that natural justice, however illusory, does inspire many people's behavior much of the time. As an ethical utterance it seems to be an attempt to define a sense of rightness which is not simply derived from some other utterance elsewhere.
>
> Now a philosopher exploring the difficult terrain of right and wrong should not be overimpressed by the argument 'a child would know the difference.' But when, let us say, we are being persuaded that it is ethical to put someone in prison for reading or writing the wrong books, it is well to be reminded that you can persuade a man to believe almost anything provided he is clever enough, but it is much more difficult to persuade someone less clever. There is a sense of right and wrong which precedes utterance. It is individually experienced and it concerns one person's dealings with another person. From this experience we have built a system of ethics which is the sum of individual acts of recognition of individual right.　　　　　(scene 14, pp. 117f.)

I have quoted this lengthy stretch of Anderson's paper for two reasons. One, it helps clarify, to a limited extent, what Anderson, and, I suppose, Stoppard, have in mind by a 'pre-linguistic' but non-God-given or non-Platonic right. Two, it completes the point, originally raised by Hollar, about what one can observe in a child regarding human rights.

Anderson was not allowed to finish his paper. The chairman, committing still another 'professional foul', has sounded the fire alarm, clearing the hall. This is convenient for the Czech officials in the play and for Stoppard, the playwright who would be philosopher. As an author he is spared having to spell out a theory of justice which would bore the audience. And, as a philosopher, he suggests that he does in fact have a theory, but by not presenting it in detail he does not open himself to as much criticism as he would if he had presented it fully. At any rate, the scene shifts to the philosophers leaving the country.

The suspense about the manuscript is finally resolved. On the flight into the country, McKendrick, when he thought Anderson's planned extra-curricular activity might be political rather than athletic, had expressed an interest in getting involved. Recalling this and correctly calculating that McKendrick would not be searched thoroughly by the authorities, Anderson commits still another 'professional foul'. Anderson, unbeknownst to McKendrick, hides Hollar's manuscript in McKendrick's briefcase. Now that they are safely airborne and the ruse is revealed, McKendrick protests. Then, inconsistently with his behavior and assertions in the play thus far, exclaims, 'Jesus. It's not quite playing the game is it?' (scene 16, p. 124). Anderson acknowledges this and notes that McKendrick was not likely to be searched. It would have been pedantic at this point, but Anderson could have pointed out that McKendrick's sense of unfair treatment was but further evidence of Anderson's newly won philosophical position that moral truths are pre-linguistic. It is not unduly pedantic of me, however, to note that Stoppard has unobtrusively made his moral theoretical point by quite naturally having McKendrick be outraged at being manipulated, and even put in danger, by Anderson's clever action. Inconsistent with his own theory of ethics, in which he would have expected a reversal of principle, McKendrick is shown to have a *sense* of injustice. He is outraged at being used by Anderson. Thus Stoppard has depicted for us the pre-linguistic (pre-theoretical?) sense of justice which Anderson (and Stoppard?) thinks is the basis for an ethical system of natural rights. As it is, Anderson defends his use of McKendrick without McKendrick's permission, but admits that McKendrick 'could be right' about Anderson having violated conventional morality. He then adds, 'Ethics is a very complicated business. That's why they have these congresses' (p. 124).

THE PLAY'S PHILOSOPHICAL STANDING

And, one might add, 'That's why they have these plays.' For it is not just in academic settings that one engages in moral philosophy. If I am right about *Professional Foul*, Stoppard carefully clarifies and evaluates, through the use of dialogue and action, the necessity of breaking moral rules on principle. To be sure, an academic moral philosopher will have much to criticize in

Stoppard's dramatically presented moral position, but he or she will recognize a seriously proposed, well thought out moral critique that is not easily dismissed. It may well be that Stoppard has only suggested a moral theory, coming up short in arguing for his own proposal. No doubt, he is better at pointing out the limitations of the views he is criticizing (the ethics of authoritarian socialism, conventional morality, McKendrick's cynicism) than articulating a moral theory of his own. One could note that a *sense* of a natural right, like a belief in God, does not prove there is such a right (or God). But since Anderson–Stoppard is not trying to establish a divinely given or Platonic right, it may be sufficient for morality to show that we have a sense of justice, even if the object of that sense is fictional. At any rate, the charge that Stoppard lacks a well-argued ethical proposal is surely not a disqualification that moral philosophers can press without risking their own disqualification from the profession. Few do more than poke holes in other philosophers' critiques. If a coherent well-reasoned moral theory is the necessary condition for professional status, many, if not most, academic moral philosophers would have ony amateur standing.

But we should not too easily dismiss Stoppard's development of the Hollar–Anderson thesis that moral truths are (1) pre-linguistic and thus (2) prior to societal rules. In addition to the explicit case of the unclever person, such as a child, who has an intuitive sense of right and wrong, there is the implicit example I identified in the final interchange between Anderson and McKendrick. Some commentators take Anderson at his word when he confesses to McKendrick that he had reversed a principle in smuggling the manuscript out of Czechoslovakia in McKendrick's briefcase. Tim Brassell, for instance, points to a discussion (in scene 8) of McKendrick's paper, 'Philosophy and the Catastrophe Theory', as the essence of the moral philosophical argument 'on which the action' of the play 'turns' (*Tom Stoppard: An Appraisal*, p. 193). McKendrick had argued that 'the mistake that people make is, they think a moral principle is indefinitely extendable'. But in real life, which is three-dimensional, a principle is curved and at some point – 'the catastrophe point' – a 'principle reverses itself' (p. 97). Thus when Anderson broke the rules – obey the laws of your host country and do not risk someone else's well-being without their explicit permission – he did so because his moral principles were not extendable to the situation in which he found himself. This is true. The rule-respecting and humanitarian Anderson was in a bind: he could not obey his host country's law and his personal code of non-manipulation of others *and* act on his justifiable outrage at the violation of Hollar's fundamental human rights. But this analysis, at best, does not go deep enough, and, at worst, is wrong. It is true that Anderson's moral code was not adequate to the crisis in Prague, but it is incorrect to infer from this that the point of the play is: sometimes you have to act against a moral rule, for morality has its limits. This interpretation ignores Anderson's lack of remorse and, as I have already pointed out, McKendrick's sense of being wronged. On my view, Anderson has come to think that no rule – be it Czech law or a rule of morality – should be observed when a fundamental human value is at stake.[4] Thus Anderson has not abandoned morality; he has revised his ethics to permit rule-breaking on principle. Anderson did not drop out of the moral life when he broke the rules; he revised his understanding of morality to account for an important exception to conventional morality. A moral rule may not be indefinitely extendable, but some moral values, which serve as the basis of some moral rules, are universal.

As a philosopher I am curious about the Anderson–Stoppard justification of these basic moral rights. I would have liked a more sustained treatment of these 'illusory' moral values, these 'ethical fictions' which serve as 'ethical foundations'. I wonder whether a sense of justice is sufficient for morality even if what we have a sense of has no reality outside our 'sensing' it. In other words, could an ethic be grounded in our outrage, even if the presumed moral truth which justifies the outrage – justice – is invented by us? It is at precisely the point where Anderson is beginning to explore the notion of a God created by us and to ask the questions

> But what is fairness? What is sense? what are these values which we take to be self-evident? And why are they values? (scene 11, p. 114)

that Stoppard as playwright shifts the action away from Anderson reading the paper, showing us instead a hungover McKendrick getting dressed (scene 12) and Anderson's room being searched (scene 13). We are given a glimpse of Anderson's exploration of these questions in scene 14, but no satisfactory development.

We must acknowledge that a play cannot sustain the sort of careful analysis that one expects in a philosophical essay or book. If Stoppard had developed in *Professional Foul* a theory of justice based on our intuitive sense of natural rights, he would have broken the play's suspenseful development. A play is not a discourse. It is suggestive and illustrative of a theory rather than a development of it. Stoppard himself once said in a review, in the same year in which *Professional Foul* was shown on television:

> the most widespread misapprehension about playwrights ... is that they set out to say something and then say it, in short that a play is the end product of an idea. It is more nearly true that the idea is the end product of a play.[5]

One primarily interested in philosophical issues could have hoped that the idea of natural rights would have been more fully realized. Perhaps Stoppard could have given us an appendix which printed the full text of Professor Anderson's 'paper'. But, of course, the idea that is the end product of Stoppard's *Professional Foul* is not a theory of justice. Rather, it is the realization that sometimes one must violate conventional morality in the service of fundamental moral values. This idea, while hardly novel, is well presented in the play.

The admission that Stoppard does not give us a theory of natural rights is not an admission that denies philosophical standing to the play. This admission only limits the degree to which the play is philosophical; it does not deny its character as a philosophical activity. As a philosophical drama *Professional Foul* is a dramatic achievement above all, but it is also a philosophical one. To admit that it is only philosophical in a limited way is not to admit that it is not philosophical at all.

CONCLUSION

Stoppard's ingenuity as a dramatist–philosopher (his skill as a playwright is not in question) lies, above all, in his use of the telling example to clarify and sustain his thesis. We were not surprised by the citation of a child's sense of natural justice. But the use of the worldly McKendrick's naive outrage is a nice touch, perhaps even elegant. In this deft stroke we see crystallized Stoppard's use of character and action to advance a philosophical point. It is not the well-turned speeches alone that justify Stoppard's standing as a philosopher. Nor is it just his ability to use clever dialogue and action to challenge the audience's assumptions about the adequacy of a given moral rule. What really makes the case for Stoppard being taken seriously as a philosophical dramatist is his ability to advance a philosophical thesis through plot, action, dialogue and character development. By crossing the line into moral advocacy and philosophy, while retaining his gift as a dramatist, Tom Stoppard in *Professional Foul* breaks rules in behalf of morality, truth and art. If we did not know it before, we now know that an artist can – with flair – simultaneously be moral, philosophical and entertaining.

NOTES

1 The most useful of the dramatic analyses is Lucina Paquet Gabbard, *The Stoppard Plays* (Troy, NY: Whitson Publishing Company, 1982), pp. 135–45; but also see Tim Brassell, *Tom Stoppard: An Assessment* (New York: St Martin's Press, 1985), pp. 189–203.

2 Three articles have appeared in the British journal, *Philosophy*, discussing the philosophical significance of Stoppard's work: Jonathan Bennett, 'Philosophy and Mr Stoppard', 50 (1975), 5–18; Henning Jensen, 'Jonathan Bennett and Mr Stoppard', 52 (1977), 214–17; and Roy W. Perrett, 'Philosophy as Farce, or Farce as Philosophy', 59 (1984), 373–81. Bennett argues that *Jumpers* compares unfavorably to *Rosencrantz and Guildenstern are Dead*. Jensen is more favorably disposed to *Jumpers* than is Bennett, but Perrett stoutly defends *Jumpers*. Using a

Wittgensteinian understanding of philosophy as dissolution through showing, Perrett argues that 'the farcical structure' of the play 'is itself an attack on the audience's presuppositions about what counts as a serious and credible statement' (p. 379). Examining several Stoppard plays, Roger A. Shiner, 'Showing, Saying and Jumping', *Dialogue*, 21 (1982), 625–46, goes beyond the preceding discussion to argue that philosophy must make better use of plays and poetry than it has. In this paper I focus on *Professional Foul*, a play Shiner does not discuss, except that he notes that it is a 'straightforwardly didactic' play in which Stoppard defends 'a theory of natural rights ... with some subtlety' (p. 626). I will also use a more widely held understanding of philosophy than those who rely on Wittgensteinian showing. In my view, philosophy is the clarification, evaluation and possible reconstruction of our basic beliefs through argument. I think Stoppard is engaged in this sort of philosophy in *Professional Foul*.

3 References are to Tom Stoppard, *Every Good Boy Deserves Favor AND Professional Foul* (New York: Grove Press, Inc., 1978).

4 Gabbard notes that 'once Anderson's perception of smuggling the thesis has come into alignment with his moral principles, stretching a small ethical point is not outside his ken' (*Stoppard Plays*, p. 143). But her correct insight is marred by her failure to speak carefully, distinguishing between rules, principles and rights, and her low estimation of moral and societal rules. Anderson is willing to break a rule if it is in conflict with his newly-appreciated principle that rights take precedence over rules. It is not that the rules, in this case, obey the law and do not manipulate people, are 'small ethical points'. Rather, they may sometimes be set aside in favor of the most fundamental human values.

5 'But for the Middle Classes', *Times Literary Supplement* (3 June 1977), p. 677. In this review of Paul Johnson's *Enemies of Society* Stoppard commits himself to 'objective truth' and 'absolute morality'.

FORUM

The puzzle of Tadeusz Różewicz's *White Marriage*

HALINA FILIPOWICZ

Why Tadeusz Różewicz's *White Marriage* (*Białe małżeństwo*) should have earned a reputation as an unequivocally feminist play is perhaps more a question for a cultural historian than a literary scholar.[1] All the same, it is an issue that can hardly be ducked in the context of current feminist debate.

The most eloquent case for *White Marriage* as a feminist work, indeed the first major feminist play in Polish, has been made by Rhonda Blair and Allen Kuharski.[2] Both Blair and Kuharski regard *White Marriage* as a play that questions the gender-based habits and assumptions imposed by a rigidly patriarchal culture. They do not subscribe to the concept of *écriture féminine* which links sex and style, hence they are hardly amazed that a man should have had such enlightened insights into what it means to live as a woman in a male-dominated, traditionally Catholic society. They arrive, however, at conclusions that are markedly different.

To Blair, the play's central character, Bianka, is a victim of the phallocratic order of things, which makes it impossible for her to find 'room for moderation or tenderness between the sexes'.[3] Bianka can cast off the shackles of conventional gender-roles only at the expense of self-deformation:

> In the course of the play Bianca is increasingly cornered by the social and sexual demands of her world as she is pushed into the role of the ultimate stereotypical woman–child–virgin–bride, that is, the appropriately passive female. She struggles to create an identity which both fits the demands of her patriarchal society and allows her to be at peace with herself, but this proves to be impossible. She finally denies her womanhood altogether and thereby lets go of her humanity. In doing so, Bianca becomes a kind of feminist tragic hero.[4]

In Kuharski's view, Bianka emerges victorious rather than victimized. There seems no way out of the gender-fix except by renouncing sex-roles as well as transcending gender itself. Bianka succeeds in doing both:

> Through Bianca's refusal to consummate her marriage with Benjamin on their wedding night, not only is her feminist revolution begun in the most fundamental way, but her spiritual marriage with Benjamin is made complete ... [T]he couple's rejection of sex also marks the death of the degrading old patriarchal

order and the start of a new era ... Against the squalor and tensions of the world around them, Bianca and Benjamin assume a blazing luminosity at the end of the play.[5]

The closing scene,[6] in which Bianka burns her clothes, cuts off her hair, and declares to Beniamin that she is his brother, signifies, to Blair, Bianka's 'spiritual death'.[7] This desperate act of Bianka's deformation of herself is an indictment of the patriarchal society which denies her full human potential. By the play's end, then, the opposition of male and female is left firmly in place. Not so in Kuharski's view. Unless I have wholly misunderstood his article, Kuharski deploys a deconstructionist strategy of undoing binary oppositions such as male versus female. He conceives of gender as a complex and shifting formation beyond all reach of reductive determinist thinking. Regarded from his perspective, *White Marriage* is a systematic process of displacement which deconstructs sex-role stereotypes and phallocentric presuppositions. To Kuharski, the final scene represents Bianka's

> inner transformation and her invitation to [Beniamin] to a new kind of life ...
> With this androgynous new 'supercouple', Różewicz challenges not only the
> duality of male and female but the very principle of dualistic thought.[8]

Blair's and Kuharski's exegeses rest on the assumptions that Różewicz has converted to feminism, that the characters in *White Marriage* always mean what they say, and that the linguistic structure of his play is a logically ordered sequence of referential assertions. Both Blair and Kuharski are willing to burke those aspects of Różewicz's creative biography that might contradict their interpretation. They do not, moreover, seem to be aware of the ways in which Różewicz's rhetorical stratagems work to complicate the ostensible logic of his argument beyond its express meaning. Although deconstruction is silently present in Kuharski's article, he finds no use for the deconstructionist ways of reading that have demonstrated rhetorical fragility of texts. In a marked departure from the deconstructive practice, Kuharski believes that *White Marriage* somehow offers a stable meaning. To him, the contradictory elements in the play invite a dialectical interpretation: he has proposed a 'resolution' of the binary opposition, or a displacement of the unresolved opposition by a third category, the 'spiritually androgynous union'.[9] But such an interpretation assumes that the oppositions are related in some scheme of hierarchical subordination, and thus a synthesis is possible.

White Marriage is certainly a treasure-house for feminist interpretation – almost too obviously. We watch Bianka destroy her trousseau, and we inevitably conclude that she rebels against the crude biological determinism of a phallocentric world. We see a wedding-feast table turn into Bianka's bride-bed, and we cannot help thinking that sexuality itself is seen as a process of ingestion. The play, no doubt, remains relevant both to ordinary life and ordinary human concerns, but this is only one part of the story.

If *White Marriage* is a statement about the politics of sexual oppression and liberation, why, then, has Różewicz filled his play to the bursting point with extraneous material, much of which is hardly feminist in nature?[10] The play is a kind of vacuum sucking in whatever phrase or fact may be nearby. Many of them are dazzling coruscations which are not backed up by any very solid content, others are marred by some rather facile mythologizing at the point where Father establishes his identity as a priapic bull, and Bianka hers as a virgin Athena. In even the most apparently simple passages there are enigmas introduced by the permeation or pervasion of everyday conversations by extended literary quotations. This situation is further complicated by a conjoining of the inherited material with Różewicz's own literary pastiches.[11] The fabric of quotations, references, and correspondences which crowd the play is, obviously, crucial to the way Różewicz experiences reality. In an age of deepening illiteracy, when even the educated have only a smattering of literary knowledge, erudition is of itself a kind of fantasy, a surrealistic construct.

When the allusions, quotations, and pastiches are juxtaposed with ordinary speech, what effect do the vagaries of the text have on our perception of the characters and their behavior? Audiences are not likely to identify all the references in Różewicz's catalogue of erudition, but they will hear the stylistic registers shift between prose and poetry, between trivial exchanges and overembellished pronouncements, between a textbook fragment and a turn-of-the-century advertisement. Blair does not acknowledge the borrowed material and considers it written by Różewicz himself. Kuharski concedes that the play is embedded in the Polish literary tradition, but he immediately cautions us that *White Marriage* is 'a bold departure from that tradition'.[12] When he does discuss the play's debt to the past, he privileges those references in the play (to Maria Komornicka and Narcyza Żmichowska) that support his principal thesis.[13]

Before we approach *White Marriage* as a play impelled by literature as well as a text of male authority that comes up against the limits of its own explanatory force, we must consider more closely the premises underlying Blair's and Kuharski's explication. There is certainly no good reason why male writers should not address themselves to issues of feminist politics. To deny this would be to subscribe to the sexist mystification that perpetrates the idea of some deep ontological divide between the sexes. However, when Blair and Kuharski declare *White Marriage* the first major feminist play in Polish and accept Różewicz as a well-meaning fellow-traveller, they are a bit too willing to indulge in their assumption that Różewicz has broken clean out of the prison-house of his creative biography. Stanisław Barańczak has pointed out the 'definitely nonfeminist sexual obsessions expressed in [Różewicz's] poetry'.[14] His plays too confront us with the male-sanctioned order of things, in which women's proper place is that of natural providers of male domestic security or of male sexual gratification.

However outspoken their respect for human dignity, the plays of Różewicz reveal a nervousness about feminism, indeed an alarming tendency toward misogyny whenever female characters are involved. Różewicz can be astonishingly cruel to the women in his plays. They are, almost without exception, mere stereotypes: the repulsive Fat Woman (in *The Card Index*) and Old Woman (in *The Old Woman Broods*); the demonic housekeeper in *On All Fours*; the lame-brained young women in *The Card Index*, *The Interrupted Act*, *The Old Woman Broods*, and *On All Fours*; the cloying wives and fiancées in *The Card Index*, *He Left Home*, and *The Trap*, for whose affectionate simplicity the male characters come to feel a cold detestation. The few intelligent, articulate women in Różewicz's plays are viewed by the male characters with suspicion and condescension.[15] Young and attractive women exist in Różewicz's work primarily as orifices: the war bride, the Secretary, and the female Journalist in *The Card Index*; Kowalski's mistress in *A Funeral Polish Style*; the Young Woman in *On All Fours*; Gretchen in *The Trap*; even the Impresario's Wife in *Departure of a Hunger Artist*. Given this context, it would not be impossible to view *White Marriage* as another flight of phallic fancy.

Yet a writer's *œuvre* need not be the ultimate criterion in judging a work at hand. Perhaps *White Marriage* indeed represents Różewicz's conversion to feminism, and he intended his work to be read as a feminist one. If so, we must also confront the perennial problem whether, and how, to honor the principle of authorial intentionality.

There is no paucity of statements by Różewicz about the genesis of *White Marriage*. The play, he said in a French interview, is firmly rooted in modern culture:

> My literature doesn't come from Freud. It is, like Freud, from our epoch. And so are the existential and feminist themes which are very obvious in *White Marriage*, for example. But the play is also a reaction against the surge of pornography in the 1970s, against the brutalization of eroticism as we saw it in Genet.[16]

It is tempting to surrender to the author's overt intention so freely dispensed. As we compare several explications by Różewicz, however, we begin to realize that we will not go very far if we take them uncritically. The proposition that *White Marriage* is an *engagé* play, conceived to counter the pornographic exploitation of sex, had already been dismissed by Różewicz himself six years before the French interview. In a conversation with his Polish scholar-friend, Józef Kelera, he had this to say about the origins of *White Marriage*:

It's impossible to tell why I've written this play. I could have come up with sham answers [*pozorne odpowiedzi*]. I could have said, for example, that by writing this play I tried to stem the tide of pornography in the world, that I tried to return the human face to eroticism and sex which have been rendered inhuman by pornography.[17]

Further, Różewicz did not diminish his 'purely playful motives [*motywy czysto zabawowe*]' in writing *White Marriage*, but he sought to explain why it 'holds a very special place' in his creative biography although 'it's not a step forward in the development of [his] dramatic technique'.[18] The theatre at the time, he said to Kelera, was shrouded in mysticism; *White Marriage* was to bring the theatre down to earth. Nonetheless, Różewicz emphatically denied that his intention in *White Marriage* was to show a conflict between biological and social aspects of human existence. Throughout the conversation, he indeed dwelled on those elements of *White Marriage* which have more to do with literary tradition than with real life. He called *White Marriage* 'a layer cake [*przekładaniec*]' of quotations and allusions.[19] He is indebted, he said, to Piotr Skarga, Adam Mickiewicz, Aleksander Fredro, Narcyza Żmichowska, Gabriela Zapolska, Maria Komornicka, Stanisław Przybyszewski, Jan Lemański, Tadeusz Miciński, and Stanisław Ignacy Witkiewicz. He compared the 'movement of the play: "up" and "down", forward and backward', to 'copulation, to the rhythm of life, to an act of conception'.[20] *White Marriage*, then, emerged as a tale of the erotic relations between master and matter, of the unique intimacy he achieved with his writing as begetter.

Such a confession of phallic authority and literary paternity may well prompt misgivings about the author who is elsewhere presented as a crypto-feminist, if not a fully fledged convert.[21] Let us turn, however, to Różewicz's explanation of the play's last scene. Bianka, he told Kelera, destroys the traditional social 'forms' that have constrained her, causing her 'complexes and obsessions':

This ending means, above all, that Bianka does exist: I am here, in this world, I am a person, I am an individual. . . Second, she doesn't say: I'm your loyal wife with whom you can do in bed whatever you want and so on, but in her innocence she says: I am. Understand that I also exist.[22]

The motives of defensive male prejudice seem to have blinded Różewicz to his best insights on the subject of gender relations when he immediately negated the second part of his explanation. Bianka's final line, he said, is a proclamation of 'her human condition, not of her gender [*płeć*]'.[23]

For her boldness Bianka must pay with her sanity. This is essentially what Różewicz told Kazimierz Braun, a noted theatre director. He chided Braun, who directed two of the early productions of *White Marriage*, for missing the point of the final scene: 'Even you didn't take Bianka over the edge of sanity.'[24] He reminded Braun that the scene had been inspired by an actual incident in the life of Maria Komornicka who, in Różewicz's explanation, went insane after declaring herself a man.[25] The original title of the play, as Różewicz tells us elsewhere, was in fact *Madness (Szał)*.[26]

In the conversations with Konstanty Puzyna as well as Kelera, Różewicz repeatedly said that it was the situation in the theatre at the time that prompted his response in the form of *White Marriage*. His diagnosis of the situation, however, changed. In 1976, when he spoke with Kelera, it was the separation of the theatre from the rest of human life that concerned him. In 1974, when he talked with Puzyna, it was the theatre's scorn for drama as literature. In no uncertain terms he rejected the theatre which favored either a collective creation or the arrogated authoritarianism of the director and the designer at the expense of the playwright. As he told Puzyna, *White Marriage* was conceived out of the desire to have the authority unconditionally surrendered to the dramatist. He wanted to write a play resistant to manipulations by theatre artists. *White Marriage*, he contended, is such a work. It can do very well without directors and designers: 'I feel like "playing it out" in a notebook and reading it to my friends . . . [in] my "one-man's theatre" at home.'[27]

If Różewicz's authorial intentionality is so hard to pin down – shifting incessantly from interview to interview – it is because he insists on his right to self-contradictions:

> I have left the door open so that I can experiment. I don't want to be held accountable for my theories. Otherwise someone will grab me by the lapels and say: You said this and that and you better stick with it.[28]

On epistemological grounds, then, it is necessary to deny that authorially determined meaning can be reliably ascertained at all. Even if an author were to follow through his or her intentions, a text inescapably exceeds the limits of what its author set out to assert. Indeed, the author's intention is a condition whose fulfillment neither the author nor the audience can know with certainty and one which cannot control the play of meaning.

Whatever Różewicz may have consciously undertaken to say in *White Marriage*, it is ultimately the play's language that speaks to us in ways often unbeknown to the author. We must therefore confront the play on its own terms. It is a procedure that both Blair and Kuharski seem to have adopted. But since their authority is the English translation, they are compelled to carry their argument at a considerable sacrifice of the Polish original's linguistic richness and complexity. Further, Blair and Kuharski regard *White Marriage* as a human document, that is, as a representation of characters who think, feel, and act in a way that is enough like ours to engage us in their experience. In their approach to *White Marriage* as a human document and a feminist critique of patriarchy as well, language is taken as a more or less transparent device conveying meaning. But, to quote the Hero of Różewicz's *The Card Index*, 'It's a lot worse with words than we think.'[29] Apart from the fact that language is never fully transparent to meaning, the imagined world of *White Marriage* is generated by literature and thus foregrounds the linguistic medium itself. This aspect of the play – its play of language – is often overlooked or insufficiently stressed.

The outpouring of quotations, allusions, and pastiches in *White Marriage* is not merely a literary stylization to convey the intellectual ambience of the Polish *fin de siècle* when the action takes place. The play's main rhetorical strategy is, in fact, that of decontextualizing rather than setting up a context, of a de-montage rather than a montage.[30] The spoken lines constantly oscillate between the language of everyday conversations and the language of borrowed or parodied fragments. When the fragments are lifted out of their context and placed in a new linguistic milieu, they merge but do not meld. This is underscored by the fact that the extraneous materials are usually either read aloud or recited rather than delivered in the style of casual conversation. The most immediate result of such a rhetorical strategy is an unsettling sense of incongruity. The recognizable details of life compete with the power of the language that draws attention to itself.

Moreover, when the action is repeatedly interrupted to allow a reading or recitation, we begin to distance ourselves from the reality on stage. And since the lines in an inherited fragment compel a character to assume a different expressive identity, the play's textual workings deny the characters any stability or psychological continuity. After the work of expressionist dramatists, it is, of course, no longer safe to assume that a play is going to present characters, each of whom has a total unity. On the contrary, one of the major achievements of modern drama has been to put that notion of selfhood in question, to present it as an aggregation of conflicting selves. This is in fact one of the unspoken premises in Kuharski's article. But *White Marriage* goes even further. The identities of the characters become functions of language rather than a preexistent given which uses language. It is not that there is no such thing as identity, but that it is a changing set of linguistic conventions.

In *White Marriage*, then, we have a dramatic text whose perfidious play of language inescapably undoes the ostensible meaning which, in Blair's and Kuharski's interpretation, has to do with a fully rationalizable conflict between individual self-assertion and society's crudely reductive, biological view of sexual difference. To discover signs of the strain and self-division in the text, let us look at the characters of Beniamin and Bianka, who are central to Blair's and Kuharski's feminist reading of the play.

Of all the characters, Beniamin is the one who rarely speaks in his own voice, and before he says any text of his own at all, before he has a chance to establish his identity, he gives a poetry recital at a soirée. He appears in six of the play's thirteen scenes; in one of them, he asks a short question, and in the remaining five he usually recites poems. His quotations occupy a rhetorically significant position: they either open a scene and prompt a response (in scene 4),[31] or they counter a preceding text as a scene draws to a close (scenes 7, 9, and 11). In scene 12 – the crucial scene of the wedding feast and the wedding night – Beniamin's own text is minimal; the linguistic centerpiece of the scene is his exchange with Bianka of excerpts from Żmichowska's *The Heathen Woman*. Once we see the character of Beniamin as generated by literary quotations, then his identity becomes precarious rather than fixed and unified, and his spoken lines can hardly be taken as a reliable source of determinate meaning.

Bianka, even more than Beniamin, emerges as a literary construct. Indeed, she describes herself, in scene 9, in the words of Żmichowska's letter to her brother Erazm,[32] and in scene 13 she assumes the identity of Maria Komornicka. Her own spoken lines are more extensive than Beniamin's, but so are her inherited fragments. As soon as the play opens, we see her read a book. The fact that it is a textbook of zoology, rather than a poem by Wincenty Korab Brzozowski, is a welcome, if unexpected, change from the point of view of Paulina, Bianka's vivaciously practical friend.[33] Bianka's identification with the precious turn-of-the-century writing, such as Brzozowski's, is confirmed in scene 2. She is present in this scene through her diary that is read aloud by her parents; the diary fragments are excerpts from Komornicka's 'Black Flames'. In scene 8, after Beniamin has proposed marriage to her, Bianka reads from the journal herself:

> I shall dwell with thee at the bottom of a lake in a golden temple like a bell, which thou wilt toll with thy strong arms like boughs... and the still heart will stir... The heart of the bell, thine heart, to hold it in my hand like a frightened little bird... The heart pounds and bursts with happiness... with my claws I shall toll thy silent bell... Oh, the bellringer of my temple! Toll the silent bell of my body with thy bronze heart, follow me to the top of Mont Blanc, wrap me with the flame of thy desire...[34]

The passage throbs with the most embarrassingly jejune emotionalism. It invites a smile at the reiterated 'bell' and 'heart'. It may even provoke a growl: heart me no such heartness. It cannot, however, be taken seriously; it is, indeed, a parody of Komornicka's overembellished poetic prose.

In scene 12, on their wedding night, Bianka declares to Beniamin:

> Have you seen a woman who is beautiful, strong in her passion, holy in her soul? Her forehead glows with the power of thought which could determine the fate of Athens. Her lips burn with desire, her gaze with irresistible seduction... Have you dreamt of her? If her eyes are downcast, 'tis only because a flame of hope or of memories is too bright and must be concealed; her blush is her blood, 'tis her life which springs forth for it cannot be contained in her body... and her love... believe me, brother, such women there are... if you meet her, you might succumb to the desire to die in her embrace, to be no more...[35]

The lines are from Żmichowska's novel; removed from their context, they strike us as extraordinarily muddled and pretentious. In the same scene farther away, Bianka turns to the imagery and the diction that filled the pages of the turn-of-the-century *Chimera*:

> My legs have grown together... from my feet up to my navel I am covered with cold fish scales... Ben... your beloved has a fish tail instead of legs... you know? I am a siren... you've married a siren... a chimera. Look! I have a lioness's head, a goat's body, and the tail of a snake...[36]

Bianka ends scene 12 with another excerpt from *The Heathen Woman*. It is in plain idiom which may be more appealing to contemporary audiences, but it nonetheless points up the stylistic instability of Bianka's language.

Throughout the play, Bianka seems in opposition to the phallocentric world that surrounds her. However, different linguistic effects in her spoken lines are at times concordant with, but most often directly subversive of, the manifest content of the play. The seemingly peripheral quotations and pastiches work to deny Bianka a psychological identity and hence credibility as a character. Locked in textual combat with Bianka's own lines, the inherited fragments rarely fail to embarrass the apparent logic of her rebellion. In no other scene is this more evident than in the penultimate scene 12. The events of this scene are, of course, the turning point of the play: Bianka refuses to consummate her marriage to Beniamin. Yet there is an insoluble antagonism between action and word. Bianka's and Beniamin's recitations provoke laughter but not without a sense of discomfort as if our laughter were inappropriate, perhaps even irresponsible. This sense of discomfort is hardly relieved by scene 13 which, unless we are familiar with Komornicka's biography, catches us unawares. The humor of the ridiculous excerpts does not eliminate an awkward sublimity in scene 12, but it does little to prepare us for the rueful pathos of the play's closing scene.

Różewicz's use of inherited material is not limited to *White Marriage*. In the earlier plays, such as *The Card Index* and *The Laocoon Group*, it was his way of recovering and re-examining the past, of evaluating its inherent cultural value through new context. But the pervasiveness of quoted and paraphrased fragments in *White Marriage* (as well as *Departure of a Hunger Artist* and *The Trap*, written immediately afterwards[37]) suggests a more radical strategy. According to Różewicz, he used the many references in *White Marriage* as a scaffolding to assure a cohesive structure. At stake for him was a closed dramatic form, as opposed to the looser, more open forms of his plays such as *The Card Index*:

> I would like ... to make sure I am contained in time and space, that I won't disintegrate into smaller and smaller pieces but that I will begin to coalesce again... My complete surrender to the open dramaturgy had become a threat in the sense that dramatic elements might continue to disperse and thus leave an empty center. I was aware of that, and so I tried to pull these elements back

to the center ... to contain them within a framework [of quotations and references], to compress them ... until they release a new energy.[38]

As we have seen, however, the inclusion of the borrowed material in the spoken lines undermines the very thing Różewicz said he was trying to accomplish: a stable form. It is not only that *White Marriage*, wavering between different linguistic registers, stubbornly refuses to yield an exact meaning. By outrageous peculiarities of language, the play also betrays an internal struggle for an appropriate language. In *White Marriage*, there is a very precise identifiable movement back and forth among many stylistic possibilities none of which, however, is decisive. The rhetorical practices within the play break the text down into contradictory elements, put in question and at times suspend an ostensibly determinate meaning, and prevent the text from being read as a unified whole, as an organic unity. It would not be too much to say that these discordant dynamics of the text are a source of the palpably disturbing effect the play has on us.

Most of the inherited material in *White Marriage* comes from the Polish modernist movement, known as the Young Poland. It was notorious for its linguistic license and stylistic liberties, which for many decades made the style of the Young Poland writers 'a synonym for bad taste'.[39] When *White Marriage* recreates this linguistic chaos, it literally makes the most of it. The world we see on stage is a world structured of fragmented visions as well as verbal fragments which clash with one another. It is a world denied a center, deprived of a single linguistic authority.

We might be tempted to conclude that the play seems to touch on feminist aesthetics precisely in its defiance of the unifying power and rigid discipline of logical reason, which, we are told, has been the domain of male power *par excellence*. Such a conclusion, however, would be based on a belief that each of the sexes has its own, essential attributes – a belief, in other words, that re-enforces the old stereotypes about gender difference. The trouble is, moreover, that while *White Marriage* may indeed not be reducible to a single interpretation, it is not reducible to interpretations taken out of context of the play's linguistic system.

NOTES

1 The play was written between May and October 1973. It was first published in 1974, and had its world première in 1975 in Warsaw.
2 See Rhonda Blair, '*A White Marriage*: Różewicz's Feminist Drama', *Slavic and East European Arts*, 3 (Winter/Spring 1985), 13–21; and Allen Kuharski, '*White Marriage* and the Transcendence of Gender' in James Redmond (ed.), *Themes in Drama*, vol. 11: *Women in Theatre* (Cambridge: Cambridge University Press, 1989), pp. 129–38. In Poland, where feminist theory has not yet arrived, critics

are generally satisfied to carve the play up into the oppositions of body/soul, culture/nature, social contract/bestial instinct, high/low, mature/juvenile. See especially Marta Fik, '*Mariage blanc*', *The Theatre in Poland*, 17 (September 1975), 13–14; Tadeusz Burzyński, '*Białe małżeństwo* po raz drugi', *Kultura* (Warsaw), 13 (12 October 1975), 13; Marek Jodłowski, 'Między *Operetką* a *Rzeźnią*', *Odra*, 15 (September 1975), 77–81, and '"He, he" Różewicza', *Odra*, 15 (December 1975), 107–8; Barbara Osterloff, '*Białe małżeństwo* inaczej', *Teatr*, 30 (1–15 December 1975), 11–12; Józef Kelera, 'Od *Kartoteki* do *Pułapki*', [introduction to] Tadeusz Różewicz, *Teatr*, vol. 1 (Cracow: Wydawnictwo Literackie, 1988), pp. 51–7. Marta Piwińska has cautiously discussed *White Marriage* as 'a historical drama' about 'a vague [*niejasna*] revolt of artists, women, and children surrounded by swinishness' (see 'Cukiernia ciast trujących', *Dialog*, 19 [March 1974], 92). No less cautiously, Tadeusz Drewnowski has described it as 'a play about the emancipation of *a woman*' (see 'Poeta zostaje sam. . .', *Polityka*, 30 [25 October 1986], 9; emphasis added). And Irena Bołtuć has, with irresistible logic, applauded the play as 'a defense of women, which is concerned not with the superficial and deceptive equality of professional and social status, but with partnership in life, including its most intimate aspect, sex' (see 'Z czym na festiwal wrocławski?', *Teatr*, 30 [16–31 March 1975], 4).

3 Blair, '*A White Marriage*: Różewicz's Feminist Drama', p. 20.

4 Ibid., p. 13. Blair's idea that Bianka is a tragic hero anticipates Kelera's conclusion in 'Od *Kartoteki* do *Pułapki*', p. 56. His essay originally appeared in *Dialog* (April–May 1985).

5 Kuharski, '*White Marriage* and the Transcendence of Gender', p. 136. He finds the ending tragic only to the extent that Bianka and Beniamin are compelled to reject physical sexuality. In Kuharski's interpretation, Beniamin appears a willing participant in Bianka's 'feminist revolution', despite that her declaration in the last scene catches Beniamin unawares. Dressed in his Sunday best, he stands speechless. Różewicz, a master of open-ended dramatic forms, would not have it otherwise. Worth noting is a significant change from the conclusion of the first edition of *White Marriage*, in which Bianka extended her arms to Beniamin in a gesture of welcoming (see *Białe małżeństwo*, *Dialog*, 19 [February 1974], 33). In all the subsequent editions, this gesture is absent, and thus Bianka appears cautious toward Beniamin.

6 Both Blair and Kuharski have conceded that *White Marriage* consists not of scenes, but of tableaux, the term adopted in the English translation (see Tadeusz Różewicz, *Mariage Blanc and The Hunger Artist Departs*, trans. Adam Czerniawski [London: Marion Boyars, 1983], pp. 5–69). The Polish text uses the term '*obraz*'; when applied to drama, it simply means a brief act or a scene, without the visual connotations suggested by 'tableau'.

7 Blair, '*A White Marriage*: Różewicz's Feminist Drama', p. 20.

8 Kuharski, '*White Marriage* and the Transcendence of Gender', p. 137.

9 Ibid., pp. 135, 136.

10 Among Różewicz's sources was Felicjan Faleński's unfinished play, *The Dances of Death* (*Tance śmierci*, c.1860–c.1885), which, in the character of Princess Febronia, ridicules emancipated women as unkempt and neurotic spinsters (see *Archiwum Literackie*, vol. 8 [Wrocław: Zakład Narodowy imienia Ossolińskich,

1964], pp. 115–293). A biography of Maria Komornicka, another source for the play, is in the same volume of *Archiwum Literackie*.

11 Jerzy Paszek has identified the following verbal fragments in *White Marriage*: a poem by Wincenty Korab Brzozowski in scenes 1 and 8; Maria Komornicka's poetic prose, 'Black Flames' ('Czarne płomienie', 1901), in scene 2; a poem by Komornicka in scene 3; poems by Stanisław Korab Brzozowski and Jan Lemański in scene 4; a poem by Tadeusz Miciński in scene 7; Juliusz Słowacki's drama, *Balladyna* (1839), and Różewicz's pastiche of 'Black Flames' in scene 8; Narcyza Żmichowska's letter to her brother and her novel, *The Heathen Woman* (*Poganka*, 1846), in scene 9; *Lives of the Saints* (*Żywoty Świętych*, 1579) by Piotr Skarga, Różewicz's pastiche of hagiographical poetry, and a poem by Stanisław Wyrzykowski in scene 11; *The Heathen Woman* in scene 12; and the diction of the leading Polish modernist journal, *Chimera* (1901–1907), scattered throughout the play. (See J. Paszek, 'Aluzja literacka w dramacie [*Białe małżeństwo* Różewicza]', in *Sztuka aluzji literackiej: Żeromski, Berent, Joyce* [Katowice: Uniwersytet Śląski, 1984], pp. 146–55.) It is worth adding that a folk song in scene 4 appears in a similar context in 'Little Frog' ('Żabusia', 1889), a short story by Gabriela Zapolska whose works were a major source of inspiration for the play.

12 Kuharski, '*White Marriage* and the Transcendence of Gender', p. 130.

13 The text of *White Marriage* does not bear out Kuharski's claim that 'Bianca's initial narcissism and excessive aestheticism can be seen as an allusion to the early life of [Zofia] Nałkowska' ('*White Marriage* and the Transcendence of Gender', p. 132).

14 Stanisław Barańczak, [an untitled review of the special issue of *Slavic and East European Arts* which carried Blair's article], *Slavic and East European Journal*, 30 (Summer 1986), 298.

15 See, for example, the scene between the protagonist of *Departure of a Hunger Artist* and the Young Woman. She interviews the Hunger Artist using the formal and respectful *pan*, but he addresses her with the familiar *ty*. He thus underscores his own position as master while relegating the woman to a position of inferiority.

16 Irène Sadowska-Guillon, 'Tadeusz Różewicz: le théâtre de la mythologie a venir' [an interview with Tadeusz Różewicz], *Europe: Revue Littéraire Mensuelle*, 61 (April 1983), 164.

17 Józef Kelera, 'Na temat i nie na temat' [an interview with Tadeusz Różewicz recorded early in April 1976], *Odra*, 16 (June 1976), 65.

18 Ibid., pp. 67, 66.

19 Ibid., p. 66.

20 Ibid., p. 66.

21 As Sandra M. Gilbert and Susan Gubar have pointed out, 'In patriarchal western culture ... the text's author is a father, a progenitor, a procreator, an aesthetic patriarch whose pen is an instrument of generative power like his penis' (see *The Madwoman in the Attic: The Woman Writer and the Nineteenth-Century Literary Imagination* [New Haven: Yale University Press, 1979], p. 6).

22 Kelera, 'Na temat i nie na temat', p. 66.

23 Ibid., p. 66.

24 Kazimierz Braun and Tadeusz Różewicz, *Języki teatru* (Wrocław: Wydawnictwo Dolnośląskie, 1989), p. 40.

25 For a biography of Komornicka, including a description of the clothes-burning episode in July 1907, see reminiscences by her sister and brother: Aniela Komornicka, 'Maria Komornicka w swych listach i mojej pamięci', and Jan Komornicki, 'List brata' in *Archiwum Literackie*, pp. 294–341, 350–3. According to Jan Komornicki, Maria Komornicka looked upon women as 'inferior creatures' (p. 352).

26 See Tadeusz Różewicz, *Przygotowanie do wieczoru autorskiego* (Warsaw: Państwowy Instytut Wydawniczy, 1977), p. 81. He later replaced *Madness* with *Black Flames*, borrowing the new title from Komornicka's 'Black Flames', which is quoted in scene 2 and parodied in scene 8. According to Paszek, *White Marriage* is a negative of 'Black Flames' (see 'Aluzja literacka w dramacie', p. 154).

27 Konstanty Puzyna, 'Koniec i początek' [an interview with Tadeusz Różewicz recorded on 23 January 1974], *Dialog*, 19 (June 1974), 122.

28 Ibid., p. 122.

29 *Teatr*, vol. 1, p. 116.

30 For a different explanation of the role of the quotations and allusions, see Paszek, 'Aluzja literacka w dramacie'. According to Paszek, they serve as cultural ornamentation to evoke the atmosphere at the turn-of-the-century, as a source of humor, and as a means of characterization.

31 In scene 4, Father recognizes that Beniamin, by leaving out the last two words ('O, death'), has turned Stanisław Korab Brzozowski's poem into an erotic verse. He picks up Beniamin's verbal game and responds with Lemański's *carpe diem* poem 'Novena xxv', to which he has added a final couplet.

32 See *Teatr*, vol. 2, p. 154.

33 Ibid., p. 109. In scene 8, Paulina once again identifies Bianka with the same poem, 'Affinité d'ombres et de fleurs en le soir' (1899) by Wincenty Korab Brzozowski (see p. 150). Incidentally, there is no evidence in the text to support Blair's and Kuharski's claims that Paulina is Bianka's sister or half-sister. By the premises of the play, her identity must remain an enigma.

34 Ibid., p. 150.

35 Ibid., p. 168.

36 Ibid., p. 169.

37 These two plays, written between 1975 and 1982, are based on Franz Kafka's fiction, diaries, and correspondence.

38 Puzyna, 'Koniec i początek', pp. 120, 123.

39 Czesław Miłosz, *The History of Polish Literature* (Berkeley: University of California Press, 1983), p. 329.

Index

Abelard, Peter, 41, 42
Adelman, Janet, 87, 88
Aeschylus, 3, 5, 6, 10, 11, 12, 13
  Agamemnon, 2, 11
  Iphigeneia Among the Taurians, 9
  Oresteia, 11
  Seven Against Thebes, 10, 31
Anaxandrides, 30
Appia, Adolphe, 143–4, 145, 146, 148, 150
Aquinas, St Thomas, 42, 48
Araros, 27
  Acharnians, 25
  Clouds, 25, 127
  Frogs, 31
  Wasps, 26
Aristotle, 1, 3, 8, 9, 10, 13, 21–32, 41, 42, 63, 139
  Ethics, 22–32 passim, 41
  Metaphysics, 41
  Nicomachean Ethics, 8, 9, 22–32 passim
  Poetics, 21, 23, 32
  Politics, 22, 23, 24, 25, 28, 29–30, 31
  Rhetoric, 9, 22–32 passim
Armin, Robert, 75
Averroës, 41–2

Bacon, Francis, 49, 88
Bakshy, Alexander, 144, 156
Baraka, Amiri, 74
  Dutchman, 74
Beaumont, Francis and John Fletcher,
  A King and No King, 107–25
Baranczak, Stanislaw, 213–14
Beckett, Samuel, 171–81
  Endgame, 172, 175–6, 177
  Film, 171
  Krapp's Last Tape, 176, 177–8
  Not I, 178–9
  Ohio Impromptu, 179

A Piece of Monologue, 179
  Waiting for Godot, 175
Berkeley, Bishop, 171
Bernard of Clairvaux, 42
Berry, Ralph, 58
Blair, Rhonda, 211, 213
Boethius of Dacia, 42
Breton, Nicholas, *Pasquil's Passe*, 79
Brook, Peter, 157
Bruno, Giordano, 171–81
Buchanan, George, 119–20
Bushe, Amyas, *Socrates*, 131–2, 133, 139

Callinus, 3
Carter, Huntly, 144, 155
Catherall, Samuel, *Εἰκων Σωκρατική; or, a Portraiture of Socrates*, 127–31, 139
Chantraine, Pierre, 2
Chaplin, Charlie, 65
Chekhov, Anton, 157
Cheney, Sheldon, 144, 145, 146, 147, 148–9, 154, 156
Chester cycle, 37, 38, 40
Cicero, 139
Coventry cycle, 37–45
Craig, Edward Gordon, 143–4, 148, 150, 157
Croo, Robert, 38, 39, 40, 44, 45

Descartes, *Meditations*, 93
Dostoevsky, Feodor, 164

Eco, Umberto, 74
Elizabeth I, Queen, 37
Epicharmus, 32
Epimenides of Crete, 73–4
Erasmus, *Praise of Folly*, 78

Euripides, 5–6, 11, 12–13, 21–2, 23, 30–1
  Andromache, 24
  Hecuba, 31
  Heracles, 24
  Oedipus, 31
  Phoenician Women, 24, 31
  Suppliants, 24

Fletcher, John, with Francis Beaumont, *A King and No King*, 107–25
Freud, Sigmund, 8

Geddes, Norman Bel, 144, 152, 153, 154, 155–6
Gödel, Kurt, 73
Goldberg, Jonathan, 109
Gorky, Maxim, *The Lower Depths*, 161–9
Grotowski, Jerzy, 157
Guthrie, Tyrone, 157

Havelock, Eric, 21
Hegel, G. W. F., 61–3, 67, 69, 70
Heidegger, Martin, 172
Heinemann, Margot, 107–8
Herodotus, 4
Hesiod, 21
Homer, 12, 14, 21
  Iliad, 5
  Odyssey, 3, 5
Hooker, Richard, 108, 118, 119–20
Huxley, Aldous, *The Devils of Loudun* 185–97

Ingram, Reg, 44

Jaeger, Werner, 21
James I, King, 109, 113–15, 119
Jerome, 1
Jones, Robert Edmond, 144, 145, 151
Jonson, Ben, 67, 118
Joyce, James, 171
Jung, Carl, 8

Komornicka, Maria, 215, 216
Kristeller, P. O., 139
Kuharski, Allen, 211–12, 213

Lugué, Gabriel, 185, 186–7
Lemański, Jan, 215
Longinus, 1

Macgowan, Kenneth, 144, 145, 146, 147, 154
Maeterlinck, Maurice, 156
Menander, 25, 27
  Dyskolos, 27
Micinski, Tadeusz, 215
Mickiewicz, Adam, 215
Moore, G. E., 93, 94
  On Certainty, 93
Muchnic, Helen, 161

Nietzsche, Friedrich, 168

O'Neill, Eugene, 144, 147, 154
  The Iceman Cometh, 161–9

Pausanias, 4
Pindar, 4, 24
Plato, 6–7, 8, 9, 10, 11, 13, 21, 127, 128–31, 138, 139
  Apology, 6, 127, 128, 134
  Crito, 127, 129
  Euthyphro, 6
  Phaedo, 6, 127, 129, 130
  Republic, 6, 7, 11
Plautus, 24, 26
  Miles Gloriosus, 24
Plutarch, 4
Pope, Alexander, 1
Przybysewski, Stanislaw, 215

Reinhardt, Max, *The Miracle*, 156
Robbe-Grillet, Alain, 172
Robinson, Lillian S., 168
Różewicz, Tadeusz
  The Card Index, 214, 217, 219–20
  Departure of a Hunger Artist, 214, 219
  A Funeral Polish Style, 214
  The Interrupted Act, 214
  He Left home, 214
  The Old Woman Broods, 214
  On All Fours, 214
  The Laocoon Group, 219
  The Trip, 214, 219
  White Marriage, 211–23
Russell, Bertrand, 73

Sartre, Jean-Paul, 171
Schechner, Richard, 157
Schopenhauer, Arthur, 60
Shakespeare, William, 47–58, 61–70
  All's Well that Ends Well, 67–9
  Antony and Cleopatra, 87–104
  Hamlet, 45–98, 91
  King Lear, 73, 74–82, 91
  Macbeth, 103
  Measure for Measure, 64–5, 66
  Othello, 91
  The Tempest, 69–70, 104
  Timon of Athens, 103
  Troilus and Cressida, 65–7
Simonson, Lee, 144, 157
Skarga, Piotr, 215
Socrates, 3, 5, 11, 127–41
Socrates Triumphant; or, the Danger of
  Being Wise in a Commonwealth of
  Fish (anon.), 135–8
Solon, 2, 5, 13
Sophocles, 5, 12, 13, 14, 31
  Antigone, 31
  Electra, 11
  Oedipus at Colonus, 31
  Oedipus the King, 2, 9, 11
Stoppard, Tom
  Jumpers, 200
  Professional Foul, 199–208

Terence, *Phormio*, 24
Theophrastus, *Characters*, 21
Theopompus, 25
Tourette, Gilles de la, 185
Towneley cycle, 38

Urban, Joseph, 144

Vico, Giambattista, 171
Voltaire, *Socrate*, 133–5, 139

Waugh, Frank A., 155
Whiting, John, 187
  The Devils, 187–97
  The Port-Royal, 187
  Saints' Day, 187
Wickham, Glynne, 44
Witkiewicz, Stanisław Ignacy, 215
Wittgenstein, Ludwig, 93–6, 97–8, 100,
  101, 102

Xenophon, 127, 129, 138, 139

Yeats, W. B., 117–18
York, cycle, 37

Żmichowska, Narcyza, 213, 215
  The Heathen Woman, 218–19